Russell Williams

Series editor: Patrick Walsh-Atkins

Cambridge International AS Level

European History 1789–1917

CAMBRIDGE
UNIVERSITY PRESS

CAMBRIDGE
UNIVERSITY PRESS

University Printing House, Cambridge CB2 8BS, United Kingdom

One Liberty Plaza, 20th Floor, New York, NY 10006, USA

477 Williamstown Road, Port Melbourne, VIC 3207, Australia

4843/24, 2nd Floor, Ansari Road, Daryaganj, Delhi – 110002, India

79 Anson Road, #06–04/06, Singapore 079906

Cambridge University Press is part of the University of Cambridge.

It furthers the University's mission by disseminating knowledge in the pursuit of education, learning and research at the highest international levels of excellence.

Information on this title: education.cambridge.org

© Cambridge University Press 2013

First published 2013
20 19 18 17 16 15 14 13 12 11 10 9 8

Printed in the United Kingdom by Latimer Trend

A catalogue record for this publication is available from the British Library

ISBN 978-1-107-61324-9 Paperback

Contents

Introduction

Cambridge International AS Level History is a new series of three books that offer complete and thorough coverage of Cambridge International AS Level History (syllabus code 9389). Each book is aimed at one of the AS History syllabuses issued by Cambridge International Examinations for first examination in 2014. These books may also prove useful for students following other A Level courses covering similar topics. Written in clear and accessible language, *Cambridge International AS Level History – European History 1789–1917* enables students to gain the knowledge, understanding and skills to succeed in their AS Level course (and ultimately in further study and examination).

Syllabus and examination

Students wishing to take just the AS Level take two separate papers at the end of a one-year course. If they wish to take the full A Level there are two possible routes. The first is to take the two AS papers at the end of the first year and a further two A Level papers at the end of the following year. The second is to take the two AS papers as well as the two A Level papers at the end of a two-year course. For the full A Level, all four papers must be taken. The two AS papers are outlined below.

Paper 1 lasts for one hour and will be based on *Liberalism and Nationalism in Italy and Germany 1848–71*. The paper will contain at least three different sources, and candidates will have to answer two questions on them. Students are not expected to have extensive historical knowledge to deal with these questions, but they are expected to be able to understand, evaluate and utilise the sources in their answers, and to have sound background knowledge of the period. In the first question (a) candidates are required to consider the sources and answer a question on one aspect of them. In the second question (b) candidates must use the sources and their own knowledge and understanding to address how far the sources support a given statement. Chapter 3 provides the appropriate level of historical knowledge to deal with Paper 1.

Paper 2 lasts for an hour and a half. The paper contains four questions, and candidates must answer two of them. Each question has two parts: part (a) requires a causal explanation; and part (b) requires consideration of significance and weighing of the relative importance of factors. A question on each of the four topics outlined in the Cambridge syllabus (for example, *The Industrial Revolution* c. *1800–50)* will appear in every examination paper.

Examination skills

Chapter 6, which is entirely dedicated to helping students with examination skills and techniques, gives guidance on answering all the different types of exam questions. Students should read the relevant section of the exam skills chapter *before* addressing practice questions, to remind themselves of the principles of answering each type of question. Remember that facts alone are not enough; they must be accompanied by a clear understanding of the questions and must employ a range of skills such as focused writing, evaluation and analysis.

All chapters have a similar structure. They key features are as follows:

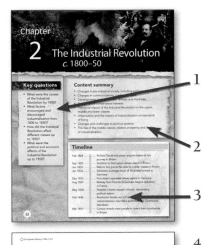

1 **Key questions** pose thought-provoking pointers to the key issues being dealt with in the chapter.

2 **Content summary** explains the essence of a chapter.

3 **Timeline** offers an overview of significant events of the period.

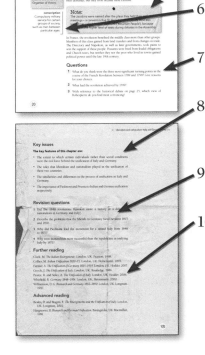

4 **Key figures** offer a detailed profile of key personalities.

5 **Notes** highlight significant points from within the text.

6 **Definitions** of key terms enhance students' understanding of the text.

7 **Questions** interspersed within the chapters help to consolidate learning.

8 **Key issues** outline the main aspects of the content that might be significant for exam preparation.

9 **Revision questions** help students assess their own understanding and skills.

10 **Further reading** provides a list of extra resources that will help with gaining a wider perspective of the topic.

1 The French Revolution and Napoleon 1789–1804

Key questions

- What were the aims and domestic problems of French politicians in the early revolutionary years?
- Why were French governments so unstable up to 1799?
- Why did Napoleon Bonaparte rise to power by 1799?
- What were Napoleon Bonaparte's domestic aims from 1799 to 1804?

Content summary

- The situation in France before the French Revolution.
- The outbreak of the revolution and the reaction of Louis XVI.
- The counter-revolutionaries and the reasons for the king's execution in 1793.
- The rule and fall of Robespierre and the aims of the Jacobins.
- The Thermidorian Reaction and the aims and rule of the Directory.
- Napoleon Bonaparte's rise to power.
- Napoleon's government of France, including his domestic aims and reforms.
- The formation of the French Empire and Napoleon's reputation in other countries.

Timeline

May 1774	Accession of Louis XVI
Feb 1787	Assembly of Notables takes place
Jul 1789	Storming of the Bastille during the revolution
Aug 1789	Declaration of the Rights of Man adopted
Jul 1790	Civil Constitution of the Clergy passed
Jun 1791	Louis XVI's Flight to Varennes
Apr 1792	French Revolutionary Wars begin
Jan 1793	Louis XVI executed; Robespierre and the Jacobins take power
Jul 1794	Robespierre executed; fall of the Jacobins
Nov 1795	Directory established
Nov 1799	End of the Directory; Napoleon becomes first consul
Jul 1801	Concordat with the pope
Mar 1804	Civil Code (Napoleonic Code) comes into force
May 1804	Napoleon becomes 'Emperor of the French'

Introduction

At its outbreak in 1789, many people believed that the French Revolution marked the dawn of an age of freedom and equality in France. However, the period was characterised by mass killings, intolerance and, eventually, the rise of the powerful **dictator** Napoleon Bonaparte. In fact, those who initiated the revolution did so in the hope of introducing only moderate changes. They did not predict that their efforts would have such an extreme and dramatic conclusion – the execution of the king and the establishment of a **republic** in France.

During the course of the revolution there were widespread changes in just about every sphere of life in France. With the overthrow of the monarchy, the power of the nobility declined. The middle class gained in both wealth and influence, while the peasantry was freed from many of the burdens that it had formerly borne. At the same time, the Roman Catholic Church lost much of its religious monopoly and power.

The French Revolution is generally divided into three distinct stages. The first stage, from 1789 to 1795, witnessed a rapid development from moderate to extreme opposition to the ruling classes. The second stage, up to 1799, marked a return to caution and conservatism. The final stage was the rule of Napoleon, who took the title 'first consul' in 1799 and established himself as the country's leader, promising to fulfil the ideals that had initiated the revolution ten years earlier. Napoleon became emperor in 1804, and although some revolutionary ideals survived, he largely failed to deliver on his promises.

dictator
An absolute ruler who controls a country without democratic institutions.

republic
A form of government in which the head of state is not a monarch, and where supreme power usually lies with a group of citizens elected by the people.

Figure 1.1 Fighting in the streets of Paris during the French Revolution, 1795

The aims and domestic problems of French politicians 1789–91

Long-term causes of the French Revolution

Before the French Revolution, France had been governed by a monarchy for most of its history. Indeed, the country was unique in Europe for the length of the reign of its kings – **Louis XIV** and **Louis XV** had governed France for more than 130 years between them (1643–1774). Their extended rule discouraged reform at a time of great change in the world beyond France.

The power of the king, the nobles and the Church

On the death of Louis XV in 1774, the throne passed to his grandson, **Louis XVI**. The new king was more enlightened than his predecessors had been, but the power and influence of the nobility remained strong, and few reforms could be implemented in the face of their resistance to change.

The king himself maintained considerable authority, and there were few limitations on the power of the monarch. Nobles enjoyed substantial privileges, including low taxes. Only a small middle class existed in France at the time, so the burden of taxes fell most heavily on the peasantry. Almost all French people followed the teachings of the Roman Catholic Church, which gave this institution immense influence. The Church used its power to support the monarchy and to oppose any reforms that might challenge the dominance of the *ancien régime*.

> **Note:**
> The term *ancien régime* ('old order') refers to monarchical governments and their strictly hierarchical societies before the French Revolution (although some historians believe that elements of these regimes continued well after the revolution). It applies particularly to France, and covers the country's system of government and administration, the structure of its society, the role of its Church, and the nature of its dominant arts and ideas.

Regional divisions and financial troubles

France was a difficult country to govern, as different regions had particular and diverse customs. Most of the population identified themselves more with their region than their country. In addition, there were significant differences in language, culture and law between the north and south of France:

- The language of the south was different from the language of the north.
- Some towns and cities had traditional rights that they guarded jealously, such as appointing local officials and voting for some taxes.
- Laws issued by the king were not applied automatically, but had to be recorded by local institutions throughout France. There were different systems of law in the north and the south.

By 1789, the most urgent problem Louis XVI faced was his country's financial debt. Continuous wars had proved expensive, especially France's intervention on the side of the Americans in their War of Independence (1775–83). Some ministers, including Viscount Calonne and Jacques Necker, tried to introduce reforms that included plans to raise money by imposing higher taxes on the wealthy. However, they were defeated by powerful groups amongst the nobility and Church, who defended their privileges against these reforms. Despite his overall authority, tradition prevented the king from imposing higher taxes without the agreement of these influential institutions.

Like many countries in Europe, France was a largely agricultural economy. Poor harvests over several years resulted in food shortages and rising food prices – a situation that forced many French citizens into poverty and starvation. Discontent grew, and there were increasing calls for change. The apparent indifference of the king and the nobles to the suffering of the lower classes created a tension that contributed significantly to the outbreak of the revolution. The rigid and unsympathetic attitude of the king's wife, **Marie Antoinette**, also added to his increasing unpopularity. The queen was regarded as wantonly extravagant at a time when many people were facing extreme hardship.

The Enlightenment

Despite these entrenched conservative structures, there were some signs of change in France throughout the 18th century – especially with the rise of the Enlightenment. This movement favoured new ideas about government and the rights of citizens, and therefore had significant revolutionary potential. The importance of the Enlightenment as a cause of the French Revolution has been much debated by historians. Some have argued that by undermining institutions such as the Church, the Enlightenment threatened the monarchy and thus played a key role in encouraging rebellion.

Note:

The Enlightenment was an intellectual movement that swept across Europe in the 17th and 18th centuries. Pioneered by thinkers and scientists such as Baruch Spinoza (1632–77), John Locke (1632–1704), Pierre Bayle (1647–1706), Isaac Newton (1643–1727) and Voltaire (1694–1778), the Enlightenment sought to place reason and science at the centre of human endeavour, pitting itself against religious irrationalism and superstition.

However, other historians have dismissed this as a romantic view, believing that practical issues such as taxation and the poor condition of the economy were the most significant causes of the revolution.

Short-term causes of the French Revolution

The main reason for the start of the revolution in 1789 was the refusal of the nobility to accept reforms that would interfere with their traditional privileges. In particular, there was friction over the French tax system, which imposed the heaviest taxes on the middle and working classes, while the upper classes and the nobility benefited from numerous tax exemptions and advantages. At a time when the French state was nearing bankruptcy from its involvement in expensive wars, this provoked widespread hostility.

In an effort to address the country's financial problems, Louis XVI agreed to call a meeting of the Estates General. This advisory assembly comprised representatives from the three classes, or 'estates', into which society was traditionally divided:

- **The First Estate:** the Church. Members in the Estates General were not ordinary clergy, but came from the upper levels of the Church hierarchy. These representatives were chosen informally by other clergy rather than being officially elected.
- **The Second Estate:** the nobility. Members of the Estates General were informally elected. A few nobles in the assembly were willing to embrace reform, but the majority resisted change.
- **The Third Estate:** everyone else. Although the majority of the Third Estate was made up of peasants, members of the Estates General were overwhelmingly from the middle class. Their demands therefore represented the interests of the middle class rather than the peasantry. The Third Estate sought change, but it did not aim to bring about revolution.

The king's decision to convene the Estates General in 1789 was a desperate measure. The assembly had last been called in 1614, and few people really understood either its procedures or the extent of its powers. Typically, each estate had the same number of votes in the Estates General. This meant that the Church and the nobility – traditional allies – could join forces to outvote the Third Estate and block any suggestion of reform. However, in 1789, the First Estate comprised 10,000 clergy and the Second Estate was made up of 400,000 nobles, while the Third Estate represented 25 million people. As such, the Third Estate demanded that voting should more fairly reflect the membership of the different classes. After three months of disputes, the Third Estate was eventually granted double its number of representatives in the Estates General, and the meeting began in May 1789.

Note:

Although some members of the Third Estate were convinced to participate in the Estates General after being granted double representation at the meeting, this turned out to be irrelevant. When it came to voting, the king upheld the traditional way that votes were counted – that is, the collective vote of each estate carried equal weight.

The start of the revolution

Louis XVI had ordered each of the three Estates to draw up a list of its grievances (called *cahiers*), which would be presented to the king and discussed at the meeting. All three groups agreed on certain matters, including the need for a constitution, liberty of the press and an end to **internal trade barriers**. However, there were many more issues on which they could not agree. Most importantly, the First and Second Estates refused to surrender their taxation privileges. The king himself proved his lack of leadership ability during the discussions, offering weak support to the First and Second Estates, but failing to take any firm decisions or enforce his own will. It quickly became clear that the situation was deadlocked.

internal trade barriers
Restrictions imposed by a government on the exchange of goods and services within a particular country.

Figure 1.2 A painting showing the opening of the meeting of the Estates General in 1789

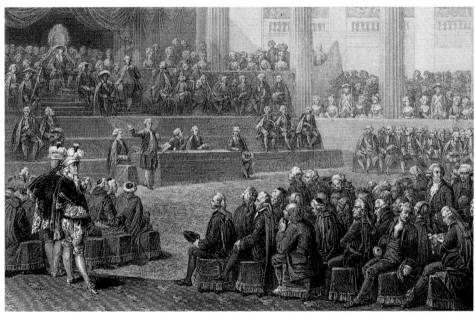

The National Assembly and the Tennis Court Oath

As a result of this impasse, representatives of the Third Estate decided to break away from the Estates General and form an independent assembly that would more fairly address the demands of the lower classes. Some clergy and nobles who favoured reform also joined this group, which called itself the National Constituent Assembly.

Although the National Assembly claimed to be working in favour of the king as well as the people, Louis XVI was angered by what he perceived to be a challenge to his royal authority. Urged on by his family and other advisors, on 19 June 1789 the king ordered that the hall in which the Assembly met should be locked. Armed guards were posted at the door and members were denied entry. Louis resolved to reassert his power by overturning the decisions made by the Assembly and dictating the few reforms that would be implemented.

Note:
The National Constituent Assembly was formed on 9 July 1789. It was dissolved just two years later, in September 1791. The group is alternatively referred to as the Constituent Assembly or the National Assembly.

Turned away from their meeting-place, members of the Assembly instead convened at a tennis court in the Saint-Louis district of Versailles on 20 June. There, 576 members swore an oath not to disperse until a new constitution for France had been established. The 'Tennis Court Oath', as it became known, was a significant moment in the history of the French Revolution. It was the first act of defiance against the king – and the first demonstration that decisions about the government of the country could be made by the people. Such defiance was exemplified by **Honoré Gabriel Riqueti, Count of Mirabeau**, a nobleman who supported the cause of the Third Estate and joined the National Assembly. Mirabeau declared: 'We shall not stir from our places save at the point of a bayonet.'

The storming of the Bastille

There were fears that Louis XVI would bring in the army to crush this unofficial gathering of the National Assembly. As a result, many French citizens flocked to the centre of Paris to show support for this new political movement that defended the rights of the people. Violence broke out and, on 14 July 1789, one of the first major actions of the revolution took place when crowds in Paris stormed the Bastille in an attempt to seize the guns and ammunition being stored there, to use against the king's soldiers. All those defending the building were killed.

Figure 1.3 A map of Paris in 1789

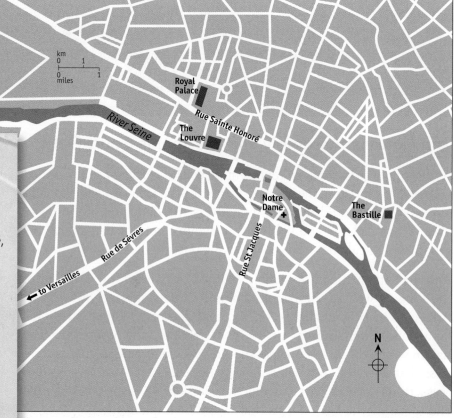

Note:

The Bastille was a fortress and prison in Paris, and was considered a symbol of the tyranny of the *ancien régime*, although at the time of its 'storming' in 1789 it housed only seven prisoners and was more important as a weapons and ammunition store. Bastille Day is still remembered every year on 14 July – a national day of celebration for the French.

The fighting grew steadily more intense. The citizens had become hardened to the gunfire. From all directions they clambered onto the roof of the Bastille or broke into the rooms. As soon as an enemy appeared among the turrets on the tower, he was fixed in the sights of a hundred guns and mown down in an instant. Meanwhile cannon fire was hurriedly directed against the inner drawbridge, which it pierced. In vain did the cannon on the tower reply, for most people were sheltered from it. People bravely faced death and every danger. Women, in their eagerness, helped us to the utmost; even the children ran here and there picking up the bullets. And so the Bastille fell and the governor, De Launey, was captured. Blessed liberty has at last been introduced into this place of horrors, this frightful refuge of monstrous despotism. De Launey was struck by a thousand blows, his head was cut off and hoisted on the end of a pike with blood streaming down all sides. The other officers were killed. This glorious day must amaze our enemies, and finally bring in for us the triumph of justice and liberty. In the evening, there were celebrations.

An extract from a French newspaper describing the fall of the Bastille, 14 July 1789.

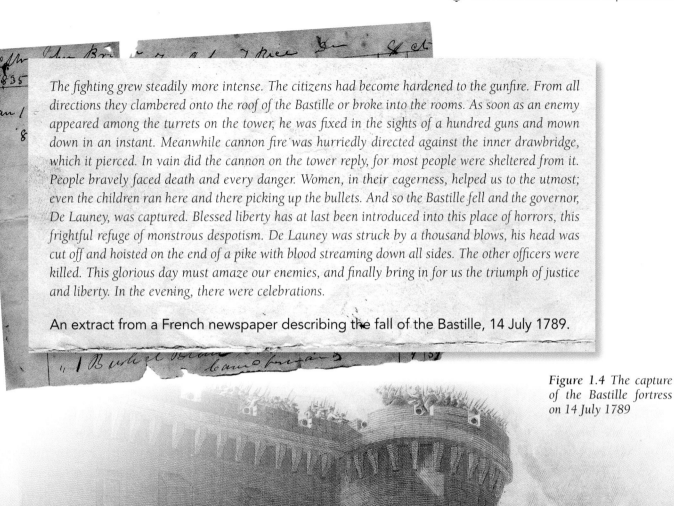

Figure 1.4 The capture of the Bastille fortress on 14 July 1789

One of the most radical groups in Paris at the start of (and indeed throughout) the revolution were the so-called *sans-culottes*. These working-class revolutionaries demanded democracy and equality, and were willing to resort to violence to achieve their aims. Amidst rumours that the king would overthrow the revolution, panic spread from Paris to the provinces and peasants began to riot. They seized property from landlords and stole food from stores; records with lists of services and taxes to be paid by the peasants were also destroyed. As the revolution gained momentum across France, some nobles – the *émigrés* (emigrants) – fled abroad to try to persuade other European monarchies to lend support in putting down the rebellion.

The August Decrees and the Declaration of the Rights of Man

feudalism
A system of social organisation that prevailed in Europe between the 9th and 15th centuries, but which persisted in some parts of the continent until the 19th century. In essence, feudalism relied on people holding land in return for service or labour to a wealthy landowner, placing them in a position of servitude.

The following month, the National Assembly issued the August Decrees – a series of new laws that effectively brought about the end of **feudalism** in France and granted many more rights to peasants and workers. The nobility agreed to abolish compulsory service by peasants, including unpaid work to repair roads, and to abandon the taxes that peasants usually had to pay their landlords at harvest time. The decrees also abolished law courts run by the nobility. In addition, the Church gave up the right to collect payments from the rest of the population, which had previously added greatly to its wealth.

On 26 August 1789, the Assembly issued the Declaration of the Rights of Man. This document was based on the American Declaration of Independence and was the first step in establishing a constitution for France. It stated that:

- all men were born free and had the rights of equality, liberty, security and property
- imprisonment without trial would be banned
- taxation was to be fairly apportioned to all people based on their wealth
- sovereignty lay with the people; no individual or group should be allowed to make decisions that went against the will of the people.

Louis XVI believed that the problems were temporary, but accepted the changes to prevent further disorder. However, unrest continued. A march headed by several thousand women went to Versailles and forced the royal family to return to Paris. Louis XVI and Marie Antoinette were greeted with cheers on their return, but the king now had to acknowledge formally the reforms introduced by the Assembly. A foreign ambassador reported that France was ruled by the Paris mob.

The situation by the end of 1789

The counter-revolutionaries (the people who opposed the revolution) included the king and the rest of the royal family, as well as almost all the nobility and the higher clergy. Outside France, several foreign governments also opposed the revolution – they were afraid that if it succeeded there, rebellion might break out in their own countries. Paris was the centre of revolutionary enthusiasm, and although the movement quickly gained a following in other parts of the country, support was not universal among the lower classes. In fact, in strongly Catholic regions such as Brittany and the Vendée in the far west, many people remained loyal to the Catholic king.

Even amongst the counter-revolutionaries there were divisions. The most hardline of them thought that the king should refuse to accept any changes to the way France was governed, and were determined to restore the *ancien régime* (see page 8) as swiftly as possible. More moderate counter-revolutionaries felt that certain reforms were reasonable and believed that the king should accept some limits on his power. However, they could not agree on the extent of these changes. The counter-revolutionaries looked to the king for leadership, but Louis was indecisive and failed to take a firm stand. As a result, those who opposed the revolution were not well-organised and had no clear programme of action for suppressing the rebellion and regaining control.

The revolutionaries also lacked strong leadership and a clear agenda for reform. The lower classes had many grievances against the *ancien régime*, but their remedies for the situation were vague at best. The people of France demanded equality, liberty, security and land ownership, but offered no detail about exactly what this meant or how it should be implemented. For some months after the royal family was brought to Paris from Versailles, the revolution moved uncertainly.

The situation required someone to act as an intermediary between the king and the revolutionaries. At first it seemed that the Count of Mirabeau (see page 12) might suit this role, but although Mirabeau was popular with the people, the king and his court distrusted him. Another moderate nobleman, **Gilbert du Motier, Marquis de Lafayette**, was suggested, but he expressed little enthusiasm for representing the demands of the more radical revolutionaries. Consequently, little progress was made by either side in the first months of the revolution.

The Civil Constitution 1790

As a symbol of the *ancien régime*, the Church naturally became a target for reformers. Some monasteries were dissolved and the Church's right to raise taxes was abolished, but these reforms were not controversial and leading clergy did not protest or appeal to the pope for support. However, in July 1790, the Assembly introduced a much more radical law – the Civil Constitution of the Clergy:

- The pope was deprived of his authority over the Church in France. He could no longer appoint archbishops and bishops (or, as a consequence, any clergy that served under them). Instead, bishops and parish clergy were to be elected by state officials.

Key figure

Gilbert du Motier, Marquis de Lafayette (1757–1834)

Lafayette was a French nobleman. He led the French soldiers who supported the American War of Independence, and returned as a national hero. When the French Revolution broke out, he favoured moderate reform and helped draw up the Declaration of the Rights of Man. However, he later came into conflict with the more radical revolutionaries, was arrested and spent five years in prison. Lafayette was released when Napoleon came to power.

- The number of bishoprics (districts or dioceses under the control of a bishop) was reduced.
- Some Church offices were abolished.
- The clergy were to be paid by the Church rather than the state, and their role was to be exclusively religious.

Even at this point, most clergymen supported the reforms, and Louis XVI accepted the Civil Constitution. However, the situation changed when the Assembly added a requirement for the clergy to sign an oath of loyalty to the Constitution. For many, this was a step too far. Only seven bishops and half the parish clergy agreed to take this oath. The pope publicly condemned not only the Civil Constitution but also all the revolutionary reforms that had been introduced. The French people were split between those who supported the Civil Constitution and its revolutionary principles, and those who remained faithful to the Church's traditional role in society.

The Flight to Varennes 1791

As the revolution continued, rumours began to circulate that the king was intending to seek safety abroad. So far, Louis had resisted advice to flee France – partly because he believed it was wrong for a king to abandon his

country in time of trouble, but also because he was afraid that if he deserted his throne, another royalist might take over in his absence. However, by 1791 the situation had changed. The pope's condemnation of the revolution stirred up further violence and the king had been largely unsuccessful in suppressing unrest across the country. Foreign monarchs – including Marie Antoinette's royal relations in Austria – had expressed disapproval of the developments taking place in France, but no one had offered any practical help in putting down the revolution. Louis felt that if he could escape abroad, he might be able to gather support more effectively.

On the night of 20 June 1791, therefore, Louis XVI and his family fled Paris. They set out for the royalist town of Montmédy, on the border with Luxembourg. There they hoped to be met by Austrian troops sent by Marie Antoinette's family. However, the flight was poorly organised and the disguises used by the king and his family were unconvincing. Their coach was halted at Varennes, 50 km (30 miles) from the border. The king and queen were arrested and taken back to Paris under heavy guard. They remained there until their executions in 1793.

Figure 1.5 Louis XVI and Marie Antoinette are arrested during the Flight to Varennes in 1791

Questions

1. What do you think was the most significant reason for the outbreak of the French Revolution in 1789?

2. Could the king, Louis XVI, have prevented the revolution from breaking out? Were there any points at which he could have halted its progress?

3. Why did the French Revolution lack a single leader?

4. In the extract from the French newspaper report of the storming of the Bastille on page 13, the writer refers to 'justice and liberty'. What specific social changes might he be referring to in these terms?

5. Source A below lists some of the accusations made against Louis XVI at his trial in 1792. How do these accusations compare to your own views on the primary causes of the French Revolution?

Source A

Louis, the French people accuse you of having committed a multitude of crimes in order to establish your tyranny by destroying its liberty …

You attacked the sovereignty of the people by suspending the assemblies of its representatives and by driving them by violence from the place of their sessions …

You caused an army to march against the citizens of Paris and caused their blood to flow. You withdrew this army only when the capture of the Bastille and the general uprising showed you that the people were victorious …

For a long time you contemplated flight and you made your escape as far as Varennes with a false passport …

You apparently accepted the new Constitution. Your speeches announced a desire to maintain it, but you worked to overthrow it before it was achieved …

Your brothers, enemies of the state, have rallied the émigrés. They have raised regiments, borrowed money, and formed alliances in your name …

You allowed the French nation to be disgraced in Germany, in Italy, and in Spain, since you did nothing to exact compensation for the ill treatment which the French experienced in those countries.

You caused the blood of Frenchmen to flow.

Adapted from the accusations made against King Louis XVI at his trial, 11 December 1792.

The instability of French governments 1791–99

In 1789, Louis XVI convened the Estates General, beginning a period of instability in France. In July the same year, the Estates General adopted the name the National Assembly as a sign of the authority that it claimed (see page 11). The Assembly lasted only two years, until 1791, when popular pressure forced it to call elections for a National Convention – an organisational structure that became official in 1792. The Convention soon came under the influence of its leading Jacobin members; the Committee of Public Safety was set up, dominated by the Jacobins (see page 20) and their leader Maximilien Robespierre. By 1795, a reaction against the Jacobins led to the fall of the Convention, the introduction of a new constitution, and the establishment of the Directory. All the governments during this period attempted to bring their own revolutionary aims to the fore, but all faced a variety of challenges.

Economic problems

Economic problems had been a major reason for the outbreak of the French Revolution in 1789, and these troubles continued into the 1790s. The state's debts remained, and so did the inefficient system for collecting taxes. Farmers began hoarding their grain rather than distributing it. The Assembly in Paris outlawed this practice, but it continued nonetheless, and food became scarce. **Assignats** were issued, but their value fell sharply as people lost confidence in the currency. As the revolution spread, the situation improved for members of the middle class, who could afford to buy land that had been seized from the nobility and the Church. However, those without any wealth at all – the peasants and the working classes in the towns and cities – suffered greatly. These problems were made worse by divisions amongst the revolutionaries. While moderates objected to the seizure of property and food, radicals demanded complete state control over them.

assignats
Paper money used instead of coins and guaranteed by the government. The value of this type of currency depended on people's confidence in it and their willingness to accept it as payment for goods.

The start of the Revolutionary Wars

In addition to internal disagreements, the revolutionaries faced a serious threat from abroad. The monarchies of Europe regarded Louis XVI as the rightful ruler of France, and were outraged by his arrest and imprisonment. The ideals of the revolution – reflected in the Declaration of the Rights of Man (see page 14) – threatened the peace in their own countries. Austria and Prussia, the strongest powers in central Europe, were particularly alarmed by the reforms. As French émigrés began gathering support in these countries, the National Assembly decided to declare war on Austria in 1792. The Duke of Brunswick, commander of the combined Austrian and Prussian forces, issued a manifesto defending an invasion of France and promising to restore Louis XVI to his full powers. Britain and Holland soon joined this anti-revolutionary alliance.

Most French army officers had been dismissed or had fled the country as royalists, and this left the French forces weak and lacking in strong leadership. When Prussian troops crossed the border and began marching on Paris, it seemed that the revolution might be crushed at last and the monarchy restored. On the advice of **Lazare Nicolas Marguerite, Count Carnot**, the Jacobin government increased French forces through conscription, and they won a surprising victory at the Battle of Valmy in September 1792. However, the danger to the revolution was not over, and there were fears of treason when Charles-François du Périer Dumouriez, a leading general, deserted and joined the Austrians. Such events only served to further weaken the government.

The rise of the radicals

From 1791, the government grew divided by suspicion. The more radical elements in the Assembly accused the moderates (the Feuillants) of collaborating with the king. In September 1791, a new constitution was introduced and the National Assembly was replaced by a new body called the Legislative Assembly. This allowed the radicals, especially the Jacobins and the Girondins (see below), to gain more influence. The 1791 Constitution benefited the middle class, but the *sans-culottes* in Paris (see page 14) and similar lower-class mobs in the provinces maintained disruptive powers that could not be ignored. The instability in the revolutionary government was shown when the Legislative Assembly was replaced by another ruling body, the Convention, just a few months later.

The Girondins and the Jacobins

The two leading radical groups during the French Revolution were the Girondins and the Jacobins. The Girondins were originally from the south of France. They supported the rights of the provinces to influence the revolutionary movement and were therefore opposed by those who regarded Paris as the centre of the revolution, including the *sans-culottes*. The Jacobins formed in Paris, although Jacobin clubs were later organised in the provinces, too. At the start of the revolution the Jacobins were relatively moderate in their demands, but they soon became more extreme.

Note:
The Jacobins were named after the place they held their early meetings – a convent in Rue St Jacques in Paris. They were also sometimes called the Montagnards ('Mountain People'), because they sat in the higher level of seats during debates in the Assembly.

The Girondins and the Jacobins were united by a hatred of the Church and a desire to end upper-class privilege. However, after the Flight to Varennes, the Girondins continued to encourage negotiation with Louis XVI – a policy that was not popular with other revolutionary groups. As a result, the Girondins lost both power and influence; many of them were arrested and some were even executed. This left power almost exclusively in the hands of the Jacobins and their influential leader **Maximilien Robespierre**.

The Jacobins had several priorities:

- **The fate of the king:** all the revolutionaries distrusted Louis XVI, but there was disagreement about what should be done with him. Some favoured further negotiation in the hope of reaching an agreement, but the Jacobins called for his execution.
- **The threat from royalist sympathisers within France:** the Jacobins used a policy of terror against anybody suspected of being a danger to the revolution (see below).
- **Progress in the Revolutionary Wars:** the fight against Austria and Prussia (and later Britain) went badly for France at first, but the Jacobins used Carnot's army and turned the tide. They were helped in this by a lack of effective co-operation between the opposing forces, which fought as individual units rather than a cohesive army. Eventually, the French revolutionary army was even able to take the initiative against Austria and Prussia.
- **The severe economic conditions within France:** problems increased rather than diminished after the outbreak of the revolution. As the administration collapsed, fewer people paid taxes. It was almost impossible to obtain loans from financiers. An absence of law and order affected trade and caused scarcities. The war was expensive.

The Reign of Terror

One of the first steps the Jacobins took once they had control of the Convention was establishing the Committee of Public Safety. This was given extensive powers to supervise military and legal affairs, and was dominated by the most hardline Jacobins under the leadership of Robespierre himself.

Between 1792 and 1794, the Jacobins used the Reign of Terror to consolidate their power. Robespierre set up a Revolutionary Tribunal in Paris to put on trial anyone suspected of being an 'enemy of the revolution'. Local committees serving a similar purpose also sprang up in the provinces, although these were often unofficial. In September 1792, a massacre of prisoners in Paris was carried out, in which more than 1000 people were killed. The justification for this was that the prisoners were conspiring to rise up and join a counter-revolutionary plot. However, although some of them were noblemen and clergy, many were common criminals with no political agenda.

Key figure

Maximilien Robespierre (1758–94)

The lawyer Robespierre was elected to the Estates General in 1789 as a member of the Third Estate. He was strongly critical of the monarchy and was one of the first to suggest that the king should be put on trial and that France should become a republic. Robespierre has become inextricably linked to the period known as the 'Reign of Terror', in which thousands of people were executed for opposing the revolution. He was eventually arrested and executed in July 1794.

Note:

Even in late 1792, it was not inevitable that Louis XVI would lose his life. There were still moderate revolutionaries who argued against his execution. They believed that the king's death would only increase the divisions between factions in France and strengthen the determination of foreign powers to intervene in the revolution.

The execution of the king

On 21 September 1792, a decree was passed that abolished the monarchy and proclaimed a republic in France. The king was put on trial and sent to the guillotine in January 1793. (Marie Antoinette met the same fate in October that year.) In celebration of a new era, a new calendar was introduced – the months were renamed and 1792 was designated Year I.

Figure 1.6 The execution of Louis XVI on 21 January 1793

Robespierre's cult

Robespierre himself was a man of high morality. He called for a 'Republic of Virtue' to replace Roman Catholicism, emphasising duty, the need for all citizens to help each other and a loyalty to democracy. Previous revolutionary leaders had curbed the power of the Church, but few had attacked Christianity itself. Robespierre now introduced the Cult of the Supreme Being to replace the worship of the Christian God. He himself led one of the ceremonial processions to introduce the cult.

Paris and many other large cities strongly supported extremist Jacobin rule, but agents sent from Paris by the Committee of Public Safety were not popular everywhere. There were still some members of the nobility who had not fled abroad, and they became the focus of loyalist activity. The clergy also commanded support in parts of the country where moderates or royalists remained dominant. The Jacobin agents sent to uncover and suppress anti-revolutionary feeling were ruthless, but their task was not an easy one.

Note:
The *sans-culottes* were the best known of the extremist groups acting in both Paris and the provinces, but several other groups emerged to enforce revolutionary law throughout the country. These included the *enragés* ('wild men'), *bras-nus* ('bare-armed') and *canaille* ('rabble').

The Law of Suspects

By September 1793, the Jacobins were facing several crises. Most significantly, the port of Toulon in the south was besieged by the British; if it fell, it would open up a base for counter-revolutionaries to make inroads into France. In response, the Convention passed a decree known as the Law of Suspects, which allowed people to be arrested on the basis of accusation rather than evidence. Guilt was defined in vague terms so that anybody who was not an active supporter of the regime could be charged. The accused were not allowed lawyers, and were tried in special tribunals presided over by Jacobin agents rather than judges. The only possible outcomes were acquittal or death.

Some historians claim that the Reign of Terror was a class war waged against the peasantry and the lower orders in the towns and cities. Certainly, victims of the Terror were not just aristocrats and clergymen. Members of the middle class also found themselves on trial, and many innocent people were sent to the guillotine simply because their accusers wanted to impress the authorities by their revolutionary zeal. It is estimated that around 40,000 people were killed during the Reign of Terror. Some believe this was necessary to ensure the survival of the revolution, and point to the fact that this violence was moderate compared to that carried out by 20th-century dictators such as Adolf Hitler and Joseph Stalin. However, the Reign of Terror shocked 18th-century Europe by its scale and lack of respect for legal institutions.

The fall of Robespierre

As the Reign of Terror swept through France, other revolutionary groups grew alarmed by just how extreme the Jacobins had become. In particular, the Law of Suspects was widely regarded as a step too far. As success in the Revolutionary Wars reduced the threat from abroad, some groups within France felt that the time was right to challenge Robespierre's rule. The disorder persuaded many people, even in Paris, that Robespierre was too dictatorial. The Committee of Public Safety was becoming overly powerful – ignoring the Convention – and the Committee itself was divided. The Jacobins were falling apart. Robespierre made plans to purge the Committee, but the Convention decided to act against him in what became known as the Thermidorian Reaction. Robespierre was arrested in 1794, and 80,000 prisoners were released from jail. After a failed suicide attempt, Robespierre was executed on 28 July 1794; around 90 of his colleagues were also killed.

Note:
The Thermidorian Reaction was named after Thermidor, the month in the new French Revolution calendar in which Robespierre fell from power.

Robespierre remains a controversial historical figure. Some commentators believe that he saved the revolution from defeat at a critical time. Others condemn the dictatorial nature of his rule and the executions that took place under his leadership. On a personal level, Robespierre was also a man of contradictions. He was known as 'The Incorruptible' and was highly principled. He firmly believed that power belonged to the people and not to governments. However, he proved himself to be a ruthless politician and would not tolerate rivals even among his fellow Jacobins, many of whom he sent to the guillotine.

We want a state of affairs where all unworthy and cruel passions are unknown, and all kind and generous passions are aroused by the laws. Ambition becomes the desire to deserve glory and to serve the fatherland. The citizen submits to the magistrate, the magistrate to the people and the people to justice. The fatherland guarantees the well-being of each individual, and where each individual enjoys with pride the prosperity and glory of the fatherland. Commerce is the source of public wealth and not only of the monstrous riches of a few people.

In our country we want to substitute morality for selfishness, honesty for honour, the rule of reason for the tyranny of tradition, the contempt of vice for the contempt of misfortune, love of glory instead of love of money, good people instead of the advantages of birth, a generous, powerful, happy people instead of despicable people – that is to say, all the virtues and all the miracles of the Republic for all the vices and all the absurdities of the monarchy.

What kind of government can realize these marvels? Only a democratic or republican government.

Jacobin leader Maximilien Robespierre, in a speech explaining his 'Republic of Virtue'.

Historical debate

One of the main areas of debate about the French Revolution concerns Maximilien Robespierre. Historians disagree about whether he was a tyrant, seeking only to fulfil his own ambitions, or whether he took extreme steps in the interests of justice for the common people of France. Below are two views of Robespierre's policies.

Source A

From the standpoint of the subordinated and oppressed, the very existence of a state is a fact of violence in the same sense in which, for example, Robespierre said ... that one does not have to prove that the king committed any specific crimes, since the very existence of the king is a crime, an offence against the freedom of the people. In this strict sense, every violence of the oppressed against the ruling class and its state is ultimately 'defensive'.

Historian Sophie Wahlich, In Defence of the Terror, 2012.

Source B

For the first time in history terror became an official government policy, with the stated aim to use violence in order to achieve a higher political goal. Unlike the later meaning of 'terrorists' as people who use violence against a government, the terrorists of the French Revolution were the government.

Historian Marisa Linton criticises Robespierre as a terrorist, in 'Robespierre and the Terror', History Today, Vol. 56, Issue 8.

The Directory 1795

The death of Robespierre marked the end of the most bloodthirsty period of the revolution and the start of a move away from the extremism that had characterised Jacobin rule. The Convention drew up a new constitution in August 1795. In order to balance power and avoid the dictatorship of one man or one group, the Directory was established, which had two councils:

- The Council of Five Hundred (with 500 members) proposed laws.
- The Council of Ancients (with 250 members) accepted or rejected the proposed laws.

In addition, there were five directors, who were selected by the Ancients from a list drawn up by the Five Hundred. They were responsible for choosing government ministers, army leaders, tax collectors and other officials. The directors and those who supported them came from the middle class, which had gained from the revolution – acquiring land and benefiting from trade. Now these men wanted to make sure they did not lose such advantages. Although they made money from their positions in the new government, claims that the directors were totally corrupt are probably exaggerated.

Note:

The Directory has received less attention from historians than the early stages of the French Revolution and the later rule of Napoleon Bonaparte. Some historians believe that the French Revolution really ended in 1794 with the death of Robespierre, but others point to the continuing work of the Directory in building on the positive reforms that had been introduced since 1789.

The Directory faced considerable problems. The treasury was empty and the government was almost bankrupt. The continuing war with foreign monarchies was expensive. Although the Reign of Terror was over, factions still existed within France, and royalists, Jacobins and moderate republicans continued to fight for their own agendas. In fact, these internal divisions helped the Directory to survive – the lack of co-operation between other political groups meant that none of them was strong enough to challenge the new government.

Importantly, the Directory had the support of the army. If the royalists won back control of France, the war against Austria would end and many soldiers would be unemployed. The Directory also needed the army to put down the uprisings carried out by dissatisfied groups. The government could not escape the opposition of the Jacobins and other radicals, who believed that members of the Directory had betrayed the revolution. Anger against the government increased after a severe winter in 1795–96 led to a shortage of food. Riots broke out and there were calls for the 1795 Constitution – by which the Directory ruled – to be abolished. The Directory called on the army to suppress the revolts and the National Guard, formerly a focus of lower-class agitation, was re-formed to bring it under control.

The Jacobins were not yet defeated, though, and in 1796 they launched a plot to overthrow the Directory and replace it with a 'Republic of Equals'. The Babeuf Plot (named after one of its leaders, Gracchus Babeuf) was well organised. The rebels issued a newspaper to spread their ideas and gather support, and began stockpiling weapons in preparation for the fight ahead. However, police spies uncovered the plot and the Jacobin leaders were arrested. Babeuf was executed.

People of France:

Never before has a vaster plan been conceived of or carried out. Here and there a few men of genius, a few men, have spoken in a low and trembling voice. None have had the courage to tell the whole truth.

The moment for great measures has arrived. Evil has reached its height: it covers the face of the Earth. In the name of politics, chaos has reigned for too many centuries. Let everything be set in order and take its proper place once again. Let the supporters of justice and happiness organise in the voice of equality. The moment has come to found the REPUBLIC OF EQUALS, this great home open to all men. The day of general restitution has arrived. Groaning families, come sit at the common table set by nature for all its children.

An extract from the 'Manifesto of the Equals', issued by the Jacobin plotters in 1796.

Although the Babeuf plot failed and the Directory survived, by 1797 it was becoming isolated. Having excluded both extreme wings of opinion (royalists and Jacobins), it now began to lose the support of the moderates, too, mainly due to its reliance on the army.

Successive elections saw the return of critics into the ranks of the Directory, including **Emmanuel Joseph Sieyès**.

The rise of Napoleon and the fall of the Directory 1799

The Directory pursued an active foreign policy, partly to satisfy the army and partly to win popular support. Two armies were sent against Austria, one in the north and one in the south to attack Austrian-controlled parts of Italy. The southern army was led by a young commander called Napoleon Bonaparte, whose outstanding success in the Italian campaign cemented his reputation and brought him to wide public attention in France.

After his victories against Austria, Napoleon was encouraged to lead an expedition to Egypt. The government hoped to weaken Britain's influence in the Mediterranean, but an underlying motive for this campaign was to keep Napoleon out of France, where his popularity made him a threat. In fact, this plan backfired, as although he was defeated in Egypt he was still welcomed back to France in triumph.

Key figure

Emmanuel Joseph Sieyès (1748–1836)

Sieyès was a priest and a politician during the French Revolution. He criticised the privileges of the Church and the nobility, and supported the Third Estate in the 1789 Estates General. Sieyès disliked the 1795 Constitution and at first refused to serve in the Directory. However, he was so popular that he eventually gave in to pressure and became a director. Despite this, he believed that the government was inefficient and self-serving, and he helped Napoleon come to power in 1799. He was made one of the three consuls (see page 28), but he resigned in protest when Napoleon declared himself emperor in 1804.

Figure 1.7 Napoleon Bonaparte as general of the army in Italy in 1795

By 1799, the Directory was in disarray. The directors were plotting against each other and against other groups, and Napoleon himself had ambitions to play a political role. Together with two of the directors, he proposed several changes to the 1795 Constitution. When these were rejected by the Directory's Council, Napoleon called on his loyal soldiers to impose his will. On 9 November 1799, he staged a coup and overthrew the Directory. In its place, he established the Consulate, with himself the chief of the three consuls who now controlled France.

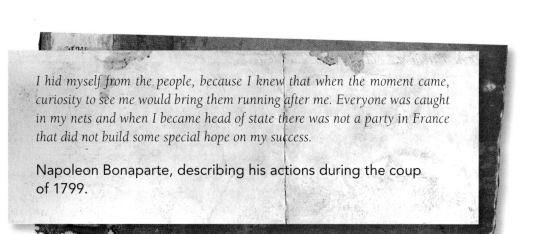

I hid myself from the people, because I knew that when the moment came, curiosity to see me would bring them running after me. Everyone was caught in my nets and when I became head of state there was not a party in France that did not build some special hope on my success.

Napoleon Bonaparte, describing his actions during the coup of 1799.

How important was the French Revolution?

The period of radical and violent revolution in France lasted only ten years, but this short period of history does not reflect its importance. Louis XVI was executed in 1793, and although kings from his family ruled from 1814 to 1848, the restoration of the monarchy was short-lived. France became a republic again and remains so today. Thus, Robespierre and the Jacobins laid the foundations of modern France. The influence of the nobility in France ended. Nobles retained their titles but they no longer dominated the politics, economy and society of France.

Indirectly, the French Revolution affected the political systems in other European countries. Absolute monarchies continued for some years, but the French Revolution launched a wave of democratic forces that eventually brought about change. Absolute rulers survived in some states – for example, in southern Italy – but only until the middle of the 19th century. The exception to this was Russia, where the Romanov family of tsars retained absolute authority until the 1917 Revolution (see Chapter 5).

In France, the revolution benefited the middle class more than other groups. Members of this class gained from land transfers and from changes in trade. The Directory and Napoleon, as well as later governments, took pains to win the support of these people. Peasants were freed from feudal obligations and Church taxes, but neither they nor the poor who lived in towns gained political power until the late 19th century.

Questions

1 What do you think were the three most significant turning points in the course of the French Revolution between 1789 and 1799? Give reasons for your choices.

2 What had the revolution achieved by 1799?

3 With reference to the historical debate on page 25, which view of Robespierre do you find most convincing?

Napoleon Bonaparte's rise to power

Napoleon's youth

Corsica is a small island in the Mediterranean Sea, closer to Italy than France. It was governed by Genoa, an Italian port, until local revolutionaries tried to make it independent. France intervened and gained control of the island by the terms of the Treaty of Versailles in 1768. Napoleon Bonaparte was born in Corsica a year later, and therefore became a French citizen.

The Bonaparte family were minor nobility, traditionally lawyers and with sufficient money to employ servants. However, their fortunes dwindled and they were poor by the time Napoleon was born. The young man showed a talent for mathematics, which was an advantage when he entered the army. He had a special interest in **artillery**, rather than the more prestigious **cavalry**. His skill at mathematics gave him insight into the important practical needs of an army, including training, supplies, map-reading and the use of guns. (A French general reported that Napoleon had 'much science and equal intelligence, and perhaps even too much courage'.)

artillery
Large weapons such as cannons or big guns, usually operated by a crew of people rather than an individual.

cavalry
Soldiers who are trained to fight on horseback.

Napoleon during the revolution

Napoleon's career survived the uncertainty of the revolutionary years. He remained loyal to his new masters when other royalist officers refused to swear allegiance to the revolutionary authorities after 1789. When Britain sent support to counter-revolutionaries in the important southern port of Toulon, Napoleon was dispatched with his artillery troops to defend the region. Although he was only a junior officer at the time, his skilful planning and courageous actions contributed to the successful defence of Toulon. It was a turning point in his career.

Napoleon was politically close to the Jacobins during the Reign of Terror (see pages 21–3), but in the turmoil of the times this was a risky allegiance. When Robespierre was executed, Napoleon was arrested but he was quickly released by the Directory, which realised that his military talents could be put to good use. Napoleon was sent to northern Italy, where he furthered his reputation by conducting a bold and successful campaign. The Treaty of Campo Formio (1797) gave France power in Italy and money for its treasury.

It was not long before Napoleon was regarded as France's best general. However, his growing ambitions began to be seen as a threat to the Directory. He was enthusiastic about a plan to take control of Egypt – a link between Britain and its eastern empire in

Note:
The Treaty of Campo Formio was important for France and for Napoleon personally. By the terms of the treaty, France gained Belgium from Austria, as well as winning parts of Italy. This was Napoleon's treaty and showed that he had become an international figure.

India – with the possibility of gaining a colony for France. Winning over this ancient civilisation would bring prestige to France and to Napoleon personally. In the event, the Egyptian campaign was a failure – the British commander, Admiral Horatio Nelson, destroyed the French fleet during the Battle of the Nile. However, propaganda about events in Egypt ensured that Napoleon returned to France a hero. Instead of harming his reputation, the Egyptian expedition only strengthened his popularity.

The coup of 1799

By 1799, the Directory was accused of inefficiency and corruption, and lost popularity due to the failure of several foreign campaigns. Support grew for a return of the monarchy, not only among the émigrés (see page 14) but also among the general population in France. On the opposite side of the political divide were the Jacobins, who demanded the return of the more radical policies that had been introduced early in the revolution. There was a real danger that civil war would break out. Napoleon saw his chance, and with the help of the army, seized power in an action that became known as the coup of 18 Brumaire, after the date it took place in the revolutionary calendar (see page 22).

Immediately after the coup, the director Sieyès – who had supported Napoleon – began moves to limit the power of the Council of Five Hundred (see page 25). This was a controversial step. Although the Council was blamed for the loss of government control in the provinces and for the failures of France's foreign wars, many people still supported it, believing that its democratic nature was true to the principles of the revolution. Napoleon encouraged members of the council to back Sieyès' reforms, but they were unwilling to relinquish their control and the plan failed. Fearing that this would damage his reputation, Napoleon and his brother Lucien rounded up military support and dispersed members of the Council by force.

Sieyès had used Napoleon's influence to serve his own agenda, but the director underestimated the ambitious general. When the Directory was replaced by the Consulate – a smaller body, intended to be more efficient – Napoleon ensured that he was appointed 'first consul'. Sieyès was also a consul, but had far less influence. This was Napoleon's first decisive step towards complete power in France.

> **Note:**
> The Consulate had three assemblies. The Council of State drew up laws and other documents related to the running of the state. The Tribunate discussed these bills, but had no power to vote on them. The Legislative Assembly voted on the bills, but was not allowed to discuss (and therefore change) them. Real authority lay with the three consuls, of which Napoleon was the most powerful.

Questions

1. Why was Napoleon able to rise to power by 1799?

2. To what extent did the Directory achieve its goals?

3. What does Napoleon's rise to power say about the weaknesses of the French Revolution?

Napoleon's domestic aims 1799–1804

Although Napoleon shared nominal power with the two other consuls, in reality he was the leader of the Consulate and had almost total control. A new constitution confirmed Napoleon's power, giving him the right to appoint ministers, as well as national and local officials, who would be responsible only to him. Within five years, he had transformed politics in France and imposed his will on the entire nation. Many historians believe that this period marked the height of Napoleon's domestic achievements.

Napoleon as first consul

ideology
A body of ideas and beliefs that forms the basis of a social, economic or political system.

Unlike Lenin in Russia, who was devoted to Marxism, or Hitler in Germany, who supported Nazism, Napoleon did not have any single **ideology**. He adopted any ideas (and used any people) that he felt would ensure order and efficiency. This sometimes meant accepting contradictions. For example, in theory Napoleon's laws guaranteed equality, but in practice they favoured particular social groups such as employers over workers, or men over women. The rule of law was proclaimed but Napoleon used his powers, sometimes illegally, to crush opposition. Napoleon claimed to rule by the will of the people – a revolutionary ideal – but he justified his government through the will of God (divine right), a claim also made by the monarchs of the *ancien régime*.

Note:

The most famous example of Napoleon's disregard for the rule of law was an incident involving the Duke of Enghien. Enghien was a royal émigré, related to the Bourbon kings who had been overthrown during the revolution. Believing the duke was a threat to his own position, Napoleon had him seized from his home in Baden (outside France), put on trial on false charges and then executed.

The Napoleonic Code

Since the start of the revolution, all governments had tried to bring order to the system of law in France, but few had made any significant progress. To address this problem, Napoleon decided to issue a unified code of law to replace the complex system that existed at the time. Many of these laws were based on ancient traditions, others came from regional customs, and still others were dictated by the Church. Moreover, the north and south of the country tended to follow different legal procedures. The south relied on Roman law – the system of written laws developed from those established during the days of the Roman Empire. The north tended to follow common, or customary, law, which interpreted the laws according to traditions and local practice. There were also differences in property laws and in the powers of courts throughout the different regions. This lack of coherence created uncertainty for governments and generated confusion among the population, particularly in areas that made use of both Roman and common law.

Napoleon asked the Council of State to design one set of laws for all parts of France and all social groups. He took a personal interest in the process, attending many of the meetings and approving other recommendations made in his absence. In developing these reforms, Napoleon used men of talent whatever their background – royalist or revolutionary – as long as they were efficient and reliable.

The outcome of this was the Civil Code of 1804, usually called the Napoleonic Code. This gave the country a common set of laws that were imposed by Napoleon and could not be challenged by traditions and local rights. The Napoleonic Code included some of the reforms that had been introduced during the revolution: there was equality under the law; privileges and feudal practices were abolished; and land formerly owned by the Church was confirmed as belonging to those who had been granted it during the era of rebellion. All these measures proved to the people that Napoleon wanted to safeguard the revolution.

Figure 1.8 Napoleon (seated on the left on the far side of the table), at a meeting of the Council of State during discussions about the Napoleonic Code in 1804

Social and economic changes

Much of the male population of France benefited in some way from Napoleon's reforms, as the same laws applied to all people, whatever their class. However, women were not considered a significant political force at the time, and Napoleon's social policies reflected this attitude:

- Many of the rights that women had been granted since 1789 were reversed. The authority of a husband over his wife and children was restored. Married women were ordered to obey their husbands and were prevented from making legal contracts.
- Women were allowed to seek divorce, but on much more restricted terms than men.

Although such reforms may seem unjust, many historians argue that Napoleon was no different from many other European rulers at the time. Apart from the most radical revolutionaries in France, few people supported women's rights, believing that the traditional structure of the family – under the rule of the husband – was the very foundation of society. Overall, women may have had fewer rights under Napoleon than they did under the revolutionary governments that came before him, but they were no worse off than most women in Europe at the start of the 19th century.

In addition to his social policies, as first consul Napoleon attempted to address France's financial problems. The revolutionary governments had recognised that the inefficient system of tax collection was a major issue. Before 1789, tax farmers were used in France – groups of financiers who had bought the right to collect taxes for the government. The tax farmers were widely unpopular among the French people because they often took a large share of the money for themselves, instead of paying it all to the government. After 1789, the corrupt system of using tax farmers had been replaced by local authorities responsible for collecting taxes, but this move had not resolved the situation. Napoleon decided to use his own officials, the prefects, to collect taxes. He also confirmed the Le Chapelier law, introduced in 1791, which banned trade unions and made strikes illegal.

When Napoleon came to power, there was no reliable banking system in France. After the revolution, four banks were created, but they did not have state backing and quickly foundered. The government-backed Bank of France was founded in 1800 and was run by the influential Swiss banker Jean Frédéric Perregaux. This helped strengthen France's finances, although debts remained high largely because of the costs of war.

> **Note:**
> The Bank of France was different from the Bank of England (which had been established more than 100 years previously), because it was supervised by the government. The Bank of England was independent – it issued bank notes, arranged loans to the government and managed the deposits made by tax collectors.

Religion under Napoleon

The Church's links with the monarchy and the *ancien régime* meant that it came under immediate attack when the revolution broke out. The changes imposed on the Church by revolutionary governments were widely popular at first. However, later religious reforms were controversial, particularly those introduced by Robespierre. His Cult of the Supreme Being and policy of de-Christianisation were major reasons for his downfall.

Napoleon was not a religious man, but he recognised the importance of religion to the French people. Priests were still influential members of society, especially the poor clergy who lived in villages and in town parishes. Napoleon saw religion as a social bond and a useful support for his government.

In 1801, he made a concordat (official agreement) with Pope Pius VII, by which Napoleon recognised Roman Catholicism in France. In return for this acknowledgement, he was allowed to nominate the men who would serve as bishops in France, which meant he could choose those who supported his regime. The concordat was soon revised without reference to the pope. Papal bulls (official statements) could only be published in France with the permission of the first consul, and bishops were placed under the authority of Napoleon's prefects. This gave Napoleon immense power. He controlled the bishops, and the bishops controlled the clergy. In this way, the Church became an important agency for Napoleonic propaganda and centralised power.

A few people believed that the pope had made a poor bargain, and some radicals opposed any deal with the Church. However, most of the population was content. They had their churches and priests, but kept the lands that the Church had forfeited during the revolution. Minority groups such as the Huguenots (French Protestants) and Jews were tolerated and allowed to practise their religion free of persecution. Napoleon extended this policy of tolerance to territories that he conquered, too.

Napoleonic propaganda

Historians generally agree that Napoleon was a skilled self-promoter. Both during his rise to power and particularly during the early years of his reign, he employed propaganda techniques to emphasise his leadership qualities and to spread his message to the French people – and to the world at large. His military actions abroad undoubtedly assisted in cementing his popularity at home and provided a key element in his later propaganda. He claimed that his aim was to break down the national barriers in Europe for the benefit of the different populations, bringing to them the advantages that France had gained from the revolution. He also made much of the claim that he was a liberator in his early campaign in Italy in 1796.

The arts and sciences

Napoleon embarked on large-scale public activities that were often intended as propaganda for his rule. When he invaded Egypt in 1798, he took archaeologists and historians with him to study and bring back ancient Egyptian records and artefacts. During his time as first consul, he encouraged the work of scientists. Famous French artists recorded Napoleon's heroism and achievements. Festivals were organised throughout France in Napoleon's honour. A well-known example of Napoleon's propaganda is the series of medals he had made to celebrate his accomplishments. One of the earliest of these was created in 1797, shortly after the signing of the Treaty of Campo Formio (see page 30). The medal showed Napoleon on his horse, holding an olive branch. It also depicted the figure of Victory carrying a statue and several manuscripts. In this way, Napoleon emphasised not only his military skills and his desire for peace, but also his role as a patron of the arts.

The press and censorship

Napoleon was keen to ensure that the French people received only positive messages about his regime, and he achieved this through policies of control and censorship. Theatres were controlled and used to gain popular support, from the Comédie Française with classic plays to the Théâtre de la Gaieté for the working classes. Newspapers and journals were censored, and Napoleon established six newspapers, designed to spread his own message to the widest possible spectrum of the French people.

The end of the Consulate

In 1804, Napoleon abandoned the Consulate and had himself crowned emperor. His coronation was a magnificent event, following the style of coronations of the French kings of the past (except that Napoleon placed the crown on his own head). Pope Pius VII was in attendance, to represent the approval of God and the Church.

The object of my dearest thoughts has always been the happiness of the French people, and their glory the object of my labours. Called by Divine Providence and the Constitutions of the Republic to Imperial power, I see in this new order of things nothing but greater means of assuring, within and without, the national power and prosperity. I take comfort with confidence in the powerful aid of the Almighty. He will inspire His Ministers to support me by all means within their power. They will enlighten their people by wise instruction, preaching to them love of duty, obedience to law, and the practice of all the Christian and civil virtues. They will call the blessing of Heaven upon the nation and on the Supreme Head of State.

Napoleon's proclamation on becoming emperor, 1804.

Figure 1.9 Napoleon crowns his wife Josephine as empress at their coronation in 1804

Although his position as emperor contradicted the idea of a republican government in France, Napoleon claimed that the change would unify the country and allow him to continue enforcing the best features of the revolution. The establishment of the empire was confirmed by popular approval through **plebiscites**, giving the impression that France was a democracy. However, these votes were arranged to result in an overwhelming majority in favour of the change. Napoleon styled himself 'Emperor of the French', perhaps to emphasise his links to the general populace.

There has been some debate about why Napoleon declared himself emperor in 1804, as he already exercised total control over France in his role as first consul. There are several possible reasons:

- The title 'emperor' simply implied more grandeur than that of consul.
- Having an emperor might reconcile royalists to the new regime.
- It would have been too controversial to declare himself king, but emperor was a title known throughout Europe and would still ensure that the succession would be hereditary, unlike the elected consuls.

plebiscites
Referendums (votes) giving people the opportunity to express their opinion for or against a proposal relating to a constitutional issue.

From this time onwards, Napoleon ruled in regal splendour. Like other emperors, he had a large court and placed an emphasis on ceremonies. His soldiers were given new uniforms and favoured followers were bestowed with imperial titles.

Who gained from Napoleon's policies?

It could be argued that almost all Frenchmen gained from Napoleon's policies. There was less corruption and inefficiency than there had been under the Directory. Laws were clear and most of the population no longer lived in fear of sudden arrest. Taxes were high but were universal – nobody was exempt as they had been under the *ancien régime*. The religious changes were overwhelmingly popular.

However, there were limits to the rule of law. Napoleon sometimes acted illegally and the police, under the minister **Joseph Fouché**, could be heavy-handed. State prisons were re-established for political crimes. In addition, some social groups benefited more than others from Napoleon's rule. Votes in elections were limited to those with an annual income of more than 150 francs – much more than peasants and the lower classes in the towns could hope to earn. Napoleon needed the support of landowners, nobles and the urban middle class. Financiers did well, and were encouraged to make profits. Manufacturers who made goods such as clothes, weapons and ammunition, which were needed by the army, also flourished.

One of Napoleon's favourites during his rise to power was **Charles Talleyrand**, a noble-born priest. However, Napoleon also won support from middle-class professionals, including doctors and teachers, who reaped the benefits. Coming from a relatively humble background himself, Napoleon was drawn to similar men, and he introduced a system in which appointments and promotions were based on talent rather than status. It was coincidence that this practice also happened to be one of the ideals of the revolution.

Napoleon operated this same form of promotion through merit in the army. Many of his generals joined the army after the outbreak of the revolution in 1789, and at first he insisted on their training in a military academy. Later, though, ordinary soldiers could earn promotion by their performance on the battlefield. Unlike those before the revolution, most of Napoleon's marshals came from families with no previous connections to the army; they were the sons of stonemasons, merchants, surveyors and even artists and musicians.

A few had served in the royal army before the revolution, and their rewards under Napoleon were considerable – some were made dukes, princes and even kings of territories that France conquered.

Key figure

Joseph Fouché (1759–1820)

An extreme Jacobin, Fouché flourished during the unpredictable early years of the revolution. After the Reign of Terror he survived Robespierre's fall, turning against him just in time. By 1800, Fouché was minister of police, in charge of an extensive policing system, but kept his contacts with royalists. He joined Louis XVIII when the king was restored, informing on those who had aided Napoleon.

Napoleon's foreign policy and empire

Historians are generally divided into two groups when considering Napoleon's foreign policy. Some believe that he wished to liberate Europe from the control of tyrant rulers and spread the high ideals of the French Revolution. Others think that he was driven by an increasing desire for power, seeking only to enhance his own prestige. The fact that, under Napoleon's leadership, France was almost continuously engaged in conflict with foreign powers lends some support to this belief.

The claim that Napoleon went to Italy as a liberator is also not wholly convincing. France's political interests were a more significant reason for French interference there than any feeling of responsibility towards the foreign-ruled Italians. The Directory saw this raid on Italy as a sideshow – the main attack on Austria was intended to be in the north and Napoleon's expedition was meant primarily to divide the Austrian army. French gains in a treaty with Austria were considered to be more important than Napoleon's successes in Italy.

His foreign policy was an important reason why Napoleon gained power as first consul in 1799 and was later able to establish himself as emperor. By 1799, the French people were comparing him favourably with the directors, whose success in governing France seemed limited. However, once he was in power, France enjoyed only one year of peace until Napoleon's final defeat in 1815.

Napoleon was an outstanding general and his victories against continental countries continued until he overreached himself. He made two major errors that proved fatal. He became involved in a long series of campaigns against Spain and Portugal and then made an even more serious mistake by invading Russia. These drained France of resources, whilst Britain – always supreme at sea – continued to resist him. Napoleon was forced to abdicate and leave France in 1814. He made a desperate but brief effort to regain power in 1815. However, his defeat at the Battle of Waterloo was followed by a permanent exile on the remote island of St Helena.

The 'Napoleonic Legend'

Napoleon may have arrived at a position of power controversially, but he soon gained the support of most of the French population. Although he ruled as a dictator and made little attempt to fulfil the revolutionary ideal of democracy, he was not a harsh leader. He encouraged people to forget the past, and only those who refused to do so were punished; the extreme royalists and republicans would never have been won over. The most convincing proof of his popularity was his return from exile in 1814. With a great deal of popular support, he drove out the restored monarch Louis XVIII and

Key figure

Charles Talleyrand (1754–1838)

The aristocrat Talleyrand was a bishop before the revolution. After 1789, he supported the revolutionary governments in their Church reforms. He helped bring Napoleon to power and to form the Consulate. However, by 1813, Talleyrand had lost faith in Napoleon and instead worked for the restoration of the monarchy. Louis XVIII later appointed him French representative at the Congress of Vienna, which dismembered Napoleon's empire. When asked later what he had done during the French Revolution, Talleyrand replied: 'I survived.'

once more assumed power himself. Ultimately, it was not a French uprising that defeated him, but foreign enemies.

Napoleon's fame and influence – often described as the Napoleonic Legend – lasted long after his death in 1821. Many of his laws and methods of administration continued even under the restored monarchies from 1815 to 1848. Successive kings, including Louis XVIII, Charles X and Louis Philippe, believed them too useful to replace, and some of them even survive to this day. In an effort to increase his own popularity, Louis Philippe allowed Napoleon's body to be buried in Paris in an elaborate ceremony in 1840. His tomb still attracts thousands of visitors – French people and foreigners alike – every year.

Figure 1.10 Pictures of Napoleon often show him in heroic poses

Questions

1. How far did Napoleon Bonaparte maintain freedom in France from 1799 to 1804?

2. How did Napoleon ensure his continued popularity in the period 1799–1804?

3. Explain the reasons why Napoleon introduced social and economic changes in France during his time as first consul.

Key issues

The key features of this chapter are:

- the origins of the French Revolution

- the reaction of Louis XVI to the revolution and how this contributed to his downfall

- the aims of different groups of revolutionaries

- the impact of war and economic problems on France during the revolution

- reasons for the instability of the revolutionary governments from 1789 to 1795 and of the Directory up to 1799

- Napoleon Bonaparte's rise to power and his policies in the early years of his rule.

Revision questions

1 How far was Louis XVI responsible for the problems of the monarchy from 1789 to 1793?

2 Was Robespierre more a success or a failure as a revolutionary leader?

3 'Napoleon's domestic policies did more to increase his power than extend liberty in France.' How far do you agree with this claim?

Further reading

Dwyer, P. and McPhee, P. *The French Revolution and Napoleon*. London, UK. Routledge. 2002.

Ellis, G. *Napoleon (Profiles in Power)*. London, UK. Longman. 2000.

Emsley, C. *Napoleon: Conquest, Reform and Reorganisation*. London, UK. Pearson. 2003.

Jones, P. *The French Revolution 1787–1804*. London, UK. Pearson. 2003.

Kates, G. *The French Revolution*. London, UK. Routledge. 2008.

Rees, D. and Townson, D. *France in Revolution*. London, UK. Hodder. 2008.

Advanced reading

Doyle, W. *The Oxford History of the French Revolution*. Oxford, UK. Oxford University Press. 2002.

The Industrial Revolution
c. 1800–50

Key questions

- What were the causes of the Industrial Revolution by 1800?
- What factors encouraged and discouraged industrialisation from 1800 to 1850?
- How did the Industrial Revolution affect different classes up to 1850?
- What were the political and economic effects of the Industrial Revolution up to 1850?

Content summary

- Changes in pre-industrial society, including early mechanisation.
- Changes in communications, roads and canals.
- Developments in steam power, railways and machines.
- Trade and the conservative interests.
- The social impact of the Industrial Revolution on the upper, middle and lower classes.
- Urbanisation and the impact of industrialisation on standards of living.
- Changes and challenges to political systems.
- The rise of the middle classes, relative prosperity and decline of industrialisation.

Timeline

Feb 1804	Richard Trevithick's steam engine makes its first journey in Britain
Sep 1825	Stockton to Darlington Railway opens in Britain
Jun 1832	Reform Act grants the vote to middle classes in Britain
Jan 1834	Zollverein (customs union of 18 states) formed in Germany
Dec 1835	First steam-operated railway opens in Germany
Aug 1837	Railway from Paris to Saint Germain begins operation in France
May 1838	People's Charter issued in Britain, demanding political reform
Feb 1848	Revolution breaks out in France, strongly influenced by industrialisation; Karl Marx publishes *The Communist Manifesto*
Mar 1851	Census reveals more people in towns than countryside in Britain

Introduction

The dates of the Industrial Revolution cannot be stated as precisely as those of political revolutions. Some historians believe that the Industrial Revolution in Britain began in the 1780s, but others claim it started much earlier – in the late 17th century. It is generally agreed that the Industrial Revolution in France and Germany began after Napoleon's defeat in 1815. Nonetheless, at the beginning of the 19th century, most people in Britain, France and Germany lived much as they had done for centuries. A few cities and regions had experienced some industrialisation, but the economy of most areas continued to be based on traditional farming.

The Industrial Revolution – a profound series of changes in trade, technology, agriculture and mining – did not just affect the process of manufacturing. It infiltrated almost every area of life and society, changing the face of Europe. The power of the nobility declined and the middle and working classes increased in importance. Urbanisation resulted in a dramatic increase in the numbers of people living in towns and cities and a corresponding drop in rural populations. Education became central in providing a more skilled workforce, while the development of the railway system transformed both personal travel and commercial logistics. The domestic sphere benefited from a new range of appliances and utilities, including (eventually) electricity and the telephone.

While the Industrial Revolution fuelled progress in areas such as manufacturing, business and medicine, it also fostered an increase in crime, deprivation and political unrest. Not everyone benefited. Nor was change uniform across Europe. Some countries, including Spain and Italy, retained their largely agricultural economies until the end of the 19th century, and even in the 21st century there are parts of the continent that can still best be described as **agrarian** rather than industrial. As a result of this, some historians prefer to distinguish between two Industrial Revolutions in the 19th century – the first centred on the use of coal and iron, and the second based on steel and electricity.

agrarian
A term that relates to the ownership, management and cultivation of land.

Figure 2.1 The landscape of Europe changed dramatically between 1800 and 1850, as the Industrial Revolution spread

Causes of the Industrial Revolution by 1800

Agrarian, or pre-industrial, societies were based on the cultivation of land. This provided a livelihood for almost all sections of society, and was the basis of both wealth and social hierarchies. Most land belonged to the monarchy or the aristocracy, and the lower classes and peasant populations had no rights of ownership over the land they farmed.

Even those people who were not directly employed on the land – craftsmen and traders, for example – still depended on it indirectly. In small towns, carpenters made simple furniture and ploughs, and jewellers supplied the wealthy with symbols of their status; the incomes of these craftsmen were also based on the state of agriculture in the region, as good harvests meant that more money was available for non-essential goods. Clergymen were also dependent on the land: their income came from tithes (taxes), and these were often **paid in kind**.

paid in kind
When goods or services are used instead of money to pay for something.

Changes in pre-industrial society

Before the 19th century, methods of agriculture changed slowly. Communications were poor and many communities were isolated. This made it difficult for new ideas to penetrate them. New methods of farming, such as better fertilisers to improve crops, developed gradually but these were very localised and often depended on individual enterprise. The peasants who worked on the land had little incentive to improve farming methods – any increase in productivity would not benefit them directly but would only fill the pockets of their already wealthy landlords. The ancient system of feudalism (see page 14) had disappeared from Britain and parts of Germany by the 18th century, but feudal taxes and forced service survived in France and were common in Eastern Europe.

Even after the decline of feudalism, the poorest peasants in Britain, France and parts of Germany came under pressure from landowners, who combined smallholdings (small farms) into larger units that could be run with greater efficiency by producing more with fewer labourers. This meant that there was not enough work to go around, and many peasants lived under the threat of starvation. One poor harvest could result in the deaths of thousands of peasants, and a prolonged period of bad harvests could be devastating.

The peasants' prospects worsened with population growth, which created more competition for work in the countryside. Rising prices, reflecting a greater demand for goods, did not benefit society's poorest.

Note:
The serfs, the lowest peasants, were tied to their landlords. Heavy burdens were imposed on the serfs, including taxes and compulsory labour service. Feudalism disappeared in Britain during the 16th century, but it was not until the French Revolution in the late 18th century that it was abolished in France. The system survived longest in Russia and other parts of Eastern Europe.

In Britain, a system existed by which the lower classes had rights over public land – they could use it to make hay or to graze their own livestock. However, in the mid 18th century, landowners began enclosing areas of common land and using them to produce a diversity of crops, not merely basic foodstuffs. They also bred livestock selectively to increase yields and to avoid diseases that might be spread from the animals kept by the peasants. The peasants themselves were often denied access to the woods and common land they had previously relied on to collect fuel and use as pasture. Their rights to this land were traditional rather than officially recorded, so it was difficult to challenge the enclosures in unsympathetic courts of law.

Changes in communications, roads and canals

In the pre-industrial societies of Britain, France and Germany, communications and transport depended on horses and river transport. The condition of most roads was poor because local communities were responsible for their upkeep and there was no incentive to maintain good roads that would benefit outsiders. Governments encouraged road-building, but this was largely met with indifference from local populations. In the 18th century, Britain began building more turnpike roads – privatised roads that people had to pay to use.

Figure 2.2 A horse-drawn wagon in the early 19th century; before the advent of the railways, this was one of the only ways of transporting goods

Rivers were used for transport wherever possible, as barges were able to carry larger loads than horse-drawn carts. Rivers were widened and deepened to take the increased traffic, but greater changes came with the widespread canal-building programmes that occurred in the 18th century, especially in Britain. Unlike rivers, canals could be specially designed and their routes planned in the interests of trade. They linked industrial centres and encouraged the expansion of villages along their routes. Mass transport made the costs of carrying goods cheaper. Investors in the canal network made huge profits, and this encouraged further investment and growth. At its height in the late 1700s, the Canal Age in Britain has been regarded as a small-scale version of the Railway Age, except that the canals were not used for passenger transport in the way that railways later were.

Population growth and the Agricultural Revolution

The population of Europe began to increase significantly from the middle of the 18th century. Although birth rates did not increase (and even decreased in Britain, France and Germany from 1800 to the 1850s), death rates fell, resulting in a net population growth. The expansion of roads and canals meant that food could be distributed more widely and more quickly, and larger areas of land were cultivated. In the first half of the 19th century, there were a number of natural disasters, including famines across Europe in 1816–17 and the Irish potato famine of the 1840s. Such events declined after 1850, and this also contributed to the falling death rates. Other changes took place that led to greater increases in populations, especially medical advances that prolonged lives. Increased prosperity resulted in bigger families.

Note:
The population of Britain increased from about 7.5 million in 1750 to 20 million in 1840 – the greatest rate of growth in Europe during this period.

Figure 2.3 A map showing the main population centres in Europe by 1820

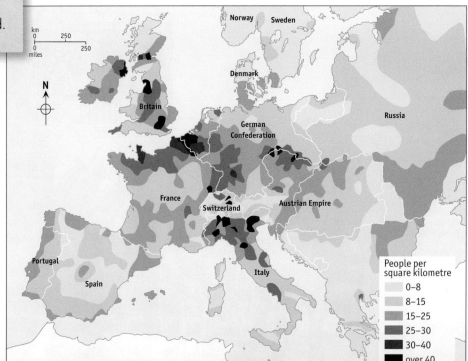

A larger population meant there was a greater demand for food and other products. More people also created a bigger labour force in towns, as many could not find employment in rural areas; more efficient farming methods in some countries were already cutting the number of jobs in agriculture. The 1851 census in Britain revealed that, for the first time, more than half the population lived in towns and cities. Over 1 million people lived in London and the same number resided on the outskirts of the capital. The number and size of British cities far outstripped those of France and Germany. Paris, the largest city in France, had a population of half a million. Berlin and Hamburg in Germany were inhabited by only around 100,000 people. The link between industrialisation and large urban areas did not apply to every country, however. In the mid 19th century, Denmark, Italy and Portugal – countries with few industries – all had towns that housed higher proportions of the population than cities in France and Prussia. The reasons for these exceptions are not clear.

The changes in food production have been called the Agricultural Revolution. The increasing population, greater demand for food, an increased labour force, the availability of money for investment and improved communications all laid the foundations for the Industrial Revolution. Railway builders, for example, used what they had learnt from the modernisation of roads and canals in surveying long and difficult distances and overcoming obstacles by viaducts and tunnels.

The Agricultural and Industrial Revolutions overlapped, and it is not easy to categorise all the many inventions that were developed during this time as belonging to one or the other. Indeed, many new machines proved useful in both agriculture and industry. These inventions largely affected workers in small or cottage industries – either making them more productive or causing unemployment because fewer people were needed to work the machines. Gradually, small centres of production declined as factories took over.

Questions

1 How did the growth in population from the mid 18th century influence the development of the revolutions in agriculture and industry?

2 Carry out further research into one of the inventors mentioned in the Note panel opposite. What specific effect did his inventions have on agriculture and industry in Britain in the 18th and 19th centuries?

Note:
The British economist Thomas Malthus made a gloomy prediction about the effects of population growth in 'An Essay on the Principle of Population', published in 1798. He forecast a shortage of food and massive social unrest because the natural methods of controlling the population – disease and famine – would be ineffective. In fact, more food was grown, assisted by more productive machinery such as steam-powered threshing machines, and Malthus's prediction never came to pass.

Note:
The best-known inventors of the mid to late 18th century include John Kay, James Hargreaves, Richard Arkwright and Samuel Crompton. Kay's Flying Shuttle (1733) allowed one weaver to do the work previously done by two. Hargreaves invented the Spinning Jenny (1764), a multi-spool spinning frame that allowed a worker to operate more than one spinning machine. Arkwright's spinning machine (1769) was powered first by water, then steam. His machines became popular with factory owners because they were simple to operate. Crompton invented a machine called the Mule (1775), which combined the previously separate tasks of spinner and weaver.

What factors encouraged and discouraged industrialisation from 1800 to 1850?

Developments in steam power

The use of steam was one of the most important features of industrialisation. Water power then steam power enabled larger and more powerful machines to be built, and this began to transform industry in the late 18th century. In Britain, **James Watt** made a vital breakthrough in developing better steam engines, and from 1800 – after Watt's patent expired – other inventors improved on the efficiency of his steam engines.

Steam power began the process of revolutionising agriculture and industry. Around the middle of the 19th century, steam ploughs and threshing machines were introduced on farms – the first step towards modern agricultural machinery. Steam power was also applied to machines in factories, where it resulted in a huge increase in both productivity and the range of jobs that could be performed by machine rather than by hand.

Steam also enabled railways to be built, carrying goods and then people more cheaply and over longer distances. Both businessmen and engineers were quick to see other possibilities for steam power, especially at sea. In 1822, the first iron steamship sailed across the English Channel and then along the River Seine to Paris. There were disadvantages to steamships: they depended on coal, which was an expensive commodity, and boiler rooms and fuel storage took up a lot of space on board. However, the benefits of increased speed and power were clear. By 1850, iron was increasingly used to construct large ships with more powerful engines, and the balance began to move away from wind power and towards steam.

Steam engines soon spread to continental Europe, where engineers developed their own inventions. Coal mines in France and Germany used Watt's steam engines, and trade went in both directions as British factory owners bought continental machines. Although a small country, Belgium had plentiful resources of coal and iron, and as result it became the first country in mainland Europe to industrialise. A system of internal tariffs (taxes) among the German states hindered industrialisation there until the Zollverein was established in 1834 (see page 53). Progress was slower in France, too, where the economy suffered from unstable governments and slow population growth.

Key figure

James Watt (1736–1819)

Watt was a Scottish engineer who developed an interest in early steam technology while studying in Glasgow. Thomas Newcomen had devised the first steam pump in 1712, to remove water from mines, but Watt produced an improved model in 1769. He received financial backing from the manufacturer Matthew Boulton, and their steam engines saw much success in Britain in many different types of machine.

The rise of the railways

The advent of the railways caused a revolution in land communications. Early railways used a primitive method of mounting carts on wooden rails, with the carts being pulled by horses. These railways were often used in mines and quarries to carry loads over short distances before being loaded on to road carts. In the middle of the 18th century, iron began to be used instead of wood for the rails. The first passenger railway – about 16 km (10 miles) long, and again using horses for power – opened near Swansea in Wales in 1806. The railway revolution, however, truly started when engineers applied steam power to transport.

Developments in Britain

British inventor and mining engineer **Richard Trevithick** has been called the 'father' of the steam railways. In 1804, he used steam from his new high-pressure steam engines to power railway locomotives at the ironworks at Penydarren in Merthyr Tydfil in Wales.

Figure 2.4 Richard Trevithick's 1808 steam engine, called 'Catch Me Who Can'

Key figure

Richard Trevithick (1771–1833)

British inventor Trevithick became interested in engineering as a young man. He built a series of railway engines, but found they were too heavy and that the rails could not support them. He realised that he could make the engines lighter and more powerful through the use of high-pressure steam. Although considered one of the pioneers of the railway, Trevithick went bankrupt in later life, and died in poverty.

The civil and mechanical engineer **George Stephenson** built some short railways with increasingly powerful locomotives before being appointed surveyor of the Stockton to Darlington Railway, in north-east England, in 1825. This line, often described as the first modern railway, was a test of his abilities to master geographical problems in the design of his engines. Its success soon showed what an impact the railways could have on economics: the price of coal dropped by more than 50% because the railways provided cheaper, faster and more efficient transport, capable of carrying larger loads, than previous methods had offered.

Figure 2.5 The opening of the Stockton to Darlington Railway in 1825

In 1830, Stephenson built a railway between the major towns of Liverpool and Manchester. This was the first railway with a twin track, which meant that trains could run more frequently. Soon, other railway engineers – including Stephenson's son Robert and **Isambard Kingdom Brunel** – were contributing to a network of tracks across England and parts of Scotland and Wales.

Key figure

George Stephenson (1781–1848)

Stephenson's father worked on engines in mines in the north of England. Stephenson followed his father's work and then developed an interest in railway engines. After working on the Stockton to Darlington Railway, he won a competition to find the best railway engine for pulling heavy loads over long distances. In his later life, he built railways in different parts of Britain. He was also consulted about railway building on the continent.

Note:

The Liverpool to Manchester line was also the first to incur a major civilian casualty, when William Huskisson, a government minister, fell under the wheels of Stephenson's *Rocket*, at the opening of the railway.

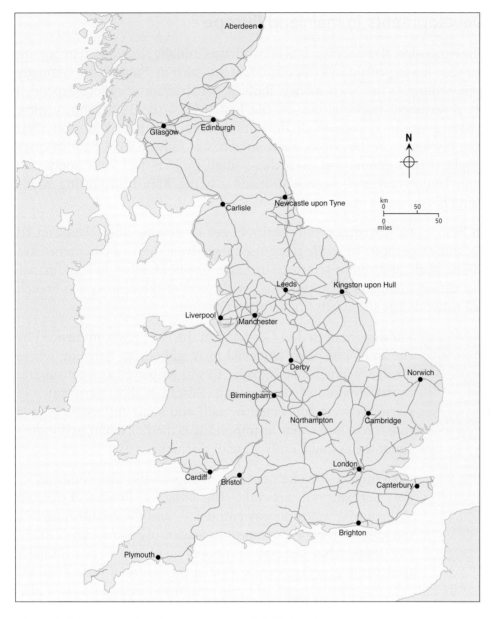

Figure 2.6 *A map showing the railway network in Britain in 1850*

The expansion of the railways in Britain was not a steady progress. There were good years, when the economy was prospering and money was available for investment, and poor years when the railways were affected by national depression.

The mid 1840s were a boom period for railway investment, which was yielding far greater profits than other traditional areas of investment. Many people assumed that profits would continue to rise, so they bought shares in railway companies. However, a financial crash towards the end of the decade caused the value of these shares to collapse, and several investors were ruined. Another cycle of 'boom and bust' occurred in the 1860s. Nonetheless, by the end of the 19th century the railway system in Britain covered most of the country, and underpinned an industrial economy.

Developments in mainland Europe

The expansion of the continental network was initially slower than in Britain, because fewer private investors in countries such as France and Germany were willing to risk their money. Railway construction therefore depended on government backing, but for the first half of the 19th century most governments in Europe made developing canal and river transport their primary focus. In the 1830s, short stretches of railway were built to carry freight (heavy goods), but even these small projects met with opposition from landowners and those who made a living from transporting goods using horses and carts.

In France, rail expansion only really began to develop after Napoleon III became emperor in 1852. He recognised the advantages of a comprehensive rail network, and authorised the state bank, Crédit Mobilier, to help finance the railway companies. Despite this, by the end of the century the French rail network was still much smaller than Britain's.

Note:

Before the railways, German trade was restricted because its only outlet to the sea was on the Baltic coast, which meant long and expensive journeys to the world beyond its borders. The rail network allowed goods to be transported through other countries.

Railways appeared in Germany in the late 1830s, influenced by the ambitious plans launched in neighbouring Belgium, where George Stephenson (see page 50) was employed as a consultant. By the middle of the century, eastern and western parts of Germany were connected by rail, and some historians believe that the railways were as important as the Zollverein in bringing about the political unification of Germany.

Government involvement also helped the development of the German rail network. The king of Prussia, Friedrich Wilhelm IV, was a railway enthusiast, and the establishment of the railways there encouraged the leaders of other German states. By 1850, the German economy had been transformed. Germany's geographical location at the centre of Europe meant that its railways provided a means of trade with many other nations; it also meant that other countries often had to make use of its railways to trade with one another. As in Britain, the railways on the continent resulted in the development of industrial centres. Ports became busier and the railway companies were major customers for iron and steel works.

The railways quickly became a significant element of the economies of many European countries, and it is no coincidence that Britain, Germany and France – the most industrialised nations in Europe – had the largest rail networks. However, the figures alone can be misleading. Britain's dense population meant that the railways played a larger role in the economy, because most places were close to a railway line. On the other hand, parts of France and Germany were still little affected because their populations were spread more thinly and many regions were almost untouched by railways. Russia boasted a large rail network, but this did not have much impact on the economy because it was such a vast country and communications were otherwise primitive.

Country	Rail network (km)	
	1840	1860
Austria-Hungary	144	4543
Belgium	334	1730
France	496	9167
Germany	469	11,089
Britain	390	14,603
Italy	20	2404
Russia	27	1626

Table 2.1 The extent of the rail network in major European countries

Tariffs and trade

Patterns of trade were changed by the Industrial Revolution. In pre-industrial times, most people relied on local trade within the provinces where they lived. Farmers earned a living selling their produce at local markets. If they happened to live near cities or large towns with substantial populations, these farmers prospered. However, most lived in more isolated areas where local markets were small affairs and there was much less demand for goods. Some would travel long distances to reach the larger markets, but transporting cereals and vegetables was slow, and livestock had to be moved on foot to city markets. There were frequent food shortages, and while wealthy people could afford to buy expensive imported goods, the poor often went hungry.

The railways opened up new markets for farmers. Cereals, meat and vegetables could be carried in large volumes to distant towns. Food shortages became less frequent and prices fell as more produce was available. The lower classes could afford better and more varied food. The upper classes still spent money on luxuries, but ships plying their overseas trade were also filled with commodities that everyone could afford.

Britain had an early advantage over foreign competitors because there were no internal charges on trade (tariffs) from the middle of the 18th century, when turnpike roads that charged for their use began to decline. In France, Napoleon Bonaparte abolished internal tariffs (taxes on goods traded within a particular country) when he became consul, in an effort to make trade within France less expensive.

In Germany, the abolition of internal tariffs was particularly significant. Previously, people had to pay when moving food or commodities between the different states. However, in 1834 a coalition of 18 German states – including the most powerful, Prussia – set up a customs union called the Zollverein, and trade tariffs between the member states were abolished. By 1850, almost all German states had joined the Zollverein. This effectively formed a single German economic market, which allowed much more rapid industrialisation.

Laws governing trade were standardised and a single currency was introduced. Industrialists now had a much larger domestic market and could compete more successfully with foreigners. In theory, the German states were equal partners in this economy, but in practice Prussia became Germany's economic leader and was responsible for making trade treaties with other countries. This economic change led to the political unification of Germany, once again demonstrating the significant influence of industrialisation on a country.

> *The Prussian and the German-wide customs union influenced the regional flow of trade and called the attention of affected states – and, indeed, of local interests in the most important cities – to the importance of transport improvements to ensure one's own share of trade.*
>
> Patrick O'Brien (ed.) *Industrialisation: Critical Perspectives on the World Economy.* London, UK. Routledge. 1998.

Capitalism

capitalism
An economic system based on the private ownership of the means of production and the accumulation of profit in a competitive market. Capital refers to funds used by businesses to produce their products and services.

The Industrial Revolution depended on **capitalism**, because it required investment in the development and use of new machines and technology. In its early years, capital tended to be kept within families, rather than being loaned to companies for investment. In France and Germany, most people who had spare funds bought land as an investment, but some were willing to consider industrial projects, especially when it became clear that large profits could be made from industry.

joint stock companies
Companies that are owned by shareholders rather than by an individual. In limited liability companies, shareholders are liable only for debts according to the amount they invest, which limits the risk they take on.

Individuals or small groups of people were unable to keep up with the investment demands of large ventures such as financing railways, but there were risks if companies or banks failed, because people might lose all their money. **Joint stock companies** protected investors from the worst losses because the organisation of these companies was such that investors had limited liability for losses, so they were not required to pay back debtors if things went wrong. As the 19th century progressed, small banks were replaced by larger banks, which were less vulnerable to collapse.

Some of the wealthiest families invested huge amounts of money in industry. One example of these 'super-financiers' was the Rothschild family. The Rothschilds began to amass a fortune in the 18th century, when they moved from Germany to Britain and lent financial support in the war against Napoleon. Over the years, they established financial centres in five different countries and invested in industry and railways, as well as making government loans. At the beginning of the Industrial Revolution, people with 'new money' (as opposed to 'old money', earned and passed down through generations) were often despised by the upper classes. By the end of the 19th century, however, financiers could rise through the social ranks, and some even became nobles.

Resistance to industrial changes

Not everyone was in favour of industrialisation. Skilled craftsmen often opposed mass production, and in Britain a group called the Luddites destroyed machines in factories, believing that they threatened their livelihoods. Members of the nobility, too, were suspicious of the effects of industrial change, as their political, social and economic interests were based on land. This was especially evident in Germany, where the landowners (*Junkers*), saw no advantage in economic reforms because their wealth depended on traditional farming systems.

Figure 2.7 Luddites wrecking a machine in a textile factory in 1812

> ### Note:
> The Luddites were a group of traditional skilled British workers that emerged in 1811. They feared unemployment because of the new machines, which meant that fewer and less skilled men and women were needed to operate them. The Luddites demanded fair wages and carried out a campaign of destruction in factories. The government responded by making the smashing of machines punishable by death.

Not even the railways were universally popular. The introduction of the early machines, including railway engines, was accompanied by a huge rise in the number of accidents. Safety measures had not been considered before the development of the railways, and were only adopted once the dangers were realised. Early engines were unreliable, often breaking down or exploding under the pressure of the steam. Some people believed that travelling by rail could harm pregnant women; others thought that these great machines rumbling through the countryside would alarm animals in the fields. Some claimed that the sparks from engines could cause fires.

Parliamentary approval of the railways did not depend on a national plan, but on the result of the lobbying of local interests. As a result, more powerful groups could sway the opinion of voting ministers. Landowners who made no profit from the railways objected to lines crossing their land. Canal owners – who believed their own profits were threatened by the rise of the railways – campaigned against them to try and delay their approval in parliament. Even when they did win approval, problems continued, as violence often broke out between gangs of workmen employed to build the rail lines and local groups stirred up by those who were hostile to the railways.

Note:

Some landowners agreed to allow trains to cross their lands only on certain conditions. In Britain, the Duke of Beaufort reluctantly permitted a railway line on his land on condition that he could require any train to stop at his specially built local station.

Questions

1. How did urbanisation result from industrialisation in Europe in the 19th century?

2. What were the main changes in trade that resulted from changes in labour and production during the Industrial Revolution?

3. Who benefited most from the Industrial Revolution? Give reasons for your choices.

The social effects of the Industrial Revolution on different classes

The Industrial Revolution had a dramatic impact on society. In industrialised Europe by the end of the 19th century, the wealthy lived in large houses with gas lighting. The urban poor were crowded into working-class districts, where several families often shared a home and where candles were the main source of light. Reports from Germany tell of up to 20 adults and children sharing a single room. In France, tall blocks of flats were more common but no less crowded. This was very different from the agricultural life led by most people 100 years earlier. Other significant changes brought about by the Industrial Revolution include the following:

- **Social mobility:** factory owners increased in wealth and influence; the children of some of these industrialists even married into noble families.
- **Voting rights:** most working-class men had the right to vote in Britain, France and Germany by the end of the 19th century.
- **Education:** by the end of the Industrial Revolution, most children were educated at least to literacy level, which was a general improvement for the lower classes compared to the situation in the 18th century.

The position of women

Women were less affected by the Industrial Revolution than men – the assumption remained that the husband/father was the head of the family. Working-class women still had jobs, but these were now often in factories rather than in cottage industries or working on the land. Many women stopped working when they married or had children. Social attitudes still prevented upper-class women from working, although more of them went on to have a university education than before the Industrial Revolution.

Health and welfare

Poor living and working conditions left the working classes vulnerable to disease. Cities were dirty and polluted by the smoke and waste from factories. Water supplies were also contaminated and spread disease. Epidemics of typhoid and cholera were frequent, whilst overcrowding and a lack of fresh air spread tuberculosis.

Note:
Cholera first appeared in Europe early in the 19th century and there were epidemics in France and Britain in 1831. At the time, no one knew that the disease was spread by dirty water, which was common in industrial areas. Smallpox and typhoid also killed many people, with little distinction between rich and poor – Queen Victoria's husband Prince Albert probably died of typhoid.

The threat from these epidemics diminished in the second half of the century, as countries installed infrastructures such as pipes to carry clean water from distant reservoirs to the cities, and sewage systems to separate waste discharge from drinking water. Britain led the way towards the reform of social conditions by the state.

In 1842, a report on the 'Sanitary Conditions of the Labouring Classes' resulted in a series of laws designed to improve the situation, including the establishment of a General Board of Health. However, these measures were not always successfully implemented as local authorities had to pay for them out of local taxes, which they were reluctant to do. This pattern was replicated in France and Germany, where local authorities resisted taking action.

Local and national governments, whether elected or not, tended to represent the rich, the property owners and the manufacturers. They did not want to either raise taxes to pay for social improvements or compel landlords to improve their houses and factory owners to treat their workers better. Governments were not expected to regulate either the social or the economic lives of their people. What little regulation there was in this period had limited effect.

The diets of rich and poor were very different. The rich ate lavishly, as food imported from abroad became more common. In contrast, in the middle of the 19th century, the working classes rarely ate meat (usually only at Christmas and Easter) and instead survived on cheap foods such as potatoes. This poor diet naturally affected their health. A lack of vitamins particularly affected children, and many suffered from diseases such as rickets (bone weakness).

Working conditions

In Britain, a series of acts of parliament known as the Factory Acts was introduced from 1833. These limited the number of hours women and children could work in factories, and factory inspectors were employed to ensure that the new laws were being followed. Although the Factory Acts were intended to improve the lives of women and children, many people objected to them. Poor families often needed to work long hours just to earn the money to survive, and the acts prevented this. Others resented the government interfering in how people raised their children.

Social traditions meant that employment of women and children in factories and coal mines was less common in Germany than in Britain. The protection of children began in Prussia in 1839 when the first legislation was introduced, and increased after Germany was unified in 1871. France lagged behind in the protection of women and children and it was only during the period of the Third Republic, from 1873 onwards, that the situation began to improve.

Figure 2.8 A child pushing a cart filled with coal through a narrow mine shaft in 1841

The social effect of the railways

By 1850, most places in Britain were within reach of a railway – and this was to have a great impact on communications within the country. News and newspapers could spread rapidly. A national postal service also began in 1840, using railways to distribute an increasing volume of letters and parcels across the country.

Diet improved, as fresh food could be quickly and easily transported to market. Labour could move more easily to where there was work, and this generated greater wealth. Travel grew more affordable, and people began making trips to holiday resorts that catered for ordinary families, as well as to sporting events.

Religious changes during the Industrial Revolution

The Industrial Revolution affected not only the physical lives of the people of Europe, but also their spiritual lives. The Church in Europe, whether Protestant or Catholic, had been a focal point for society for centuries. Now, church traditions and beliefs seemed old-fashioned and unexciting compared to the ideologies of profit-making capitalism and atheist **Marxism**. At the same time, religious beliefs were being challenged by the great leaps in scientific discovery and thought that took place in the 19th century.

> **Note:**
> The clearest proof that railways could provide mass travel in Britain was the Great Exhibition of 1851, a celebration of British culture and industry. It was visited by 6 million people. Thomas Cook first organised a railway journey for a small group of people from the Midlands to London to visit the exhibition. The idea proved popular, and ultimately Cook arranged for more than 150,000 people to do the same. Others quickly followed his example, and the travel agency industry was born.

Marxism
A political system based on the ideas of the German philosopher Karl Marx, who wanted the industrial working classes to bring about a revolution in order to achieve a socialist and then a classless society based on greater freedom and wealth for all.

Note:

Methodism, founded in the 18th century, was a Protestant religious movement that broke away from the Church of England and gained a large number of followers in the new industrial towns. Its message helped workers tolerate economic hardship, and encouraged thrift and hard work in the hope of a better life. Methodism also gave women real status, and proved to be much more conscious of the needs of the new industrial working class.

Religious movements

Church leaders were generally slow to adapt to changing industrial conditions. Many church buildings had been constructed at a time when societies were largely agricultural, and the areas served by most churches reflected this. There were few churches in the densely populated industrial towns and cities. In Britain, this led to the rise of Protestant groups that operated outside the official Church of England, many of them catering for the poor in districts that had no spiritual focal point. The Methodists were particularly successful in gaining members in these areas, and the Salvation Army was established around this time to help those poor workers who had fallen victim to the evils of alcohol. The Catholic population of England increased during the Industrial Revolution due to an influx of immigrants from Ireland, who came to work in the coal mines and factories.

Church attendance

More churches were built in industrial Britain than in France and Germany. Some were funded by poor people in the localities in which they were built, but others were built from donations made by wealthy patrons. Church attendance in Britain in the early to mid 19th century was traditionally thought to have been high. However, a later study of the census carried out in 1851 revealed that almost half the population did not regularly attend church services, and that only a quarter attended an Anglican church. Modern historians largely conclude that church attendance was patchy – more frequent in some areas than others. There is evidence that Sunday schools remained popular, particularly amongst the industrial poor, as they provided a basic education as well as Christian teaching.

In Britain, France and Germany, there were some religious thinkers who criticised the effects of industrialisation, claiming that it was driven by greed and pointing to the growing gap between rich and poor. The attitude of the Catholic Church towards modern society only began to change when Leo XIII became pope in 1878. He followed the Catholic Church's tradition of defending private property and condemning Marxism, but wanted the Church to come to terms with industrial conditions by showing a greater concern for the poor. Catholic trade unions were set up and the Church supported Catholic socialist parties to appeal to the lower classes.

In France a Catholic university was founded in the industrial city of Lille. Attempts were made to make Catholic worship more popular and the middle classes were reminded of their responsibilities to the poor.

Workers' societies were set up in France and Germany. More churches were built, although many of these were constructed in the wrong places – often outside industrial areas so that working-class families were still unable to attend.

The Industrial Revolution and the arts

The Industrial Revolution influenced the arts, especially fiction. In Britain, writer Elizabeth Gaskell considered the change from an agricultural to an industrial society in *North and South*. Her novel *Cranford* also showed an agricultural community threatened by the spread of industrial changes such as the railways. The great Victorian novelist Charles Dickens set many of his works in industrial England, including *Bleak House, Hard Times* and *Little Dorrit*, while Thomas Hardy still used agricultural societies as the context for his novels, looking at the threats posed to agriculture by industrialisation. The French writer Émile Zola wrote critically about the conditions of the working class in France.

Note:
Charles Dickens (1812–70) was one of the greatest English novelists of the 19th century. Some of his most famous novels, including *Hard Times*, *Bleak House* and *A Christmas Carol* highlighted the terrible conditions experienced by the poor in England.

Figure 2.9 Charles Dickens' novel Little Dorrit *was a commentary on industrial society*

Questions

1 In what ways did the Industrial Revolution improve life for the lower classes and in what ways did it make life worse?

2 What were the positive effects of the Industrial Revolution and how did they benefit Britain, France and Germany?

3 Read Sources A and B below, which discuss the social effects of the Industrial Revolution. What do these two sources have in common?

Source A

These machines are set up, and their expense does not appear very great. 20 girls do the work previously done by 2,000 women and children. Large numbers confined together in one room cannot make them so strong and healthy. If they marry, they can neither teach their children to work, or spin, or bring in any earnings to maintain them. Who then shall patch the clothes and mend the shoes?

Shut up from morning till night, except when they are sent home for their meals, these girls are unskilful at every domestic employment, whereas if she is at her spinning wheel in her mother's cottage, the girl assists in every occupation of the family. She lights the fire, nurses the young children, collects the harvest, takes charge of the house in her mother's necessary absence to do the shopping and becomes an assistant to her parents in sickness and old age. A girl taken from six years old to sixteen, and employed at the machines, can learn none of these habits.

An extract from a report about female factory workers, 1794.

Source B

Any man who has stood at the single narrow door-way, which serves as the place of exit for the people employed in the great cotton-mills, must acknowledge that it would be impossible to collect in a smaller space an uglier set of men and women, of boys and girls. Their complexion is pale. Their stature is low – the average height of four hundred men, measured at different times, and different places, being five feet six inches. Their limbs are thin and ungraceful. There is a very general bowing of the legs. Great numbers of girls and women walk lamely or awkwardly. Nearly all have flat feet. Their hair is thin and straight – many of the men having but little beard, and that in patches of a few hairs.

Factory labour is a type of work which is very unfitted for children. Confined up in a heated atmosphere, lacking the necessary exercise, remaining in one position for many hours, it cannot be doubted that its effects are harmful to the physical growth of a child.

An extract about the physical condition of factory workers in Britain, from a book called The Manufacturing Population of England, *published in 1833.*

The political effects of the Industrial Revolution up to 1850

In the 18th century, few people could have imagined that one day the masses would have the right to elect governments. Nor would they have believed that those governments would make every effort to introduce policies that would be approved by the people. At that time, power was held almost exclusively by kings and landowners, and while the monarchy in Britain was subject to some limited controls, the rulers of France and the German states exerted absolute authority over their domains. To a significant degree, democracy grew out of industrialisation. The middle classes who made their money out of industry began to demand a share of political power. At the same time, industrial workers realised that having the right to vote would enable them to secure reforms to improve their living and working conditions.

Political effects in Britain

The 1832 Reform Act

In Britain, the Reform Act of 1832 was the first proof that industrialisation could have important political effects. Since the defeat of Napoleon in 1815, there had been growing dissatisfaction with the old political systems. Although some limited reforms were introduced in the next few years, such as allowing Roman Catholics to vote and become members of parliament, many people felt these did not go far enough. The changes that came about by the 1832 Reform Act seem modest by 21st-century standards, but they were considerable in the context of the time.

One of the most significant parts of the act was the abolition of 'rotten boroughs': seats in parliament for **constituencies** that had few or no voters. Parliamentary seats were extended so that 22 new boroughs, mostly industrial towns, were represented in parliament, but there was no attempt to make sure that every MP represented the same number of voters. Several pocket boroughs – small constituencies controlled by the wealthy – survived.

> **constituencies**
> The group of people from particular districts who elect their representative for parliament.

Note:
Examples of 'rotten boroughs' include Old Sarum, which was represented by two MPs but contained no houses, and Dunwich, which also had two MPs but only 32 residents with the right to vote. There had been no elections in many constituencies for years because the local landlord, often a nobleman, nominated an MP whom nobody would challenge.

Voting was not by secret ballot as it is today, and landowners still influenced elections. However, the franchise (the right to vote) was granted to property owners, which included most of the middle class. This meant that about 20% of men could now vote – double the number able to before the Reform Act. At the time, people believed that this was where the extent of the franchise would remain, but in fact it marked the start of a process that ended in universal voting rights.

The Chartists

The lower classes gained almost nothing from the 1832 Reform Act, and the Factory Acts (see page 58) were not improving industrial conditions quickly enough to keep the working class happy. As dissatisfaction spread, groups began to form to campaign for more political rights for the poor; these eventually united as a movement known as Chartism. In 1836, **William Lovett** formed the London Working Men's Association, a club designed to help educate skilled workers to broaden their opportunities. In 1838, Lovett and a fellow political reformer, Francis Place, drafted a parliamentary bill that became the basis of the People's Charter. The charter demanded:

- universal franchise for men
- that MPs should not have to be property owners
- that parliaments should last for one year only
- that parliamentary constituencies should be of equal size
- payment for MPs
- voting by secret ballot.

Note:

In the 19th century, a parliament remained in control for seven years. This was reduced to five years in 1911, and remains so today. However, prime ministers can call elections before the end of a five-year period if the monarch consents.

Figure 2.10 A cartoon from 1848, showing a working-class man presenting the People's Charter to the prime minister

The aims of the Chartists went beyond electoral reform. They believed that political change was imperative if living conditions were to improve, and that the People's Charter would ensure 'free trade, universal peace, freedom of religion, and national education'. This became a rallying cry for the working classes in many towns. Chartism spread rapidly, inspired by leaders such as **Feargus O'Connor**, who issued pamphlets and had his own newspaper, the *Northern Star*, to spread the Chartist message.

As a result of the Chartist movement, a 'People's Parliament' met in London in 1839. This was an unelected body and had no legal power, but it drew up a series of demands for reform that backed the six points raised in the People's Charter. A petition in support of these reforms eventually gathered 3 million signatures.

The government was afraid that the Chartists might inspire a nationwide revolution. However, the movement declined quickly. The main reason for this was disagreements among Chartist leaders. Some, including Lovett and Place, wanted to use only persuasion, or moral force, but others felt that violence was necessary to achieve their aims. After the authorities suppressed a Chartist uprising in Wales, many of its leaders were arrested and imprisoned. By 1848, the movement was losing influence and a mass rally in London that year proved to be the last serious action by the Chartists. While France, Germany, Italy and the Austrian Empire were aflame with revolution, the British working-class rebellion was successfully crushed.

Later developments

Chartism might have failed as a movement, but most of its ideas survived and were to become law. Soon, working-class men were granted the vote and sent radical and reforming MPs to parliament. Parliamentary seats were redistributed to even out the size of the electorate for each seat, and corrupt practices in elections were outlawed. Voting in secret also became the law. Chartism, perhaps the first radical working-class movement in British history, told the ruling classes that the industrial working class was a force to be reckoned with and placed working-class issues firmly on the nation's agenda. Politicians now knew they had to focus on all classes, not just landowners and the factory owners.

In addition to these developments, the working classes gained political power in other ways – in particular through trade unions. At the beginning of the 19th century, governments and employers were hostile to unions of employees, and these had been made illegal. Although skilled workmen continued to form groups to campaign for better treatment, it was more difficult for unskilled workers in factories and the countryside. Employers there could and would dismiss them, knowing there were plenty of other workers to take their place.

Note:

Many people were prosecuted for belonging to trade unions, which were illegal. The most famous example of this was that of the Tolpuddle Martyrs in 1834. These agricultural labourers from a small village in the south of England were put on trial for membership of an unlawful organisation, and sentenced to be transported to Australia for seven years. There was outrage at this harsh punishment, and public protests led to their pardon two years later.

Establishing trade unions in industry proved difficult even after laws against combinations or unions were repealed in 1824. In 1831, miners went on strike over reduced wages, but they lost support after some strikers resorted to violence. Nonetheless, efforts to organise trade unions in Britain were more successful in the second half of the century. They eventually became powerful organisations for representing working-class grievances and ambitions.

Political effects in France and Germany

France

On the continent, the working classes also began to demand political reform in the first half of the 19th century. There were three revolutions in France after the fall of Napoleon Bonaparte: the July Revolution of 1830 saw King Charles X removed from power; in 1848, King Louis Philippe was driven out; and in 1870, there was a revolution against Napoleon III.

Economic conditions were a major factor in the 1830 revolution. Poor harvests led to social distress, and industrial workers lost jobs because of increasing competition. The middle classes also had grievances about voting rights and the lack of free trade. Despite attempts to keep power in the hands of the upper classes, the king, Charles X, was removed from power and replaced with Louis Philippe.

Figure 2.11 Rebels defeat royalist troops in the streets of Paris during the July Revolution in 1830

Louis Philippe faced opposition from the industrial lower classes in cities such as Paris and Lyon. The government allowed some social reforms, but refused to extend the franchise even to the lower middle classes, much less to the industrial working class. In 1848, with France again suffering economic distress, unrest spread across the country, and Louis Philippe fled to Britain.

The period that followed was known as the Second Republic (1848–52) and it seemed to be a triumph for the industrial classes. All men over 21 were able to vote, and there were reforms in employment conditions. However, the victory was short-lived. Wealthier people were alarmed at the developments, especially by the attempt of the socialist **Louis-August Blanqui** to seize power in 1848. It was widely felt that Louis Napoleon – the nephew of Napoleon Bonaparte and president of the French Republic – could restore order to the country. He was invited to become Emperor Napoleon III in 1852.

Germany

The political effects of the Industrial Revolution in Germany accompanied the development of the country from a collection of provincial governments into a unified state under Prussian control. Before unification, some German states had their own constitutions, but these favoured the middle classes far more than the industrial working classes. Social reforms were introduced to benefit children through education and limits on working hours.

After the 1848 revolutions, changes were made to the political system in Prussia, and the lower house of parliament (the Landtag) was elected by universal male franchise. However, the powers of the Landtag were limited, and in practice Prussia remained an authoritarian state, with real control exerted by the king and the landowners who dominated the upper house in the Prussian parliament. The brief Frankfurt Parliament (see page 82) established during the revolution gave the impression of being democratic, but it was really dominated by the middle class. Only one peasant had a seat in the parliament, and no industrial labourers were represented.

In Germany, as elsewhere in Europe, the working classes made few obvious gains immediately after 1848. However, German politicians – Bismarck (see page 84) in particular – became much more aware of the needs of the industrial workers. Fearing an alliance between a hungry and dispossessed working class and a rising middle class against the ruling class, he took great care to ensure that a welfare state was created and that working-class men got the vote. Yet again, major economic change in the form of industrialisation led to social and political change.

(see page 82)
(see page 84)

Key figure

Louis-August Blanqui (1805–81)

Blanqui studied law and medicine before becoming politically active in the 1820s. He quickly became an outspoken supporter of republicanism. He took part in the July Revolution of 1830 and the revolution of 1848. He developed a theory of revolution called Blanquism, and his followers staged a number of uprisings. Blanqui spent his life in and out of jail, but continued to fight for a French republic until his death.

Note:

A series of mass demonstrations and rebellions spread across Europe in 1848 and it became known as the Year of Revolution. In Germany, students and intellectuals led uprisings of both the middle and working classes, demanding such rights as freedom of the press and freedom of assembly, as well as German unity. However, the revolution became divided along class lines and by 1849 it had been suppressed by the nobility and the army.

Trade unions in France and Germany

Trade unions made little or no progress in either France or Germany in the first part of the 19th century. In 18th-century France, there had been several 'Friendly Societies', which had aimed to improve working conditions and to help those who lived in extreme poverty. However, they existed mainly amongst the skilled and better-paid workers, and acted more as insurance organisations to assist in cases of illness or unemployment. All attempts to gather the unskilled and low-paid into organisations that might improve the lives of the working classes failed.

In 1791, the revolutionary government passed a law known as 'Le Chapelier Law', which banned any form of trade union from existing in the country. Napoleon I, who ruled France as emperor until 1815, renewed the ban. Clearly the 'liberty and equality' of the French Revolution was not to apply to the working classes.

Repression by both employer and government continued until well after the Revolution of 1848. In both 1831 and 1834, workers in the textile industry in Lyon attempted to improve their pay and working conditions. However, their demands were refused and the government began a campaign of brutal repression. Troops were sent in to break up the workers' organisations and many people were killed. One of the reasons why there was a further revolution in France in 1848 was because a hungry working class saw no other outlet for its despair. Forbidden to organise peacefully, they turned to violence.

There is little or no evidence of any trade union development in Germany until the second half of the 19th century. The fact that Germany was broken up into many different, and often small, separate states made any national organisation difficult. As large-scale industrialisation did not occur until after 1850, and most industry before then was carried out only on a small scale, there was no requirement for what trade unions could offer during this period.

Note:

Marx became the most prominent member of a group of writers and thinkers that spanned Europe, including Louis Blanc and Claude Henri de Rouvroy, Count of Saint-Simon in France, and Robert Owen in Britain. Profoundly influenced by the Industrial Revolution, these men realised that industrialisation was changing society and politics. They developed new social theories based on the modern world.

The rise of Marxism

Karl Marx, the founder of Marxism, was born in Germany but lived in France and Belgium before settling in Britain after the 1848 revolutions. In 1848, he wrote the *Communist Manifesto* with Friedrich Engels, another German living in Britain. They were strongly influenced by French socialist ideas and the working-class involvement in the revolutions of 1848.

In this famous work, Marx put forward his theory that economic forces were fundamental to society, and that history followed an inevitable pattern dictated by economic change.

Private property had replaced primitive societies in which there was no private ownership. Capitalism replaced the feudal economy of the Middle Ages, giving power to the moneyed middle class, or bourgeoisie. Marx called for a revolution by the lower classes – whom he referred to as the proletariat or wage-slaves – to overthrow the capitalist system. A dictatorship of the proletariat would lead to a classless society. National boundaries would disappear and state governments that suppressed workers would no longer exist. Marx's rallying cry was: 'The proletariat have nothing to lose but their chains. Workers of the world unite.'

Marxism had a stronger influence in Germany and France than in Britain, the first industrial country. Marx might have been puzzled that the most successful Marxist revolutions were not in industrial countries but in agrarian Russia in the early 20th century and, later, China. Marxism had very little impact on the USA, the most industrial country in recent history and the home of capitalism.

Figure 2.12 German philosopher Karl Marx in 1860

Historical debate: who gained most from the Industrial Revolution by 1850?

Most historians agree that while the upper classes did not make many practical gains from the Industrial Revolution, they also lost very little. Land retained its value and some noblemen grew wealthier because they owned estates situated at the centre of industrial developments. In addition, the upper classes largely maintained their political influence.

There is also general agreement that the middle classes made some gains overall. Many of them became wealthier as a result of the Industrial Revolution – either directly (as factory owners or industrial inventors) or indirectly (as bankers, investors and merchants). Their economic rise was accompanied by growing political power. In Britain, the middle classes won the vote and some became members of parliament. In France and in some of the German states, they could influence government policy.

However, there is more disagreement amongst historians about the overall effects of the Industrial Revolution on the lower classes. Those who lived on the land probably lost out, as their livelihoods were threatened by wealthier landlords who could take advantage of changing conditions. Many migrated to towns where men, women and children worked in factories. Some did so voluntarily, but others were forced to move because factory work was the only way to make a living. The conditions in which most of them lived and worked were squalid. However, some historians argue that their living conditions may not have been any worse than they had been before industrialisation took hold.

Although diseases such as cholera spread in towns, slowly improvements began to be made in health, and the size of the population grew. Men who lived together in large groups in towns were better able to organise themselves into groups that could campaign for change. Women and children had to work in factories, but even when agriculture had been the main industry in Europe, they had put in long hours on the land or in their cottage industries. Gradually, governments introduced measures to limit working hours for women and children. More children were given a basic education by 1850. By the middle of the century, there were also some opportunities for leisure activities in large towns and cities. Publishers produced cheap magazines and novels aimed at the mass market. Theatres attracted new audiences with popular entertainments, including music halls and melodramas.

Questions

1. What were the most significant challenges to political structures during the Industrial Revolution, 1800–50?

2. Why were traditional politics regarded as outdated or irrelevant by many people by the early 19th century?

3. What were the differences between capitalism and Marxism?

4. Based on the information given in the historical debate section above, do you think the working classes benefited overall from the Industrial Revolution?

Key issues

The key features of this chapter are:

- the extent to which European agriculture and industry were transformed through mechanisation from 1750 to 1850

- the most significant inventions of this period

- the effects of industrialisation on the lower, middle and upper classes in European society from 1800 to 1850

- the political effects of the Industrial Revolution during this period, including the rise of communism and democracy

- the way in which Europe was reshaped by the development of the railways and improved forms of communication.

Revision questions

1 How far did the social changes of the Industrial Revolution benefit the working classes during the 19th century?

2 Why did cities and large towns grow in size during the Industrial Revolution?

3 'The development of steam power was the most important cause of the Industrial Revolution.' How far do you agree with this statement?

Further reading

Chapple, P. *The Industrialisation of Britain 1780–1914*. London, UK. Hodder. 1999.

Henderson, W. O. *The Industrial Revolution in Europe, 1815–1914*. London, UK. Times Books. 1961.

MacDonald, F. *Britain in the Industrial Revolution*. London, UK. Franklin Watts. 2008.

Advanced reading

Cipolla, C. M. *The Industrial Revolution (Fontana Economic History of Europe)*. London, UK. Fontana. 1973.

Evans, E. *The Forging of the Modern State*. London, UK. Pearson. 2001.

Chapter

3 Liberalism and nationalism:
Italy and Germany 1848–71

Key questions

- What were the main problems faced by nationalists before 1848?
- Why did Prussia and Piedmont lead the unification of Germany and Italy?
- How did Bismarck achieve the unification of Germany?
- How did Italian leaders achieve the unification of Italy?

Content summary

- The problems faced by nationalist groups in Germany and Italy.
- The post-Vienna settlement of Germany and Italy.
- Regionalism and different ideas of nationalism.
- The failure of the revolutions in 1848–49.
- The roles played by the powerful states of Prussia and Piedmont in Germany and Italy.
- Bismarck's aims for Germany in 1862, internal policies and the wars of unification.
- The contributions made by leaders such as Cavour, Garibaldi and Mazzini to unification.
- The importance of foreign intervention and the stages of unification.

Timeline

Jun 1815	Congress of Vienna concludes
Jul 1831	Giuseppe Mazzini founds 'Young Italy'
Jun 1846	Pius IX becomes pope
Jan 1848	Revolution begins in Italy
Feb 1848	Revolution begins in Germany
Mar 1849	Victor Emmanuel II becomes king of Piedmont
Mar 1850	Erfurt Union of German states formed
Nov 1852	Cavour becomes prime minister of Piedmont
Jul 1858	Plombières Agreement between Cavour and Napoleon III of France
Jan 1861	Wilhelm I becomes king of Prussia
Mar 1861	Victor Emmanuel II becomes king of Italy
Sep 1862	Bismarck appointed prime minister of Prussia
Jun 1866	Austro–Prussian War begins
Jul 1870	Franco–Prussian War begins
Jan 1871	German Empire established

Introduction

In the first half of the 19th century, Europe – particularly Germany and Italy – became a battleground for the ideas of nationalism and liberalism against traditional political structures. In September 1814, a congress of European nations met in Vienna to discuss the problems caused by the Napoleonic Wars and the fall of the Holy Roman Empire, and to establish new boundaries on the continent. Although many small nations were represented at the Congress of Vienna, the major decisions were made by the most powerful states: Austria, Britain, Prussia and Russia. French delegates attended the congress, but had no decision-making powers. The decisions made at this meeting changed the face of Europe. Most significantly, the number of German states was reduced from 230 to 39, in an effort to create larger, stronger unions that would be better able to resist future aggression. The parts of Italy that had been seized by Napoleon during his time in power were returned.

At the time, Germany and Italy were made up of a series of states with their own leaders and laws. Both became unified countries in 1870–71. Other similarities between these nations are that both suffered violent revolutions in 1848, and unification for each depended on one dominant state: Prussia in Germany and Piedmont in Italy. In order to achieve unity, both countries had to overcome the influence of a powerful Austria, and unification was only eventually achieved through war. In both cases, there were internal struggles involving groups of **liberals** and **nationalists**.

Note:

The Napoleonic Wars had their roots in the French Revolutionary Wars. They started in 1803, when various countries formed alliances against Napoleon Bonaparte's French Empire. To begin with, French forces won significant victories, but the tide began to turn after a failed invasion of Russia in 1812. Napoleon was finally defeated in 1815. (See page 39 for more information on the fall of Napoleon.)

liberals
People who favour the reform of traditional beliefs and structures to the benefit of individual freedoms. Liberalism is often characterised by open-mindedness and tolerance.

nationalists
People with a common bond such as nationality, culture or language, who want the right to govern themselves rather than be ruled by another country or culture.

Figure 3.1 Delegates at the Congress of Vienna in 1814

The rise of nationalism in Germany and Italy

Liberalism and nationalism in the early 19th century

Liberalism is based on the idea of individual freedoms, such as freedom of speech and rule by consent, laws to guarantee trial by jury, and institutions of government like parliaments, which represent the people. The ideas of liberalism began to develop in Britain in the 17th century, notably in the writings of **John Locke**.

However, early 19th-century liberals in Britain and Europe were usually unenthusiastic about a form of democracy in which everyone had a vote. This view was mainly a reaction to the French Revolution, where mob violence and an absence of law and order did not make governments inclined to extend the franchise to the lower classes. Most liberals were middle-class professionals – lawyers, merchants, manufacturers and teachers. They defended property rights against authoritarian rulers from above and disorderly crowds from below. They believed that governments should represent responsible, educated people with property or trade interests, and claimed that the illiterate and uneducated classes had no notion of what sensible government involved. Liberals tended to seek change through peaceful means, not revolution.

Liberal economics were based on a belief in *laissez-faire* (literally 'let it be') – a system of trade that was free from government interference. Competition was regarded as beneficial, because it led to lower costs and higher profits. Tariffs on trade and monopolies that protected individuals or small groups were felt to be harmful. The most efficient producers and merchants would drive out the least efficient, and consumers would benefit from lower prices and better-quality goods. Liberals opposed trade unions and believed that guilds which protected small-scale workers and traders – popular in some parts of France and Germany – should be banned, as they restricted the freedom of employers.

Key figure

John Locke (1632–1704)

The British philosopher Locke is regarded as the father of classical liberalism. He believed that all men should have the right to independence and liberty, and that this right should be defended by revolution if necessary. His ideas had a great deal of influence in Europe and beyond.

protectionism
The policy of placing high tariffs on imports in order to protect domestic industries from foreign competition. Protectionism is the opposite of free trade.

Note:
The most important book about economic liberalism was Scottish philosopher Adam Smith's *The Wealth of Nations*, first published in 1776. Smith endorsed the policy of *laissez-faire* and criticised **protectionism**, which restricted trade between different states. Smith's book was hugely influential in Europe and America.

Alongside a rise in liberalism came an increase in **nationalism** in many countries as the 19th century progressed. At the start of this period, a nobleman had more in common with the nobles of another country than with the peasants of his own country. These peasants – the majority of the population – were concerned simply with survival; they had little interest in general ideas of government. Support for national unity was limited to small sections of the population such as the educated middle classes, who were inspired as much by the writing of poets and thinkers as by the ideals of the French Revolution. The conservatives of the ruling élites were suspicious of nationalism because it threatened to bring about change.

The post-Vienna settlement of Germany and Italy

Prussia, the strongest of the German states, had played an important part in the defeat of Napoleon by 1815. It was therefore a leading member of the Congress of Vienna. Together, Prussia, Britain, Austria and Russia signed a treaty called the Quadruple Alliance, which was intended to ensure international peace. Although previously Prussia did not have as much international influence as the other nations in this alliance, the fact that it was accepted as a signatory indicated the growing respect they had for this German state.

The Congress of Vienna reorganised Germany into a confederation (*Bund*) of 39 states under the control of Austria, the most powerful state in Europe, to make it stronger and easier to defend against any future aggression. **Klemens von Metternich**, the Austrian foreign minister, presided over this group. The confederation was not a formal organisation with political powers, and member states remained independent rather than being united as a political entity.

Figure 3.2 A map showing the German states in 1815

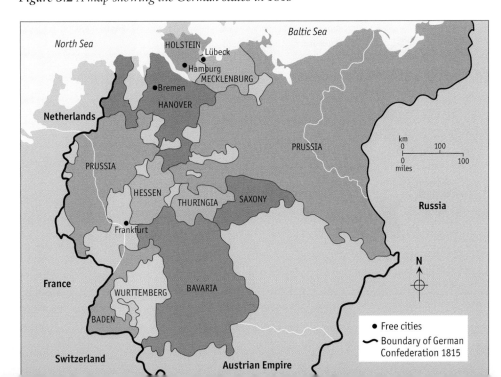

nationalism
The belief that one's own country is superior to other countries, and that its needs and interests should take priority over those of other nations.

Key figure

Klemens von Metternich (1773–1859)

Metternich was the Austrian foreign minister and an important delegate at the Congress of Vienna in 1814–15, where his priority was to maintain international order to protect Austria's interests in Germany and Italy. He was determined to suppress any signs of liberalism and nationalism. He used Austrian soldiers to put down uprisings in Italy in the 1820s and 1830s. Metternich was responsible for a repressive regime in Germany, but fell from power when the 1848 revolutions broke out.

Italy did not have any representatives at the Congress of Vienna because it was not a single country and its individual states had little power. The northern state of Piedmont was the strongest, with a significant army by Italian standards (strong enough, at least, to prevent most uprisings against its kings, other than the forced abdication of Victor Emmanuel I in 1821). However, for the most part Italy was weak compared to the rest of Europe – Metternich referred to it as merely a 'geographical expression'.

Note:

Piedmont's full name was the Kingdom of Sardinia-Piedmont. Sardinia is an island in the Mediterranean Sea, while Piedmont is in mainland Italy. Writers and historians have usually used the general term Piedmont to refer to both locations.

At the Congress of Vienna, most land that had been taken from Italy by Napoleon was restored to its traditional rulers. Austria gave up the Austrian Netherlands to Holland, but was restored to power in Italy, ruling directly or indirectly the state of Venetia in the north-west and the central states of Parma, Modena and Tuscany. The pope was restored to the Papal States around Rome in the centre of Italy. Naples and Sicily in the south were to be ruled by kings of the same Bourbon family as in France. Most of the rulers of Italy governed small or poor princedoms with underdeveloped economies.

Figure 3.3 A map showing Europe after the Congress of Vienna in 1815

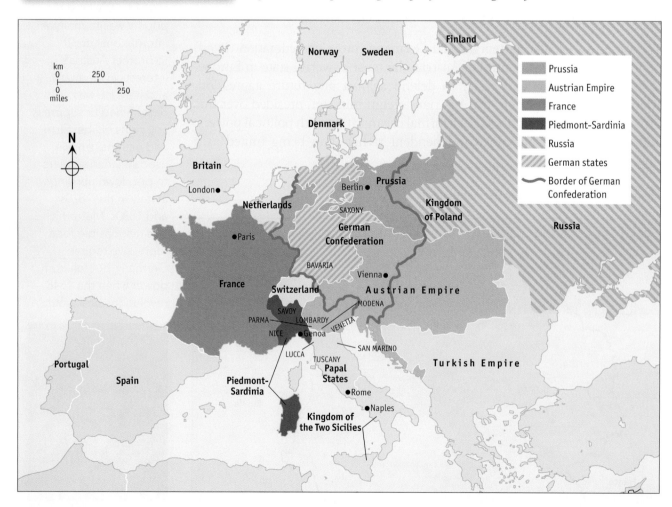

Regionalism and different ideas of nationalism

In the 19th century, the inhabitants of many parts of Europe did not feel a strong sense of national identity. Communications were poor, and people were usually born, lived, married, worked and died in the same villages or neighbouring towns. Languages varied, especially in Italy. Even when the same language was spoken, the dialects were often so different that people had trouble understanding one another. Each region had its own traditions and customs. North German states tended to be Protestant, while those in the south practised Catholicism. Although most Italians were Catholic, there was little else that united them, and people in the south did not even consider themselves part of the same country as people in the north. As a result of all these factors, most people were loyal to their region rather than their state or country. Where central governments existed, they were disliked (usually because they imposed taxes on the population) and were believed to interfere with civil liberties.

Nationalism in the Austrian Empire

Many European statesmen were wary about the growth of nationalism. The Austrian government in particular began to fear the increase in nationalist sentiment. The Austrian Empire contained a large number of **ethnic groups**, including Austrians, Germans, Hungarians, Czechs, Poles and Slavs – all of whom had different histories and traditions. This diverse empire was held together by the power of the Austrian emperor, but nationalism threatened to weaken the country. Metternich (see page 75) was determined to stamp out nationalism not only in his own country, but also in other parts of Europe because it might affect the stability of Austria.

ethnic groups
Groups of people of the same race or nationality who share a common culture or language.

Some historians have written about the 'Metternich system', but in fact little was systematic in his policies apart from a determination to protect the interests of the ruling Austrian Habsburg family. Metternich's opposition to nationalism in Germany and Italy was therefore a part of his defence of Austria. He used the army to maintain control throughout the country and in Austrian-controlled parts of Italy, selecting his soldiers from different places so that their loyalty could not be challenged. Metternich also relied on spies to bring him reports of anyone suspected of stirring up nationalist feeling. Mail was intercepted and checked for signs of nationalist activity.

Metternich was not alone in his opposition to nationalism. In 1815, Alexander I of Russia, Francis I of Austria and Friedrich Wilhelm I of Prussia signed the Holy Alliance to safeguard the power of the monarchy and Christianity in their countries. In private, Metternich dismissed this alliance as a 'high-sounding nothing', but he gave it his public support because he depended on the co-operation of these countries to prevent the spread of nationalism.

Throughout the 1820s and 1830s, a series of revolutions took place across Europe, beginning in Spain and spreading to Belgium, Germany, Poland, Switzerland and France. In 1830, the autocratic French king, Charles X, lost his throne to Louis Philippe (see page 66), who introduced a more liberal constitution. His reign did not satisfy the demands for widespread reform but it encouraged those who sought change, and this eventually led to the events of 1848 – the 'Year of Revolutions'. A poor harvest and widespread unemployment sparked unrest among the poor, and middle-class discontent over a lack of political power reached its peak. In France, the 1848 revolution overthrew Louis Philippe and established the Second Republic. Although this lasted only four years before the monarchy returned under Emperor Napoleon III, the revolution in France encouraged people elsewhere in Europe to challenge the monarchy.

Unrest in Austria during the 1848 revolution drove Metternich into exile. In the German states, the threat of rebellion forced leaders to establish constitutions. The Frankfurt Parliament (see page 82) tried unsuccessfully to bring about a national government and a freer, more unified Germany. There were also uprisings in Italy, where the middle classes drew inspiration and hope from the revolutions elsewhere on the continent.

Nationalism in Germany

For rulers in Germany – as in many other states – nationalism was negatively associated with the excesses of the French Revolution and the period of Napoleon's rule, when people had been encouraged to rise against the orderly traditions of government. A few educated Germans had more liberal ideas, inspired by writers such as Johann Wolfgang von Goethe, philosophers such as Georg Hegel and painters in the Romantic tradition who celebrated the history and traditions of German civilisation. These 19th-century German liberals imagined the Middle Ages as a time of freedom and unity and wanted to revive a national spirit that they believed Germans had shared in the past.

Note:
Liberals in 19th-century Germany did not pursue the political unity of the German states. For the most part, they simply supported the rights of individual states that shared a common feeling of being 'German'.

Liberal ideas were more widespread than nationalism, but most people retained a respect for their existing rulers. Governments in Germany varied in political style, with more liberal systems in the south than in the north. However, the princes who ruled the northern states were not unpopular. They retained an alliance with the *Junkers* – the great landowners – which ensured stability, and they governed differently from the inefficient and oppressive rulers in southern Italy, for example. In the south of Germany, there was greater freedom of the press and religious toleration. Most German states had constitutions.

However, some developments alarmed Metternich, notably the murder of the anti-liberal writer August von Kotzebue in 1819 by a mentally ill member of a liberal student association. Partly in response to this, Metternich took a leading role in asserting the authority of conservative powers. After a meeting with representatives of several German states, he issued the Carlsbad Decrees, which were intended to control radical groups through censorship.

From 1830, however, liberalism took a stronger hold across Germany. Press censorship and the supervision of schools and universities were relaxed. A group called Young Germany was established, calling for political reform. Members of this organisation were a minority – mostly young and middle class – but their influence was enough to worry Metternich and other conservative leaders. In 1832, Metternich persuaded German princes to accept the Six Articles, which curbed political meetings. Further restrictive measures were introduced after a brief outbreak of violence in Frankfurt, although it had attracted little support. After this, censorship of the press and supervision of educational establishments were increased once again.

> **Note:**
> The Carlsbad Decrees were introduced on 20 September 1819 after a conference in the town of Carlsbad, Bohemia. Universities and schools came under close scrutiny and student societies were dissolved. Many liberal teachers were dismissed and some were imprisoned. Censorship of the press increased. Many historians have argued that the Carlsbad Decrees were an overreaction. Kotzebue's assassin acted alone and there was no real danger of a large-scale nationalist or liberal uprising in Germany.

The economy and the Zollverein

Although Metternich believed that he and the German rulers were in control of the political situation, economic developments in the first half of the 19th century proved fatal to his policies. At the start of the century, the German economy was largely based on agriculture. However, just as in Britain, the Industrial Revolution in Germany caused considerable changes. Food output increased as farmers employed new methods, including new machines and fertilisers. Urban changes brought about a more prosperous middle class and a larger working class. Traditional economic structures came under strain. Guilds that formerly protected skilled workers found it impossible to resist the impact of machine-made products.

During the 1830s, German industry developed, with growth in textiles, iron and steel. Prussia led the way in these changes, building new roads and crucially investing in railways. Coal – the fuel of the Industrial Revolution – was plentiful. Prussia was also responsible for many reforms in trade and customs. In 1818, it abolished its 67 internal customs barriers because they hindered trade, and encouraged other German states to do the same. The next stage was to abolish customs barriers between states. With the establishment of the Zollverein in 1834 (see page 53), Germany found itself with the largest free-trade area in Europe, as well as the means to pursue effective trade and economic relationships with other countries.

> **Note:**
> Austria did not join the Zollverein. Most of its politicians failed to appreciate the importance of economic change. Austria also directed much of its trade towards the Mediterranean regions and underestimated the significance of what was happening in Germany. Some historians think that Austria's refusal to join the Zollverein was a significant mistake, and ultimately resulted in it losing control of Germany to Prussia. In fact, Metternich predicted that this would happen, but he was overruled.

Although Prussia was the most influential member of the Zollverein, the other states were not always willing to be dictated to by their powerful neighbour. They insisted that decisions had to be unanimous and that economic affairs should be kept separate from political issues. Although Prussia reaped the greatest rewards, other states enjoyed economic expansion, particularly in factories that produced textiles, iron and steel. The railway system grew rapidly, making trade between states and with other countries easier. Germany's geographical situation at the heart of Europe was an advantage, because it could trade easily with both east and west. Later, the railways played an important role in unification, making it possible to carry soldiers and armaments more quickly over longer distances.

Following the establishment of the customs union, German states adopted a common currency and uniform trade laws, but the Zollverein was not intended to be a political development. The states that joined it were anxious to retain their independence.

Figure 3.4 A map showing membership of the Zollverein 1818–88

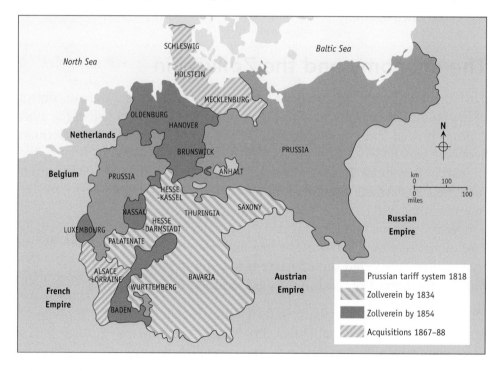

Questions

1. What signs of future German and Italian unification were evident in the first half of the 19th century?

2. To what extent could politics in Germany and Italy in the first half of the 19th century be described as a tension between nationalism and liberalism?

3. What were the principal forces behind nationalism in Germany and Italy?

Prussia and the unification of Germany

The 1848–49 revolutions in Germany

Germany did not escape the wave of revolutions in 1848, and riots spread throughout many states. These involved both the middle and lower classes, but their respective demands were different. Middle-class liberals wanted freedom of the press, jury trials and greater representation in government; some extreme middle-class revolutionaries wanted to establish a republic. The working classes were suffering from a lack of food due to poor harvests. Like the Luddites in Britain (see page 55), traditional tradesmen and workers destroyed the machines in factories that deprived them of a living.

The authorities in the various German states reacted in different ways. Some hastily granted concessions in the hope of appeasing the revolutionaries. In Prussia, the king sent soldiers to suppress the uprisings, but ordered them to withdraw when it became clear that this was only leading to further violence. He then promised to introduce a new liberal constitution.

Figure 3.5 Revolutionaries storming the royal palace in Berlin during the 1848 revolution

The revolutionaries were disorganised and their demands were vague and often contradictory. Some called for a united Germany, which they believed would strengthen the region's economy, political structure, international standing and armies, while others favoured continued government by state authorities. A few were Marxists, following the call for a socialist revolution.

In 1848, a step was taken towards greater unity when a parliament was established at Frankfurt that claimed to represent all Germans. However, the Frankfurt parliament implemented few meaningful reforms. Debates became more important than decisions, with arguments raging over what 'Germany' meant. In particular, there were disagreements about whether or not Austria should be included in a united Germany.

> **Note:**
> Some people favoured a large Germany (*Grossdeutschland*), which would include German-speaking regions of Austria, and which would be dominated by Austria. Others preferred a small Germany (*Kleindeutschland*) without those regions, which would therefore be dominated by Prussia.

There were also arguments about whether or not this united Germany should be a monarchy or a republic, and whether Germans living in other countries should be included. There was no easy answer to this question because it was difficult to define who classified as a German. The people of Alsace in eastern France spoke German, as did many people in Switzerland. Some Austrians were German-speaking and the nobility of the Baltic regions of Russia commonly spoke German. Geography was thus not a defining issue. There were reasonably clear boundaries in the west and to the south, but the east was more problematic, lacking clear river or mountain boundaries with Austria and Russia.

The Frankfurt parliament had minority support among Germans. It faced violence from republican crowds and there was always a chance that authoritarian powers might take action against it. Other mini-parliaments sprung up claiming authority. The *Junkers* were alarmed by rumours that the Frankfurt parliament proposed to end their tax exemptions and redistribute their lands.

After almost a year, the Frankfurt parliament adopted a constitution with a monarchy. Realising that Prussia was the only state with a strong enough army to withstand an attack in the event of Austrian disapproval of this decision, the crown was offered to the Prussian king, Friedrich Wilhelm IV. He rejected it, saying that the crown of Germany was 'shaped out of the dirt and dregs of revolution, disloyalty and treason'. Friedrich Wilhelm's decision destroyed the faint hope of German unity – none of the other states had the power to force unification in the face of opposition from Austria and Prussia.

Historians disagree about the significance of the Frankfurt parliament. Many have dismissed its members as impractical intellectuals who did not understand the real world of politics. They were also unrepresentative of the German people. The aristocracy opposed them and the masses had other, more practical, demands. Some historians feel that it was certain to fail, given the military strength of Prussia and Austria. Yet the Frankfurt parliament was not a complete failure. For liberals, it represented a heroic venture rather than a humiliating failure. They continued to spread their ideas and became a significant force in the coming years. Conservative landowners and industrialists learned that the grievances of the people could not be ignored and were more willing to concede social reforms.

Questions

1 What does Source A below reveal about the attitude that some Germans had towards the relationship between Austria and Germany?

2 How do Sources A and B differ in their views of German unification and government?

Source A

We cannot conceal the fact that the whole German question is a simple alternative between Prussia and Austria. In these states German life has its positive and negative poles. In Germany, all the interests are national and reforming. In Austria, all interests are conservative and destructive. The German question is not a constitutional question, but a question of power. The Prussian monarchy is now wholly German, while that of Austria cannot be. We need a powerful ruling house. Austria's power meant lack of power for us, whereas Prussia desired German unity in order to supply the limits of her own power. Already Prussia is a model for Germany.

German politician and historian Johann Gustav Droysen, in a speech to the Frankfurt parliament, 1848.

Source B

I am not able to return a favourable reply to the offer of a crown on the part of the German National Assembly [meeting in Frankfurt], because the Assembly has not the right, without the consent of the German governments, to bestow the crown which they tendered me, and moreover because they offered the crown upon condition that I would accept a constitution which could not be reconciled with the rights of the German states.

Proclamation from the Prussian king, Friedrich Wilhelm IV, after being offered the crown of Germany, 1849.

Key figure

Otto von Bismarck (1815–98)

Bismarck began his political career as a conservative opponent of the liberals. In 1862, he became minister-president of Prussia, and when the German states were united in 1871, Bismarck was the first chancellor of Germany. He helped expand the German Empire, and had great power until Kaiser Wilhelm II dismissed him in 1890.

Prussia under Wilhelm I

Wilhelm I became regent of Prussia in 1858 when his brother, Friedrich Wilhelm IV, fell ill. He ascended the throne in his own right in 1861. Wilhelm was not a liberal, but he accepted the constitution.

One of his priorities was to reverse the humiliation that had occurred at Olmütz in 1850, when Austria insisted on intervening in Germany to crush disturbances, instead of leaving the task to Prussia. Relations between Austria and Prussia had cooled further when Prussia refused to follow Austrian policy towards the Crimean War (1854–56). When Austria proposed that the Zollverein be expanded to include Austria and its territories in eastern Europe, Prussia refused – fearing that this would allow Austria to become the centre of European trade. These events strengthened the position of the liberals in Germany. Wilhelm I may not have shared their political views but they had a common distrust of Austria, and Wilhelm was willing to appoint moderate ministers in his government.

Growing nationalism in Germany was encouraged by developments in Italy, where Count Camillo di Cavour (see page 97) was working to unite the country. One German politician made a speech congratulating Italy for its moves towards unification and praised Cavour in particular. He said that he looked forward to the rise of a 'German Cavour'. His wish was soon fulfilled, in the form of the statesman **Otto von Bismarck**.

The rise of Bismarck

Few men have directly shaped a country's history for as long as Bismarck in Germany. He came to power in 1862 and governed for almost 30 years. During that period, Prussia became part of a united Germany, which in turn became one of the most powerful countries in the world. Bismarck's influence has been widely debated. Some see him as the greatest politician of the 19th century; others believe that he was responsible for the international tensions that led to the First World War, and a style of government in Germany that allowed the eventual development of Hitler's totalitarian rule.

The budget crisis

By 1860, the Prussian government was facing a threat from the liberals. This came about after a mobilisation of the army revealed serious military deficiencies, convincing the government that the army needed to be strengthened and its budget increased. The liberals – the majority group in the Landtag (the lower house of parliament) – objected because they believed that a stronger army could be used to suppress them and raise taxes without their consent. An election in 1862 resulted in an increased vote for the liberals.

Wilhelm I faced a dilemma: he believed that funds were needed urgently for the army, but the constitution required that taxes be agreed by parliament, and the liberals were unlikely to approve them. A minister sent a telegram to Bismarck, who was in Paris at the time: 'The Fatherland is in danger. Hurry home.' Wilhelm was reluctant to use Bismarck because of his extreme views, but Bismarck persuaded the king of his loyalty and was appointed minister-president in the hope that he could bring the situation under control. In September 1862, Bismarck delivered a powerful speech on this crisis.

Public opinion changes, the press is not [the same as] public opinion; one knows how the press is written; members of parliament have a higher duty, to lead opinion, to stand above it. We are too hot-blooded, we have a preference for putting on armour that is too big for our small body; and now we're actually supposed to utilise it. Germany is not looking to Prussia's liberalism, but to its power; Bavaria, Württemberg, Baden may indulge liberalism, and for that reason no one will assign them Prussia's role; Prussia has to coalesce and concentrate its power for the opportune moment, which has already been missed several times; Prussia's borders according to the Vienna Treaties [of 1814–15] are not favourable for a healthy, vital state; it is not by speeches and majority resolutions that the great questions of the time are decided – that was the big mistake of 1848 and 1849 – but by iron and blood.

Otto von Bismarck, in a speech given on 30 September 1862.

Bismarck's speech referred to 'blood and iron', and this phrase has often been used to support the view that Bismarck was a ruthless soldier-politician who favoured war more than peace and absolutism more than government by consent. He was careful not to insult the liberals in the speech, but pointed out that they had failed in 1848. He argued that he and the king shared the liberals' aims and that only their methods were different. While the liberals refused to be pacified, Bismarck's position was strengthened because the upper house in the parliament, dominated by the *Junkers*, was in favour of the budget.

Figure 3.6 Otto von Bismarck (standing) and other German ministers in 1862

Early problems

When he was first appointed minister-president of Prussia, Bismarck faced several challenges. The most significant of these were how to deal with the changing social and economic conditions that resulted from the Industrial Revolution, problems with foreign policy, and masterminding the unification of a region made up of different states with different leaders.

Bismarck himself was a *Junker* – a member of a wealthy landowning family. As such, he accepted the traditional views of his class and was not wholly in favour of granting more rights to the middle and working classes. However, Bismarck was also better educated than many *Junkers* and was something of an intellectual. He knew that he had to adapt to changing conditions in order to stay in power and to keep Prussia strong.

Bismarck felt that Prussia's interests were best served by trying to isolate Austria, but not yet waging war on it. To this end, he had campaigned against Austria's inclusion in the Zollverein. He also began promoting nationalism, not because he believed in its ideals but because he felt this was a way of advancing Prussia's power. He could not do this alone – throughout the period of his rule he had to rely on Prussian, then German, military power as well as support for his policies from the king. Despite this, Bismarck soon earned a reputation for governing alone, without consulting other ministers.

From 1863, Bismarck struck hard at the liberals, dismissing unreliable civil servants and increasing censorship of the press. His free-trade policies and determination to exclude Austria from the Zollverein also weakened the liberals' position, because they favoured these policies. Some historians believe that this was an attempt to provoke the liberals so that he could then accuse them of being disloyal. At the same time, Bismarck worked to increase his appeal to other social classes. He could be sure of support from the *Junkers*, but he also tried to win over the lower classes by promising social reforms.

Note:

Bismarck's conversations with Disraeli should be treated with caution as evidence of his political vision. It is unlikely that the German minister would reveal accurately his long-term plans to a British politician whom he knew only slightly. Bismarck may simply have been trying to impress Disraeli in the course of a casual conversation.

Bismarck: planner or opportunist?

Historians disagree about the extent to which Bismarck set out from the first to unify Germany. Some have judged that this was always his intention, but others claim that he was an opportunist who took advantage of successive crises that he did not plan, but which ended in German unification.

The first view sees Bismarck as both a visionary and a ruthless planner. Much depends on his remarks in 1862 to Disraeli, the British politician and future prime minister. Bismarck said that his first task was to reorganise the army and after that he would 'take the first opportunity to declare with Austria, break the German Confederation, bring the middle and smaller German states under control, and give Germany a national union under Prussia's leadership'. These comments suggest that Bismarck did indeed plan events over the long term. In a later conversation with Disraeli, he claimed that he had always planned the stages by which Germany was unified.

The second view depends on an awareness of the problems facing German unification. This is shown in Bismarck's message to a German diplomat in 1869, after he had set up the North German Confederation of states. The message called for patience – Bismarck did not believe that complete unification would be achieved whilst he was in office. Again, Bismarck's words must be treated carefully. Although this was an official document, Bismarck might have intended to calm fears of further Prussian expansion in Austria and especially France.

The Prussian army and the Wars of Unification

Prussia had a strong military tradition, dating back to the reign of Friedrich II in the mid 18th century. Friedrich's victories, his expansion of Prussian territory and his domestic government earned him the title 'the Great'. By the middle of the 19th century, Prussia's standing army was not large, but the state had a well-organised system of reserve soldiers ready to reinforce the army in times of war. The Prussian military was well-respected and it was considered an honourable occupation for men of noble families. The training of army officers was well organised, requiring their attendance at a military academy for three years. Elsewhere in Europe, wealthy young men could buy their commissions to become officers and received little further training as they were promoted.

Bismarck was assisted in his battle for unification by two outstanding army leaders – Field Marshal **Helmuth von Moltke**, chief of the general staff, and **Albrecht von Roon**, the minister of war. These two men made a formidable team, and it is unlikely that Bismarck would have achieved his aims without their significant contributions.

There were three wars that eventually led to the unification of Germany:

- In 1864, the German states secured a swift victory over Denmark.
- In 1866, the Austro–Prussian War resulted in the creation of the North German Confederation of states under Prussian control.
- In 1870–71, the Franco–Prussian War ended with the final unification of all German states.

Some historians have concluded that Prussian success was largely due to the weakness of its enemies, but this underestimates the advantages of the Prussian forces – training and transport helped them to victory. Denmark had a weak army, but the armies of Austria and France were strong, and few would have anticipated their defeat. The Austrian army had better heavy guns,

Key figures

Helmuth von Moltke (1800–91)

Moltke made his name as a skilful battlefield commander, and cemented his reputation with his reorganisation of the Prussian army in the 1860s. He modernised methods of training, and understood how important railways could be to transport soldiers and supplies. After unification he served as a member of the new German parliament.

Albrecht von Roon (1803–79)

Roon helped persuade Wilhelm I to appoint Bismarck, and his partnership with Bismarck and Moltke was key to Prussia's success in the Wars of Unification. He raised a large and well-trained army in Prussia with an efficient system of military reserves. Roon was also briefly minister-president of Prussia in 1873.

but the Prussians had more modern rifles with faster rates of fire than their opponents' weapons. The Austrian army, combined with its south German allies, was as large as the Prussian army. The French army had high-quality rifles but the Prussians had improved their heavy guns by 1870. Ultimately, the most decisive factors were that the Prussian army was well trained and had better officers, and that it could move quickly to take decisive positions on the battlefield.

War with Denmark 1864

The king of Denmark ruled the north German duchies (regions) of Schleswig and Holstein. Most of the people of Schleswig spoke Danish and were loyal to their Danish ruler, whereas the population of Holstein was mostly German-speaking and thus had stronger pro-German feelings. The Congress of Vienna (see page 75) had limited Denmark's influence over these regions, but in 1864 the new Danish king, Christian IX, revived an old claim to extend Denmark's power over Schleswig-Holstein.

Denmark's big mistake was to believe that Austria and Prussia would not co-operate with each other, even in the face of a common enemy. However, Bismarck did not want to provoke Austria by acting alone, and Austria wished to maintain the terms of the Congress of Vienna that limited Denmark's influence over the duchies. At a time when Austria was under pressure in Italy and elsewhere, its priority was to maintain international agreements, even though it had no direct interests in Schleswig-Holstein. Thus, the two states joined forces to wage a swift war against Denmark in 1864. By October, the Danes were defeated and control of Schleswig-Holstein fell to Prussia and Austria by the Treaty of London.

Figure 3.7 Prussian soldiers in Duppel, after the storming of Danish defences during the Schleswig-Holstein conflict in 1864

Note:

Some historians claim that the war against Denmark was proof that Bismarck planned and executed his aims carefully – using Austria as an ally when needed, but turning against it later. In fact, Christian IX instigated the crisis and Bismarck came under great pressure within Prussia to take decisive action. He embarked on the war without a clear idea of the settlement that would follow, and the terms of the treaty were largely a result of Denmark's refusal to compromise.

War with Austria 1866

Unlike the war against Denmark, Bismarck was largely responsible for the Austro–Prussian War of 1866. While more states were admitted to the Zollverein, Austria continued to be excluded. In addition, Bismarck set up a free-trade agreement with France, knowing that this would anger Austria. He also made no effort to conceal the disagreements that arose over the government of Schleswig-Holstein, hoping to stir up anti-Austrian feeling in Prussia.

Knowing that war with Austria was inevitable, Bismarck began to seek foreign allies in the hope of isolating his enemy. While Russia would only promise to remain neutral in any conflict, Bismarck did succeed in making an alliance with Italy. The Italian army was small, but Bismarck felt that it might still provide a useful distraction during a war, preventing Austria from focusing its entire force on Prussia.

Bismarck was sufficiently concerned about which side France might take in an Austro–Prussian conflict that he travelled to France himself to meet with the emperor, Napoleon III. Napoleon decided to remain neutral but, seeing himself as a champion of the new Italy, promised to hand Venetia (at the time governed by Austria) to Italy after the war. The French emperor expected that a war between Austria and Prussia would be prolonged, and he believed that France would benefit by acting as a peacemaker. Bismarck's anxiety that France should not ally with Austria led him to make some vague promises about French concessions on the Rhineland, an area along the border between France and Germany. It is not clear whether he intended to deliberately mislead Napoleon, but certainly Bismarck made no attempt to concede any land after the war was won.

Figure 3.8 The Battle of Sadowa – a decisive Prussian victory in the war against Austria in 1866

Most of Europe, including the German states, shared Napoleon III's opinion that the war would be a long one, and public opinion in Prussia was against the conflict. Some believed that Prussia could not win against the strength of Austria; others did not want to fight against the German states (mostly in the south) that would support Austria. Moltke was uncertain about the chances of victory and Bismarck himself expressed doubts about Prussian success. Surprisingly, when the war finally broke out in 1866 the Prussians took only seven weeks to secure a victory. The Battle of Sadowa (also known as the Battle of Königgratz), in particular, became part of the Bismarck legend.

The peace terms were established in the Treaty of Prague, but they were not harsh. Bismarck had no desire to humiliate Austria by seeking concessions other than granting Venetia to Italy. Although defeated, Austria was still a powerful state and Bismarck did not want to make it a permanent enemy of Prussia:

- The treaty allowed Bismarck to replace the German Confederation that had been established in 1815 (and which was dominated by Austria) with the North German Confederation. This was not an association of free states, but a political union in which northern states joined Prussia.
- The king of Prussia had control over the Confederation's foreign policy and decisions about war and peace.
- Whilst the parliament was theoretically democratic and given some powers, the reality was that Prussia dominated, under Bismarck's direction.
- The independence of the southern German states was guaranteed in the Southern Confederation.

Bismarck openly stated that he had no plans to incorporate the southern states and unify all of Germany. However, he took steps to strengthen the links between north and south. Most importantly, he set up an elected body to represent both parts of the country in matters of trade, but Prussia retained control through its presidency of the Zollverein.

> **Note:**
> The Treaty of Prague was one of the most important settlements of the 19th century. Prussia became a major power, and Austria's influence in western Europe declined. Instead, it focused its priorities on eastern Europe and the Balkans. France began to fear further expansion of Prussian power. These two factors eventually contributed to the outbreak of the First World War in 1914.

War with France 1870–71

Relations between Prussia and France deteriorated after the Austro–Prussian War. Many of the south German states were predominantly Catholic, and they saw Catholic France as a potential ally against Prussia's growing power. Austria also sought an alliance with France, and the Austrian emperor, Franz Josef, met with Napoleon III to agree terms in which they would form a united front against Prussian expansion. In addition, Napoleon maintained friendly relations with Russia. However, Bismarck became aware of France's negotiations to build an alliance against him, so when Napoleon attempted to buy Luxembourg from Holland, Bismarck made the news public. The south German states – still independent at the time – were horrified and turned against France.

These developments alone may not have made war between Prussia and France inevitable, but unexpected events in another country played into Bismarck's hands. In 1870, the Spanish queen, Isabella II, was forced to abdicate by politicians who wanted an end to Bourbon rule in their country. They selected Prince Leopold of Hohenzollern as their new monarch. Leopold was from a south German state and a Catholic, like the Spaniards, but he was also related to the Prussian royal family. Encouraged by Bismarck, Leopold accepted the offer – a move that was certain to incite French anger as a further example of Prussian expansionism.

King Wilhelm I of Prussia was doubtful about the wisdom of Bismarck's policy, and persuaded Leopold to withdraw his acceptance of the Spanish throne. The king sent Bismarck a telegram describing a meeting he had just had with the French ambassador about the issue of the Spanish succession. When he received the Ems Telegram (as it is now known), Bismarck saw an opportunity to portray France as the unreasonable party in the negotiations. He changed the original wording of the telegram to make it appear that the French were demanding a humiliating reversal of Prussia's decision to support Leopold's rights in Spain. He then released the telegram to the public.

> After the news of the renunciation of the Prince von Hohenzollern had been communicated to the Imperial French government by the Royal Spanish government, the French Ambassador in Ems made a further demand on His Majesty the King that he should authorize him to telegraph to Paris that His Majesty the King undertook for all time never again to give his assent should the Hohenzollerns once more take up their candidature. His Majesty the King thereupon refused to receive the Ambassador again and had the latter informed by the Adjutant of the day that His Majesty had no further communication to make to the Ambassador.

Bismarck's version of the Ems Telegram, published in Prussia on 14 July 1870.

The result of this manoeuvre was public outrage in both Prussia and France; resolving the situation became a matter of national honour. There were signs that Napoleon III and his government favoured negotiations – perhaps a European conference – to encourage Prussia to accept a compromise, but Bismarck would not agree. Urged on by public opinion, Napoleon decided on war. This was a risky decision: despite attempts to establish alliances, France was relatively isolated. Britain refused to offer support, believing that France was not justified in going to war over the Spanish throne. The Italians also refused to come to France's aid while French soldiers were still present in their country, defending Rome on behalf of the pope (see page 99). Austria and Russia declared their neutrality. Ultimately, France was seen as the aggressor while Prussia claimed only to be defending itself.

The Franco–Prussian War began in July 1870. Although the French army was smaller and less organised than the Prussians, German generals were still surprised by the ease with which they defeated their enemy. By May the following year, Napoleon III could no longer continue the war and sought a peace treaty with Bismarck.

Figure 3.9 Bismarck reading the French reply to the Ems Telegram to Wilhelm I in 1870

The German Empire

As a result of the war with France, Germany was fully united. However, this was not entirely a triumph for German nationalism:

- Prussia remained the dominant state in the new Germany.
- Some southern states were still reluctant to be part of a 'Greater Germany' and thus come under Prussian control. Bismarck had to make some concessions to persuade them to join the union.
- Bavaria, the largest southern state, sought special powers to retain a degree of independence.

It was not only the southern states that were concerned about the unification of their country. The *Junkers* feared that Prussia would have less power and influence in a larger Germany, and Wilhelm I expressed little enthusiasm for taking on the role of emperor of Germany. However, despite these objections all parties were eventually persuaded to follow Bismarck's policies and support a united Germany.

Napoleon III abdicated and was replaced by a republican government. Bismarck took advantage of France's weakness to impose harsh peace terms. The French provinces of Alsace and Lorraine were conceded to Germany, and France was required to pay heavy **reparations**; a German army was posted in northern France until they were paid. France's humiliation was completed by the fact that Wilhelm I was proclaimed emperor of the new united Germany at the Palace of Versailles near Paris – the ancient court of French kings.

reparations
Money that one country has to pay another as compensation for war damage.

Note:
The moderate treaty at the end of the Austro–Prussian war led to peaceful relations between Prussia and Austria. The harsh treaty with France resulted in hostility that was an important cause of the First World War and contributed to the outbreak of the Second World War in 1939. What does this tell us about the difficulty of making peace settlements?

Questions

1 The table below outlines some of the problems Bismarck faced in his campaign to unify Germany. What do you think was the most serious problem? Give reasons for your choice.

German liberals	Austria	France
Disadvantage Opposed Bismarck's budget to increase Prussia's army. Objected to his influence and methods. **Advantage** Agreed with idea of German nationalism. Lacked ability to carry out policies.	**Disadvantage** Traditionally held power in Germany. Represented stability in the country. **Advantage** Disliked by many German states. Faced problems elsewhere by the 1860s.	**Disadvantage** Determined to prevent expansion of Prussia after 1866. Supported by south German (Catholic) states. **Advantage** Poorly led by Napoleon III.

2 What does Source A below reveal about Bismarck's attitude towards Austria before he came to power in 1862?

Source A

Because of the policy of the Congress of Vienna in 1815, Germany is clearly too small for both Prussia and Austria. As long as an honourable arrangement concerning the influence of each in Germany cannot be reached, we will both plough the same disputed land. Austria will remain the only state to whom we can permanently lose or from whom we can permanently gain. I am convinced that, in the not too distant future, we shall have to fight for our existence against Austria. It is not within our power to avoid that. The course of events in Germany has no other solution.

Otto von Bismarck, in a letter to a friend written in 1856.

Italian leaders and the unification of Italy

In the mid 19th century, Italy as we know it today did not exist. It was made up of self-governing states or kingdoms, some of which were under the control of foreign powers. States in the north generally had more advanced industries and were therefore more prosperous than states in the south, whose economies were largely based on agriculture. While the north had a middle class of reasonably well-educated merchants and lawyers, the south was populated by farmers and had the highest rate of illiteracy in western Europe. All across the country, people spoke a wide variety of regional dialects. Loyalties were local, not national. One of the few unifying features of the Italian people was their religion: almost all of them were Roman Catholics. This fact also contributed to a lack of demand for change for many years as – apart from a brief period at the start of **Pius IX**'s papacy – the Church favoured the established authorities.

Italy shared a common feeling with Germany: hatred of Austrian authority. When the forces of nationalism began to emerge after 1815, therefore, they were often founded in the desire of separate regions to be free from Austrian influence rather than a wish to achieve a politically unified Italy.

Figure 3.10 A map of Italy showing the various states before unification

Nationalist groups were divided about their aims. Should they fight for a limited monarchy or a full republic? Did they want a central government or a federal state in which the different regions retained a certain amount of power? They also argued over the methods by which change should be brought about – gradually or by revolution? Different groups suggested various cities for the capital of the new Italy once it had been established; Florence, Milan and Turin were all proposed. Rome was the historic capital of Italy, but as the home of the papacy, which opposed a united Italy, Rome did not seem a likely candidate to be the heart of this new country. Such dissent made it easy for the authorities to isolate and defeat the forces of change.

Italian nationalist leaders

King Charles Albert

When King Charles Albert succeeded to the throne of Piedmont in north-west Italy in 1831, he was already known to have liberal sympathies, although he personally favoured a strong monarchy. As regent during the reign of his predecessor, he introduced a constitution (the *Statuto*) that was much more liberal than any other in Italy. By the 1840s, he was supporting the nationalists and declared war on Austria in 1848, but some suspected him of wanting to increase Piedmont's power more than achieving a united Italy. After a defeat at the Battle of Novara in 1849, Charles Albert abdicated. However, his reign marked the start of an association between the royal family of Piedmont and the cause of Italian unification.

Mazzini and Garibaldi

Giuseppe Mazzini was one of the key figures in the Italian nationalist movement in the first half of the 19th century. While other nationalists were attempting to unite certain regions of Italy, Mazzini called for the unification of the whole country, or *Risorgimento*. Radically, he believed this would be the first step towards an even broader unification – that of Europe and, eventually, the whole world. Mazzini was an idealistic visionary, but he was also a man of action, constantly planning risings and revolutions to unify Italy. His republican views and his outspoken criticism of the Church naturally angered authorities not just in Italy, but also in many of the countries in which he lived during his periods of exile.

As a member of the secret nationalist society the Carbonari, Mazzini believed that such unification could only be achieved by revolution. After being expelled from Genoa, he went to France. There, he became disillusioned by the failures of the uprisings organised by the Carbonari. In reaction to this, Mazzini founded another nationalist group, Young Italy, which dispensed with the secrecy that the Carbonari insisted on and instead openly called for support for a united Italy.

Note:
Young Italy was founded in 1831. Mazzini hoped to create a united Italy by promoting unrest, discord and violence in many of Italy's reactionary states. He believed this would lead to many people wanting a peaceful and united Italy.

Mazzini's most significant moment of leadership came during the 1848–49 revolutions (see below), where he fought alongside his most dedicated follower, **Giuseppe Garibaldi**, who later won the south for a united Italy. Although the revolution failed at this time, it inspired many Italians and won them over to the nationalist cause. Mazzini was crucial in the campaign for unification because he appealed to intellectuals in Italy, as well as winning their support in other countries. He kept the issue of Italian unification alive and persevered in the face of every setback.

Mazzini did not accept the united Italy that developed after 1860 because it was a monarchy dominated by Piedmont and the middle classes. He refused to accept a position of honour in the new country and died in hiding in Italy – an isolated figure who believed that he had been betrayed.

Cavour

Mazzini's refusal to compromise brought him into conflict with another leading nationalist, **Camillo Benso, Count of Cavour**, who favoured a more limited form of unity through a monarchy rather than a republic. Cavour first strengthened Piedmont internally, expanding the railways, making trade agreements with foreign countries, and curbing the power of the Church. To begin with, he was not enthusiastic about Piedmont's intervention in the Crimean War as an ally of Britain and France against Russia, but he came to realise that it would be helpful in the expansion of Piedmont. His priority was to enlarge his own state, and in this he was successful. However, he was forced to accept the unification of the entire country after Garibaldi's success in the south (see page 102). He was appointed prime minister of the Kingdom of Italy, and was forced into accepting a number of Mazzini's policies before his death in June 1861.

The 1848–49 revolutions

Several revolutions occurred in Italy throughout 1848–49, most of them entirely separate from each other and without any agreed plan among the revolutionaries in each region. The first uprising took place on the island of Sicily, and this soon spread to Naples – both regions governed by Ferdinand II. At the start, the rioters mainly came from the middle classes, and they therefore did not make any demands that would benefit the masses. When violence increased and the revolutionaries invaded estates, the landowners – who sought reforms that would benefit themselves – were equally determined to deny them to the peasantry and townspeople.

Key figures

Giuseppe Garibaldi (1807–82)
Garibaldi joined Mazzini's Young Italy and was soon involved in violent risings for the nationalist cause. After their failure, he spent 12 years in South America. He returned to Italy to play a leading part in the 1848–49 revolutions. Some people believe that Garibaldi's influence was limited, but he was responsible for incorporating Sicily and Naples into a unified Italy.

Camillo Benso, Count of Cavour (1810–61)
Piedmontese Cavour entered politics after the 1848 revolutions. He was prime minister from 1852 to 1861 except for a brief period when he resigned. Cavour was a monarchist, but favoured limiting the power of the king through parliament. He became the first prime minister of the new Italian state in 1861.

Figure 3.11 Barricades being erected in the streets during the 1848 revolution in Naples

Key figure

Daniele Manin (1804–57)

Manin was born in Venice and was deeply patriotic. He was imprisoned in 1848 after presenting a petition for Venetian home rule to the Venetian Congregation, and in March 1848 was made president of the short-lived Venetian Republic. Banished from Venice following Austrian military victories in 1849, he died in Paris in 1857.

Protests against Austrian rule in Milan, the chief city in the region of Lombardy, developed into armed resistance and an Austrian army was driven out. The people of Venice then rose up in rebellion and established a moderate republican government under **Daniele Manin**. Other states in the north were inspired to join Piedmont in its fight against Austria. Having to deal with uprisings in Germany as well as within its own borders, Austria was in a difficult position. However, its army was much stronger than the military forces that the individual Italian provinces could raise, and the Austrian commander-in-chief, Joseph Radetzky, was an experienced general. He planned carefully, withdrawing at first to strong fortresses in northern Italy (known as the Quadrilateral) to gather his forces, and then advancing when he was sure he could outnumber and out-manoeuvre the Italian troops. This allowed the Austrians to defeat Piedmont at Novara, and after a heroic siege the republic of Venice was forced to surrender.

At the same time, there was a violent uprising in Rome. Pope Pius IX appointed Pellegrino Rossi as minister for the interior, hoping to satisfy the discontented masses, but Rossi was assassinated. The pope refused to join the fight against Austria – a leading Catholic country – and instead fled from Rome with several high-ranking clergymen. The city fell to the extremists, who declared it a republic in its own right. An assembly was elected by a wide franchise and Mazzini became one of the leaders of the new republic. Considerable reforms were introduced, including the abolition of unpopular taxes and the seizure of Church land for peasants. However, as the majority of Rome's population remained loyal to Catholicism, the republicans lost support when they attacked the Church. Mazzini also had little support from other Italian provinces, where his extreme views made him unpopular.

At this point, France saw an opportunity both to defend the Church and to weaken Austria by leading an attack on the Roman republic. Garibaldi led the Italian resistance when Rome was besieged. The rebels were heroic, but they were a small minority compared with the French army and its allies from the south of Italy. Garibaldi had to withdraw, although he managed to take many of his soldiers with him.

The outcome of the revolutions

Ultimately, the revolutions of 1848–49 failed to achieve their aims in Italy. Austria retained its commanding position and France showed its strength in the face of revolutionary change. The Italian states remained divided – more concerned with their own interests than those of Italy as a whole. Despite these failures, however, nationalist feeling did not die, and those who sought a unified Italy learned several important lessons:

- Italy could not free itself from foreign control, but needed diplomatic and military assistance from more powerful countries.
- The activities of the masses needed to be controlled. Many peasants in the north and some in the south lost confidence in the nationalists and liberals, and supported the returning Austrian soldiers.
- The republicans had been discredited within Italy and they would have to work hard to gain future support.
- The pope was a powerful political figure and the question of Rome had to be handled carefully.

The importance of Piedmont after 1849

There are several reasons why Piedmont played a significant role in the unification of Italy. Under the leadership of Count Cavour and king **Victor Emmanuel II**, Piedmont was seen as a combination of a modernised state and a monarchy with a constitution – a situation that reassured France and Britain, and made Piedmont seem less radical than other states in Italy. The king was also anxious not to make an enemy of the papacy. When prime minister **Massimo d'Azeglio** introduced the Siccardi Laws to limit the Church's power in Piedmont, the king modified them and then opposed a proposal to introduce civil instead of Church marriages. He also stopped a bill to suppress some religious orders and seize their wealth. This further reassured those who opposed radical measures.

The Crimean War

The Crimean War broke out in 1854, with Britain and France allied against Russia. Piedmont had no interest in the balance of power in the Near East, and certainly had no quarrel with Russia. However, Victor Emmanuel II saw the advantage of an alliance with Britain and France, especially when Austria remained on the sidelines. He hoped to gain powerful friends in

Key figures

Victor Emmanuel II (1820–78)

Victor Emmanuel became king of Piedmont in 1849. He was more devoted to pleasure than government, but he supported Cavour. Once believed to be little more than Cavour's puppet, historians now praise Victor Emmanuel for his leadership during Italian unification. He became the first king of Italy in 1861.

Massimo d'Azeglio (1798–1866)

D'Azeglio became prime minister of Piedmont after the 1848 revolution. He believed that Piedmont should take the lead in unifying Italy because it was the only state strong enough to challenge Austria. He recognised Cavour's abilities, and invited him to join the government. He later recommended that Cavour should succeed him.

Europe and weaken the power that controlled much of Italy. At the end of the conflict in 1856, Piedmont's small contribution did not entitle it to any territorial gains, but its intervention proved worthwhile because the Italian state had made allies of the victorious powers.

Cavour worked hard to win the support of Britain and France in his fight against Austria, but at first he earned only expressions of sympathy rather than definite commitments. Surprisingly, events turned in his favour when the Italian nationalist Felice Orsini tried to assassinate the French emperor, Napoleon III, in 1858. While in prison awaiting execution, Orsini wrote several impassioned letters to Napoleon, begging him to help Italy in its fight for independence. Napoleon responded positively, declaring his admiration for Orsini's courage and publishing his last request.

The Treaty of Plombières

> **Note:**
>
> The nationalist leader Giuseppe Garibaldi was born in Nice, and he and other nationalists felt that Cavour had betrayed their cause by promising it to France in the Treaty of Plombières. However, the agreement demonstrated Cavour's realistic assessment of the situation: he needed French assistance and was willing to pay for it.

Cavour met Napoleon at Plombières and they agreed a treaty by which France would aid Piedmont if it was attacked by Austria. Piedmont was promised Lombardy, Venice and some papal lands; France would gain Nice and Savoy – a controversial concession by Cavour. A marriage was arranged between the daughter of Victor Emmanuel II and a cousin of the French emperor. Neither Cavour nor Napoleon III considered actions that would threaten the pope or the rulers in southern Italy. Britain and Prussia were sympathetic to Cavour's cause, but they chose to remain neutral because they did not want to see the balance of power disturbed by an Austrian defeat.

Cavour's task was to ensure that Austria declared war first so that it would be regarded as the aggressor. To incite this, he ordered Piedmont's small army to mobilise in the hope that this would provoke Austria into making preparations for war. This was a huge gamble, because Cavour could not be sure that Napoleon III would honour his promise to come to Piedmont's aid. In fact, Cavour was on the verge of cancelling the mobilisation when Austria declared war in 1859, marking the start of the second Italian war of independence.

War with Austria

The French and Piedmontese armies won decisive victories at Magenta and Solferino. Cavour had been correct in his understanding of the need for foreign support, but he was also right in his suspicion that Napoleon III would not be a reliable ally. Although he fulfilled his promise at the start of the action, the victories involved heavy French casualties and the emperor grew afraid that Britain, Prussia and Russia might turn against him. As a result, within a few months he agreed a peace with Austria – the Treaty of Villafranca – without consulting Piedmont. Ultimately, Piedmont gained Lombardy but not the other lands agreed at Plombières. Napoleon's hopes of increasing French power in central Italy came to nothing, although France was granted Nice and Savoy as Cavour had agreed. Cavour resigned briefly in protest at Napoleon's failure to honour his side of the bargain, but he returned after a few months to take advantage of unrest in other states.

In 1860, plebiscites (see page 36) were arranged in Emilia, Modena, Parma, Romagna and Tuscany over the issue of unification with Piedmont. The result was in favour of the northern states joining together. Mazzini's protest at the creation of a larger monarchy in Italy was dismissed. The Kingdom of Italy was declared in 1861, comprising all states except Venice and Rome.

Figure 3.12 The people of Bologna vote to join the united Italy in March 1860

Italy is free and nearly entirely united. The opinions of civilised nations are favourable to us. The just and liberal principles, now widespread in the governments of Europe, are favourable to us. Italy herself, too, will become a guarantee of order and peace, and will once more be an effective instrument of universal civilisation. These facts have inspired the nation with great confidence in its own destinies. I take pleasure in announcing to the first parliament of Italy the joy I feel in my heart as king and soldier.

An extract from a speech given by Victor Emmanuel II, king of Italy, in 1861.

Stages of unification: Garibaldi and southern Italy

Garibaldi (see page 97) had previously been a supporter of the republican Mazzini (see page 95), but in 1860 – with northern Italy at peace – he declared that he was going to win the south in the name of Victor Emmanuel II. The two men had met on several occasions throughout the previous year, and had agreed that Garibaldi should launch an invasion of the papal states. However, the king later changed his mind, deciding that his attentions were better focused on extending the power and influence of Piedmont than on securing full unification for Italy.

The 'Expedition of the Thousand'

Undeterred by this lack of support, Garibaldi gathered a small force of 1000 soldiers and set off for the island of Sicily in May 1860. Waiting offshore until French patrol boats left the port at Marsala, Garibaldi moved in amongst the British ships in the port. Once there, the French could not fire on him for fear of damaging the British vessels and inciting an international incident.

Having found his way in, Garibaldi led a whirlwind campaign across the island in what became known as the 'Expedition of the Thousand'. The king of Naples sent forces against him, but Garibaldi won a decisive victory at the Calatafimi garrison, and by the end of May he had succeeded in capturing the Sicilian capital of Palermo. In large part, Garibaldi's success in Sicily was due to a popular rising in his favour, as the Sicilian people flocked to welcome their liberator.

Figure 3.13 Garibaldi leads the 'Expedition of the Thousand' in Sicily in 1860

Naples and Rome

Like Victor Emmanuel, Cavour's priority had been to strengthen Piedmont's position in the north – something he had now achieved. Although encouraged by Garibaldi's capture of Palermo, Cavour remained concerned that the southern expedition was forcing him to go further than he intended. Garibaldi was too popular for Cavour to oppose his campaign openly, but he did nothing to aid him.

With Sicily safely under his control, Garibaldi turned back to the mainland. He and his 'redshirts' entered the city of Naples in September 1860, and Garibaldi declared himself 'Dictator of the Two Sicilies'. Naples rapidly agreed to unification with Piedmont. This opened the road to Rome, but Cavour realised the dangers Italy now faced from abroad. European Catholic countries (as well as Russia) were already alarmed by the dramatic events unfolding in Italy; they would not stand for an assault on the spiritual centre of Catholicism. To pre-empt this reaction, Cavour announced that Rome would become the capital of a united Italy – but not yet. When the Kingdom of Italy was declared in 1861, Turin, the chief city of Piedmont, was named as its capital.

Unification: the final stages

Some historians have argued that rather than being unified, Italy was in fact taken over by Piedmont. Piedmont's laws were introduced into the rest of the kingdom and its officials were placed in charge of other regions. They claimed this was necessary because much of Italy was lawless, with untrained and corrupt officials. There was a backlash against this in many parts of the new Italy, from people who had lost their posts, demobilised and restless soldiers – and by those who felt that the new policies of free trade threatened their livelihoods. There also remained republicans who disliked the fact that they were still under the rule of a monarchy.

The new state had large debts after the war against Austria. Taxes were raised and **martial law** was declared. The north–south divide caused many problems. The more advanced north despised the backward south, whilst the south resented the wealth and control exerted by those in the north. Some historians have claimed that rather than benefiting the south, unification actually harmed it, because the population became even poorer.

martial law
The temporary imposition of military rule over a civilian population, usually at a time of civil unrest.

Venice and Rome were added to the union by events outside Italy's control. Bismarck's Prussia prepared for a war against Austria in 1866 by establishing a series of alliances. Napoleon III agreed to remain neutral on condition that Venice became part of the Kingdom of Italy. The Prussian victory resulted in an expansion of Italy by incorporating Venice. In 1870, France and Prussia went to war. Napoleon III called back French soldiers from Rome and it fell quickly to the Italian army. Pius IX refused to concede Rome to Italy and withdrew to the Vatican City, which became an independent state. Other than this small area of land, Italy was now a single political entity.

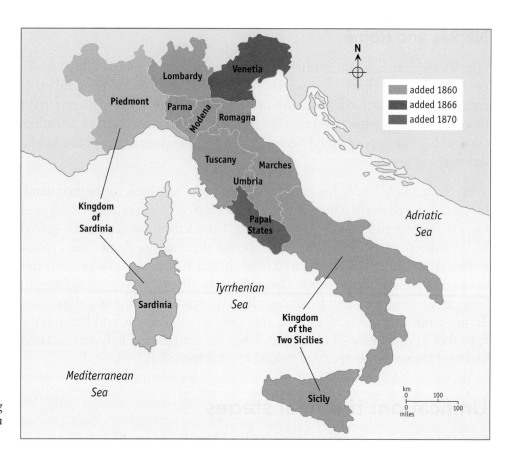

Figure 3.14 A map showing the final stages of Italian unification, 1860–70

Although united politically, Italy was far from united socially. The *Risorgimento* (see page 96) represented not one movement but a series of local risings and struggles between different groups. The old classes resisted the ambitions of the new rulers, whilst the lower classes played little part. Their resistance was suppressed both by traditional authorities and by those who achieved change. Old loyalties remained strong. The pope in the Vatican and local parish priests maintained an influence that politicians in the united Italy could not ignore. Mazzini's dream of a united Italy had been realised, but his hope of a fully democratic and non-religious republic was not achieved. Cavour's model was adopted: a respectable monarchy that was led by Piedmont and dominated by the middle classes.

Questions

1 Which of the following turning points was the most significant in achieving Italian unification? Explain your answer briefly.

- the revolutions of 1848–49
- the appointment of Cavour as prime minister of Piedmont in 1852
- the 1858 Plombières agreement between Cavour and Napoleon III
- the Franco–Prussian War of 1870–71

2 Which Italian leader contributed most to Italian unification – Mazzini, Cavour or Garibaldi? Give reasons for your choice.

Key issues

The key features of this chapter are:

- the extent to which certain individuals rather than social conditions were the real force behind the unification of Italy and Germany

- the roles that liberalism and nationalism played in the unification of these two countries

- the similarities and differences in the processes of unification in Italy and Germany

- the importance of Piedmont and Prussia to Italian and German unification respectively.

Revision questions

1 Did the 1848 revolutions represent more a victory or a defeat for nationalism in Germany and Italy?

2 Describe the problems that the liberals in Germany faced between 1815 and 1870.

3 Why did Piedmont lead the movement for a united Italy from 1848 to 1871?

4 Why were monarchists more successful than the republicans in unifying Italy by 1871?

Further reading

Clark, M. *The Italian Risorgimento*. London, UK. Pearson. 1998.

Collier, M. *Italian Unification 1820–71*. London, UK. Heinemann. 2003.

Farmer, A. *The Unification of Germany 1815–1919*. London, UK. Hodder. 2007.

Gooch, J. *The Unification of Italy*. London, UK. Routledge. 1986.

Pearce, R. and Stiles, A. *The Unification of Italy*. London, UK. Hodder. 2006.

Whitfield, R. *Germany 1848–1914*. London, UK. Heinemann. 2000.

Williamson, D. G. *Bismarck and Germany 1862–1890*. London, UK. Longman. 1997.

Advanced reading

Beales, D. and Biagini, E. *The Risorgimento and the Unification of Italy*. London, UK. Longman, 2002.

Hargreaves, D. *Bismarck and German Unification*. Basingstoke, UK. Macmillan, 1991.

Chapter

4

The origins of the
First World War

Content summary

- The reasons for the establishment of the Triple Alliance and the Triple Entente.
- The relationships between members of these alliances.
- The consequences of the alliances on international stability.
- Increasing armaments and the reasons for and consequences of the naval race.
- War aims before 1914.
- The condition of the Balkans at the turn of the century.
- Balkan nationalism and Austrian and Russian attitudes to the region.
- Reactions to the assassination of Archduke Franz Ferdinand.
- The invasion of Belgium and declarations of war.

Timeline

May 1871	Treaty of Frankfurt – France loses Alsace and Lorraine to Germany
Oct 1873	Three Emperors' League formed (Austria, Germany and Russia)
Oct 1879	Dual Alliance formed (Austria and Germany)
May 1882	Triple Alliance formed (Germany, Austria and Italy)
Jun 1887	Reinsurance Treaty between Germany and Russia
Jun 1888	Wilhelm II becomes Kaiser of Germany
Jan 1894	Franco–Russian alliance formed
Apr 1904	Entente Cordiale created (Britain and France)
Mar 1905	First Moroccan Crisis begins
Aug 1907	Triple Entente established (Britain, France and Russia)
Oct 1908	Balkan crisis – Austria annexes Bosnia
Jul 1911	Third Moroccan Crisis begins
Jul 1914	Outbreak of First World War

Introduction

In June 1914, the Austrian archduke Franz Ferdinand and his wife paid a state visit to Sarajevo in Bosnia. Bosnia had recently become a province of Austria, but the combination of tradition and nationalism in the region made the visit controversial. The majority of the population were ethnic Serbs, who resented being ruled by Austria and who looked to neighbouring Serbia for leadership. The Bosnian capital, Sarajevo, was a hotbed of Serb activism, and extreme nationalists (some of them terrorists) used it as a base for anti-Austrian agitation. The Austrians accused Serbia of encouraging this, but the politically weak Serbian government could do little to restrain these extreme elements. Public opinion prevented it from taking a strong stand; some leading politicians and members of the military and the police force even sympathised with the extremists. It was a tense situation, and during the archduke's visit he and his wife were assassinated by a Serbian nationalist, Gavrilo Princip.

The assassination triggered a series of events that led to a world war. Yet the killing itself was the culmination of political and social tensions that had been building for many years within Europe. These tensions had resulted in the most powerful European nations forming a series of defensive alliances, which resulted in two opposing groups: the Entente Powers (Britain, Russia and France) and the Central Powers (Germany, Austria-Hungary and Italy). These alliances put in place the conditions for a war that would eventually involve virtually the whole of Europe – and much of the world beyond.

> **Note:**
> Historians vigorously debate the relative importance of the factors that led to the First World War, which killed more than 30 million people between 1914 and 1918. Some see it as a failure in diplomacy; others as an inevitable product of an international arms race. Still others blame the severe ethnic and racial tensions within Europe at the time.

Figure 4.1 Archduke Franz Ferdinand and his wife Sophie, moments before their assassination in 1914

Note:

From 1867, Austria was known officially as Austria-Hungary because of its federal system of government. The ruler – from the powerful Austrian Habsburg family – was both the emperor of Austria and the king of Hungary.

Key figure

Wilhelm II (1859–1941)

William II became Kaiser of Germany in 1888, and almost immediately came into conflict with his chancellor, Bismarck. Boastful and impetuous, Wilhelm was determined to increase German power despite Bismarck's warnings that this would lead to the country's downfall. Wilhelm's popularity dwindled in the early years of the 20th century, and he abdicated in 1918, towards the end of the First World War.

The development of the alliance system

Europe in 1900

At the start of the 20th century, Europe was dominated by six major powers, each of which sought to establish alliances with other countries in an effort to increase both their power and their security.

Austria-Hungary

Austria was governed by a monarchy. A declining power, it had been defeated by Prussia in 1866 (see page 90). However, the moderate peace settlement that concluded the Austro–Prussian War meant that it now regarded Prussia's successor, Germany, as its best ally. Austria-Hungary had growing interests in the Balkans and faced Russia as a rival there.

Britain

Britain was governed by a parliament, and a monarchy with limited power. It was more interested in its extensive overseas empire than in the European continent. Britain had a long-standing distrust of France. It also regarded Russia as a threat to British interests in the Mediterranean, especially the Suez Canal and the route to India. Russia had land borders near India and was suspected of having ambitions to expand in that region.

France

France was the only major power to be governed by a republic. Although France lost the Franco–Prussian War in 1871 (see page 92), the economy recovered quickly. However, the French government was threatened by internal rivalries. Most political parties wanted revenge against Germany, but the socialists did not favour war. France had recently signed a treaty of friendship with Russia. It also distrusted Britain and Austria-Hungary.

Germany

Germany was ruled by a monarchy. Its parliament, the Reichstag, had limited power, but popular opinion could influence government decisions. For much of the latter half of the 19th century, Germany had been controlled by Otto von Bismarck (see page 84), whose priority in international affairs had been to isolate France. He had been dismissed in 1890 by the German Kaiser, **Wilhelm II**, whose aim was to make Germany a leading world power. Germany feared being encircled by Russia in the east and France in the west.

Russia

Nicholas II, the tsar of Russia (see page 138), was an absolute monarch with unrestricted power. In terms of foreign policy, he maintained friendly relations with Germany until Wilhelm II refused to renew a treaty with Russia. Russia faced Austria-Hungary as a rival in the Balkans.

Turkey

The Turkish (Ottoman) Empire was governed by an absolute monarchy. It was in decline by 1900, losing control over many regions – including the Balkans – and being described as 'the sick man of Europe'. Britain and France wanted to assist Turkey to avoid Austria-Hungary and Russia gaining more power.

Bismarck's alliances

For most of the 19th century, there were four great powers in Europe: Austria, Britain, France and Russia. After the unification of Germany was completed in 1871, it joined the ranks of these great nations. Germany had a large population, a thriving and rapidly modernising economy, and an army that had proved itself superior to those of Austria and France. Germany also had Bismarck – one of the cleverest and most ruthless statesmen of his era.

In the ten years leading up to German unification, Bismarck had changed the European balance of power. At the end of the Franco–Prussian War, he had forced France to concede the provinces of Alsace and Lorraine to Germany. He justified this by claiming that there were large numbers of German-speakers in these territories, but in truth they were overwhelmingly French in 1871. The provinces were also economically valuable, with mining, textile and metal industries, and prosperous agriculture. In addition, Germany forced France to pay a vast sum of money in reparations. Resentment at the loss of its land, and fear of this powerful new German nation, influenced French foreign policy for many years to come.

Bismarck knew that the French would eventually seek payback for their humiliation, so he set about trying to isolate France, preventing it from securing allies that would make it a threat to Germany in the future. Britain had little interest in European affairs, and while it was unlikely to be a strong supporter of Germany, it was equally unlikely to become close partners with France. This left Bismarck with two possible allies: Austria-Hungary and Russia. A German alliance with these two countries would leave France in a weak minority. The problem for Bismarck was that Austria-Hungary and Russia were rivals in the Balkans; it would take all of the German chancellor's diplomatic skills to persuade them to come to an agreement. From the 1870s to the 1890s, Bismarck's attempts to ensure German security led to a series of alliances.

> **Note:**
> Russia and Austria-Hungary had rival claims to parts of the Balkans, an area of southern Europe. Austria-Hungary argued that the region was part of the Habsburg Empire. Russia was keen to gain access to a warm-water port on the Black Sea.

The Three Emperors' League (*Dreikaiserbund*) 1873

In 1873, Bismarck negotiated an agreement between Tsar Alexander II of Russia, Emperor Franz Joseph I of Austria-Hungary and Kaiser Wilhelm I of Germany. In addition to isolating France, Bismarck hoped that regular meetings between the three monarchs would help to reduce disputes between Austria-Hungary and Russia over the Balkans. The Three Emperors' League (*Dreikaiserbund*) was largely unsuccessful, mainly because of ongoing disputes between Germany's two allies. By 1879, the league had effectively collapsed.

The Dual Alliance 1879

Bismarck still hoped to maintain a three-country alliance, but he believed that a firm agreement with Austria-Hungary was more valuable than a riskier one with Russia, and so the two nations formulated the Dual Alliance in 1879. By the terms of this alliance, Germany and Austria-Hungary agreed to come to the other's aid in the event of an attack by Russia. They also pledged to remain neutral if either was attacked by another country, such as France. Bismarck was unwilling to alienate Russia completely, so he kept this alliance a secret.

The Triple Alliance 1882

This was, in effect, an extension of the Dual Alliance. Germany, Austria-Hungary and Italy agreed to offer each other mutual support in the event of an attack by any of the other great powers. Italy's reasons for joining the alliance were partly to preserve its own national security, but also anger at France for seizing Tunisia the previous year. Italy had harboured its own aspirations for taking control of this area. Bismarck believed that Italy would not play an important role if war did break out, and saw its involvement only as a useful tool for isolating France. Italy insisted that the Triple Alliance should exclude action against Britain, and offered no guarantees that it would help Austria-Hungary if war broke out.

Figure 4.2 A German cartoon from 1889, commenting on the Triple Alliance; it was captioned 'The Fearful Governess'

The Reinsurance Treaty 1887

Despite the existence of the Triple Alliance, Bismarck's plan to isolate France had not been effective. Austria-Hungary and Italy were traditional enemies, and neither could boast a strong army to come to Germany's aid in the event of a French attack. More importantly, the loss of an effective alliance with Russia meant that Germany remained vulnerable to attack from both west and east if France and Russia should form an alliance of their own. In an effort to avoid this possibility, Bismarck signed the Reinsurance Treaty with Russia in 1887.

The two countries agreed to remain neutral unless Germany attacked France or Russia went to war with Austria. Bismarck encouraged each country to concentrate its foreign policy on different regions so that they would not clash – Germany in the west and Russia in the Balkans.

By this time, however, Bismarck's influence was beginning to wane. The year after the Reinsurance Treaty was made, Wilhelm II became Kaiser of Germany. He was more anti-Russian than his predecessor and began listening to his army generals, many of whom were in favour of war against Russia. Bismarck resigned in 1890 and the Reinsurance Treaty collapsed.

Opposition to Germany

All these alliances, so carefully negotiated by Bismarck, were entirely defensive in character and were intended to preserve peace. However, they were formed by treaties whose terms were secret, and this naturally gave rise to suspicion amongst the powers not involved in the negotiations. These suspicions intensified when Germany began to adopt a more aggressive approach to foreign affairs.

The Franco–Russian Alliance 1894

When the Reinsurance Treaty lapsed in 1890, Russia felt threatened. Despite the political differences between France and Russia, the two countries had enjoyed steadily improving relations. From 1888, France – desperate to avoid being isolated and fearing Germany's increasing power – provided Russia with cheap loans to finance improvements in its military capabilities. Both countries were afraid of what might result from the Triple Alliance, so they began negotiations for an alliance of their own. Like the Triple Alliance, the resulting agreement (the Franco–Russian Alliance) was a defensive one. It stated that if either country was attacked, the other would come to its aid. It was agreed that the Franco–Russian Alliance would remain in place as long as the Triple Alliance existed.

> **Note:**
> An alliance is a formal agreement between countries. An entente is the name given to a friendly understanding between countries. The agreements that developed in the years leading up to the First World War took both these forms.

Note:

One notable example of conflicting interests abroad came in the Boer Wars (1880–81 and 1899–1902). These were fought between the British and Dutch settlers in the Transvaal Republic of South Africa, as a result of land ownership disputes. Germany sided with the Boers against Britain. The British eventually defeated the Boers, and the Boer republics became part of the British Empire.

Britain: 'splendid isolation'?

British foreign policy at the end of the 19th century has often been described as one of 'splendid isolation' – in which Britain focused on expanding and controlling its far-flung empire rather than on events closer to home. However, this description is not entirely accurate. Britain did not have formal alliances with other European nations at the time, but it came to favour an agreement with Germany that would help to resolve rivalries over land abroad, especially in Africa. Several attempts were made to secure such an agreement but they all failed, partly because Wilhelm II insisted on maintaining an expansionist policy that brought Germany into conflict with Britain.

Figure 4.3 A map showing the extent of the British Empire in 1914

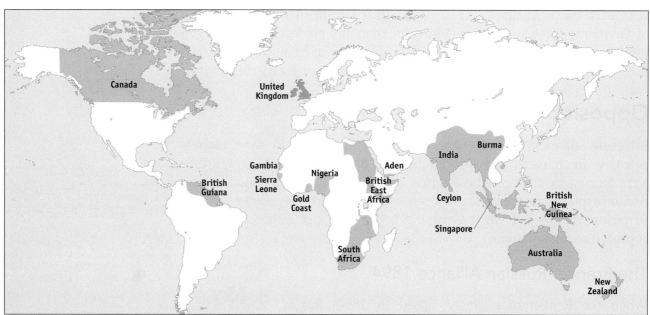

Concerned by the reaction of European powers to its involvement in the Boer Wars, Britain began to depart from its isolationist policies. It made its first treaty with Japan in 1902, which offered some protection to British interests in the Far East, especially against Russian ambitions in the region.

At the turn of the 20th century, it was unclear which partner Britain preferred on the continent – France, Germany or Russia. Many British politicians and members of the military supported friendship with Germany for the following reasons:

- Like Britain, Germany was a monarchy.
- The German Kaiser, Wilhelm II, was Queen Victoria's grandson.
- The queen's husband, Prince Albert, had been German – reinforcing the connection between the two countries.

- Germany had a thriving economy, which provided Britain with profitable trading opportunities.
- German writers, philosophers and scientists were highly regarded in Britain.

A British alliance with France seemed much less likely:

- France was a republic and seemed less politically stable than Germany.
- In Britain, memories of war with Napoleon were still strong.
- Although Britain and France had formed a brief alliance during the Crimean War (1853–56), historically the two countries had followed a pattern of hostility and mistrust.
- France's defeat in the Franco–Prussian War highlighted both its political and military weaknesses.
- France was considered a bigger threat than Germany to Britain's colonial ambitions.
- France was diplomatically closer to Russia, a country that Britain distrusted.

A British alliance with Russia seemed equally unlikely:

- Russia had an underdeveloped economy and offered few opportunities in trade.
- It was militarily weak.
- Russia wanted to expand its influence in India and China, which would put it into competition with Britain.

Taking all these factors into consideration, Britain's choice of pursuing increased co-operation with France came as a surprise to many people. In large part, this decision was based on Britain's fears of Germany, particularly the expansion of its navy and army (see page 117). As a result, Britain and France signed the Entente Cordiale in 1904.

This series of agreements was designed to settle a number of disputes that had long soured relations between the two countries. For example, France finally recognised British control of Egypt (a region that had been the cause of dispute for many years) in exchange for Britain's recognition of French control in Morocco. The Entente Cordiale provided France with additional security against the threat from Germany and its Triple Alliance cohorts. For Britain, concerned by the massive growth in Germany's military capabilities, it offered an end to European isolation.

The agreement with France sent an indisputable message that Britain was aligning itself in opposition to Germany. It was clear that the international situation was changing.

Note:
In 1903, the British king Edward VII visited Paris, and the following year the French president visited London – a sign of the developing relationship between the two countries. Some historians have credited Edward VII with making a major contribution to the Entente Cordiale, but it was mainly the result of extensive negotiations between French and British politicians.

The Anglo–Russian Entente 1907

Just like France and Britain, Russia had become increasingly fearful of Germany's intentions, and regarded the Triple Alliance as a major threat to its security. Russia was concerned that Austria-Hungary and Germany intended to take over large parts of the Balkans, threatening Russian access through the Dardanelles – a vital trade route that accounted for 40% of Russian exports.

Note:
The Dardanelles was a strait between the Black Sea and the Mediterranean Sea. With most of Russia's own ports iced up for large parts of the year, access through the Dardanelles was essential for Russian trade.

Russia was a vast country, and potentially had the largest army of all the major European powers. However, it was economically underdeveloped and militarily weak. Its defeat in the Russo–Japanese War suggested to Britain that it was no longer a serious challenger to Britain's own imperial ambitions in the Far East. Germany was now a far bigger threat. In 1907, therefore, an Anglo–Russian Entente was agreed. It was a marriage of convenience for both countries, and the agreement did not stipulate that Britain and Russia would support each other in the event of a European war.

Consequences of the alliances for international stability

By 1907, the powers of Europe had thus divided into two clear camps: the Triple Alliance and the Triple Entente. Neither of these was a union of equals. Germany was clearly the strongest power in the Triple Alliance, for example – Austria-Hungary usually followed its lead, while Italy was regarded as an unreliable partner right from the start.

Note:
At the end of the 19th and beginning of the 20th centuries, Austria-Hungary and Russia became rivals to replace Turkish control in the Balkans. Germany had no direct interests in the region but became involved because of its alliance with Austria-Hungary. Similarly, Britain and France had no direct involvement in the Balkans but were drawn in because of their growing friendship with Russia. The Sarajevo crisis in 1914 particularly concerned Austria and Russia, but it affected Britain, France and Germany because of their rival alliances.

The members of the alliances also had different interests and ambitions. In 1900, Germany saw itself as a world power, but had no vital interests in the Balkans. Austria-Hungary was not a world power, but focused on the dangers of instability in that region. However, Germany had to support Austria as its only ally in Europe. Italy was not concerned with the Balkans, but joined the Triple Alliance when deprived of territories in North Africa by France.

The term 'Triple Entente' can be misleading, suggesting a cohesive union between Britain, France and Russia. In fact, it was little more than a series of loose associations between Britain and France, Britain and Russia, and France and Russia. The agreement did not make clear what would happen if a country was attacked by Germany or Austria. This uncertainty was one of the factors that must be taken into account when considering how far the system of alliances was responsible for the outbreak of the First World War.

In 1914, it was likely (but not certain) that France and Russia would support each other in the event of a war. British policy was less clear. Britain had long enjoyed cordial relations with Germany – far more so than it had with France. Furthermore, Britain did not share any interests or ambitions with Russia.

The most significant long-term reason for Britain's break with Germany was German naval development, and the race that ensued between the two nations to build the most powerful navy in the world. The most significant short-term reason was Germany's violation of Belgian neutrality. Until German troops marched into Belgium in August 1914, there was no certainty that Britain would side with France against Germany.

The alliances failed to secure peace in the long term, but they worked reasonably well for some time. Generally, the agreements were built on the belief that countries would be more secure if they had friendly partners to consult in the case of foreign aggression. This worked during a series of crises in Africa and the Balkans in the first decade of the 20th century, which were defused before a major war broke out. However, the situation was different in 1914. Too many countries were willing to go to war to achieve their objectives. Instead of guaranteeing peace, these alliances ensured that the war swiftly involved all the nations that had joined them. While Britain could have ignored Austria-Hungary's attack on Serbia, the alliance system meant that it could not ignore Germany's attack on Belgium and then France.

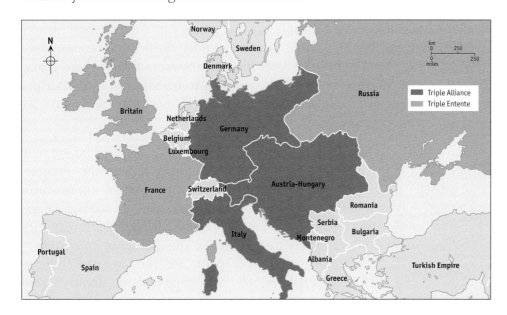

Figure 4.4 A map showing the alliances at the outbreak of the First World War in 1914

Questions

1 There were many causative factors that led to the outbreak of the First World War. In your opinion, which factor was the most important?

2 Could the outbreak of a world war in 1914 have been prevented?

3 Why did the system of alliances that developed fail to ensure peace in Europe?

Militarism and the naval race

Between 1900 and 1914, there was a dramatic increase in the amount many European countries spent on their armies and navies. The German army budget increased from almost £50 million in 1910 to almost £90 million in 1914. Other major countries also spent more on their military forces, including Britain, which concentrated most of its spending on its already powerful navy. What began as a gradual increase in armaments developed into a rapid arms race in the years leading up to the First World War.

Increasing armaments

The army had a more important place in Germany than in any other European country. Frederick the Great had expanded Prussia through war in the middle of the 18th century (see page 87), establishing it as the most powerful of the German states. In the next century, Bismarck relied on his strong army to win the wars that would unify Germany. As a result, German army generals were widely respected and had more influence over political affairs than elsewhere in Europe. By the start of the 20th century, the German army was well financed and led by highly trained officers.

From 1913, the size of the army was increased, but despite this, many in government and military circles grew concerned that with only the militarily weak Austria-Hungary as a reliable ally, the balance in army strength would favour France and Russia. In 1913, France extended the period of compulsory military service for ordinary soldiers in the army from two to three years. Some predicted that the French army would also be enlarged by conscripts from its colonies. Germany was concerned that France might soon have an army strong enough to defeat it.

Note:

The Russo–Japanese War (1904–05) grew out of rival Russian and Japanese ambitions in Korea and Manchuria. In 1904, Japan attacked Russia's fleet at Port Arthur in China. The Russians were not expecting an attack, so the ships were poorly defended and the reaction was disorganised. They were rapidly defeated. Much of the Russian fleet was destroyed, which had severe financial repercussions for the country.

The Russo–Japanese War had highlighted major weaknesses in the Russian military, and the Russian government accepted that it now needed to urgently modernise and extend its army and navy. Russia was a huge country and had a large population from which to draw its military manpower. However, the quality of its officers – mostly noblemen – was poor, and they resisted changes to the armed forces. As first steps towards improving its military system, Russia began adopting more modern weaponry and improving its transport system to allow for more efficient movement of soldiers and arms.

The Austro-Hungarian army was dominated by tradition in its appointment and training of officers as well as in its methods of fighting. Once a great power and a significant military threat in Europe, its strength and influence had seriously declined. If a war was confined to south-eastern

Europe, Austria-Hungary might achieve victory against Serbia and the other small Balkan countries. However, success against other European nations was much less likely. In particular, if Austria-Hungary faced Russia, its only chance lay with German support.

As an island nation, Britain had long relied on a large navy, and at the start of the 20th century its army was comparatively small. It was the only one of the **Great Powers** not to have a system of conscription or compulsory military service before the First World War. The size of the British army was usually sufficient to deal with unrest in its overseas empire (although even there it struggled on occasion, notably in the Boer Wars, where victory took longer than anticipated).

Great Powers
States that are able to influence international events, generally through political, economic and military strength. The Great Powers change over time and there is no authoritative list.

Country	Size of army
Austria-Hungary	3 million
Britain	1 million
France	4 million
Germany	4.5 million
Russia	6 million

Table 4.1 The size of the armies of the major powers in 1914

The naval race: Britain and Germany

The naval race between Britain and Germany began in 1906, when Britain launched the first of its Dreadnought battleships – which were larger, faster and better armed than any that existed at the time. Germany responded by immediately embarking on a naval development programme that seriously alarmed the British. The Germans maintained that this was necessary to protect their overseas trade and empire, and that Britain should not interfere in a matter that concerned only Germany. However, Britain claimed that Germany's overseas colonies were not sufficient to warrant such military expansion, and argued that the development of its navy posed a threat to peace in Europe.

Note:
Conscription was not introduced in Britain until 1916 – 18 months after the war began. Although by this point the British army was in desperate need of reinforcements, conscription was still controversial. Many British generals claimed that conscripted soldiers would be poorly trained and unprofessional. Some within the governing Liberal Party felt that conscription would be unpopular with the voting public.

Note:
In 1897, Admiral Alfred von Tirpitz convinced the Kaiser that Germany needed a large navy to protect its empire and defend its European coastline from attack. The following year, the first of a series of Navy Laws authorised a massive expansion of funds for the German navy.

Figure 4.5 The Dreadnought battleship, which revolutionised naval warfare

As the naval race gathered pace, Britain built a new naval base on the east coast of Scotland, clearly designed to counter the danger at sea from Germany. An attempt to reach an agreement about the size of their respective navies failed. Public opinion in both countries gave enthusiastic support to their governments' naval policies.

By 1914, the British Royal Navy was still stronger than that of Germany – including in its ranks 29 Dreadnought class battleships. However, it had to cover an immense area, ranging from the coastal waters of the English Channel and the North Sea to the Atlantic, Indian and Pacific oceans. All these regions required a naval presence to keep vital trade routes open.

Superiority at sea is essential to the security of the British Empire. The development of the German fleet during the last fifteen years is the most striking feature of the naval situation today.

The naval expansion of Germany has not been provoked by British naval increases. The German Government have repeatedly declared that their naval policy has not been influenced by British action, and the following figures speak for themselves:

In 1905 Great Britain was building 4 large warships, and Germany 2.
In 1906 Great Britain reduced to 3 large warships, and Germany increased to 3.
In 1907 Great Britain built 3 large warships and Germany built 3.
In 1908 Great Britain further reduced to 2 large warships, and Germany further increased to 4.

It was not until the efforts of Great Britain to reduce the naval rivalry had failed for three successive years that the Admiralty was forced in 1909 to ask Parliament to take exceptional measures to ensure the safety of the Empire against all possible hazards.

A memorandum from the British government to the Canadian government, October 1912.

By comparison, the German High Seas Fleet – although smaller in size (it had 17 Dreadnoughts in 1914) – was able to concentrate on preventing a blockade of domestic ports because Germany did not have an extensive overseas empire. It could use the protected harbours at Cuxhaven, Wilhelmshaven and Kiel as bases for raids into the North Sea, to keep the British at bay and allow merchant ships to enter German waters in safety. At the same time, individual warships or independent squadrons could venture into the oceans of the world to attack British trade from the colonies.

Our fleet provided security for Germany's flourishing political and economic expansion. By creating a fleet we strengthened our claim to sea-power, without which the German Empire must disappear. But we remained a thorn in the side of the British, and their ill-will was the constant accompaniment of our growth. Britain was never willing to grant the freedom of the seas, even if it had to come to a world-war.

We never wished to replace British world power. Our aims were limited to a small number of ships, which nowhere approached the British total. Nevertheless Britain considered herself threatened and saw in us a rival who must at any cost be destroyed.

It is not disputed that through our fleet-construction there was more tension in our relations with Britain than would have resulted from peaceful competition alone. However, it is not a fair judgment if the disaster of the world war is simply blamed on the building of the German Fleet.

Admiral Scheer, commander of the German navy in the First World War, in his memoirs, published in 1920.

Britain had a clear strategy for its navy if war broke out: its overriding duty was to protect the country from invasion. By contrast, the German government had no clear idea of how its navy would be used in the event of war, other than hoping it could limit British intervention. In addition, a large navy was a comparatively heavier expense for Germany, which was also supporting a large army.

Warships	Britain	Germany
Dreadnoughts	29	17
Other battleships	40	20
Battle-cruisers	34	9
Cruisers	74	41
Destroyers	167	130
Torpedo boats	49	0
Submarines*	75	21

Table 4.2 The size of the British and German navies in 1914

* Submarine figures can be misleading. Few in the British Admiralty took submarines seriously. Most believed that the danger to surface ships from submarines was exaggerated. Many believed that they were an immoral method of fighting wars. The German submarines were generally of a better quality.

Rivalries overseas

From the late 19th century, rivalries between European powers were no longer confined to the European continent. They also began to play out in lands far away, as the Great Powers sought to expand their influence and establish colonies overseas. **Imperialism** had developed in the 16th century, as Spain, Portugal, England and France began claiming land in the newly discovered Americas.

The 'scramble for Africa' and the struggle for concessions

Around 1870, a new wave of imperialist expansion began, as Britain, then Germany, France, Belgium and Italy, looked to Africa to fulfil their desire for more land and resources. In 1870, little of the 'Dark Continent' was controlled by Europeans. By 1914, the only parts of Africa that retained their independence were Ethiopia and Liberia. Competition in Asia between European countries, including Russia, focused mostly on China and has been termed the 'scramble for **concessions**'.

Each country had its own reasons for pursuing expansionist policies:

- **Britain** already had an empire that contained India, and included modern Pakistan and Bangladesh, Australia, New Zealand, Canada, Malaysia and Singapore, islands in the West Indies and South Africa and parts of central Africa such as present-day Zimbabwe, Malawi, Uganda, Kenya and Tanzania. In the 19th century, Britain became eager to develop its colonies in Africa and to gain new ones in the Far East. The British Empire was larger in size and population than any other empire.

- **France** had suffered a severe defeat in its war with Prussia in 1870–71. There was no immediate prospect of regaining its losses in Europe, but expansion in North Africa and the Far East would confirm that France still had the right to call itself a Great Power. France gained Algeria in north Africa and Senegal in west Africa.

- **Germany** embarked on a policy of *Weltpolitik* ('world policy') under Wilhelm II, in contrast to Bismarck's preference for concentrating on Europe. Germany thought it deserved a 'place in the sun'. Colonies would provide raw materials and markets for its industries. German colonial success in the late 19th century was limited to small regions such as part of Tanzania, Rwanda and Burundi in east Africa, German Cameroon in west Africa, and some small islands in the Pacific Ocean.

imperialism
The policy of extending a nation's power by gaining political and economic control over more territory. This is sometimes referred to as colonialism.

concessions
Areas that involved trading rights between different countries. The term is especially applied to parts of China.

Note:
The expression 'Dark Continent' was widely used by Europeans in the 19th century to describe Africa – not because of the skin colour of its inhabitants, but because of the mystery surrounding the continent. Europeans knew very little about Africa, other than that it seemed to be a dangerous and inhospitable place.

- **Italy** was unified in 1870 and had imperial ambitions to claim a place among the Great Powers, although its economy was less advanced. Its main focus was on Africa. An attempt to annex Abyssinia (modern Ethiopia) failed in 1896. Italy gained part of Somaliland and a trade concession at Tientsin in China.
- **Russia** was divided between its aims to expand at the expense of Turkey in the south towards Persia (now Iran) and Afghanistan, and in the Far East at the expense of China.

All these conflicting aims and ambitions naturally caused tension between the major European powers at the end of the 19th century. Britain and France both claimed rights in Egypt and neighbouring Sudan, and in 1898 soldiers from these nations faced each other at Fashoda, near the source of the River Nile. All-out war was only averted by a compromise that satisfied the honour of both countries.

In South Africa, Britain's desire for expansion brought it into conflict with Germany, which had territories in south-east and south-west Africa. The adventurer **Cecil Rhodes** led the way in establishing British influence from the southern Cape of Good Hope northwards to Rhodesia (now Zambia, Zimbabwe and Malawi). The Boers, descendants of the Dutch settlers at the Cape of Good Hope, moved to the Transvaal and declared it an independent republic. Some British settlers already had aspirations for a line of territories from the Cape to Egypt, but this situation was transformed when gold was found in the Transvaal. In 1899, the Second Boer War broke out. Britain saw this as an internal affair – an uprising in one of its colonies that had to be suppressed. Germany sided openly with the Boers, and after a successful Boer defence against a British attack known as the Jameson Raid, the Kaiser sent a telegram of support to Paul Kruger, the Boer president of the Transvaal, congratulating him on defeating the British 'bullies'.

The Moroccan Crises

During this period of imperial rivalry, the most serious crises took place in Morocco in north Africa. In theory, Morocco was independent, but Britain and France both had rival trading interests there. In addition, France claimed that the borders of Morocco had not been clearly determined and that its proximity to French Algeria gave it a claim to the region.

In 1905, Kaiser Wilhelm II visited the area and declared that Germany favoured an independent Morocco. Germany's interference in this matter was a clear challenge to Britain and France, in the hope of dividing them over the issue and improving German prestige on the world stage. The Kaiser's plan failed. The crisis was defused in 1906 by a conference at Algeciras, during which only Austria supported Germany. Italy – the other member of the Triple Alliance – backed France's claim over Morocco. In the end, Morocco's independence was confirmed but France was recognised as the controlling power.

> **Note:**
> Fashoda became a turning point in Anglo–French relations, because the politicians of both countries showed they were willing to settle their differences. One result of this was that it allowed the development of the Entente Cordiale in 1904 (see page 113).

> **Key figure**
>
> **Cecil Rhodes (1853–1902)**
> Rhodes was a British-born businessman who made a fortune from the extraction of diamonds in South Africa. He was prime minister of Cape Colony between 1890 and 1896, and a strong supporter of British imperialism in Africa. However, he believed that British settlers and local governors in Africa should be in charge, rather than being ruled from London.

The Second Moroccan Crisis in 1908 was resolved quickly by France and Germany. However, the third crisis in 1911 threatened to cause a war. In 1911, the *Panther*, a German gunboat, was sent to the Moroccan port of Agadir to undermine French power in the region. Britain was not involved directly but saw the incident as a dangerous use of the German navy. Even British politicians who favoured moderation towards Germany were concerned by this action. Some German politicians and generals were in favour of going to war, but the Kaiser backed down, agreeing to a minor concession from France in the Congo. Ultimately, Britain and France drew closer, and Germany suffered an embarrassing diplomatic defeat.

Questions

1 Why did Britain and Germany expand their navies in the early years of the 20th century?

2 Compare Sources A and B below as evidence of German policy towards Morocco.

Source A

The question is whether we should build single naval bases or colonies. I prefer colonies because colonies will directly affect Europe in the event of a war. We should raise demands for colonies in the press and in public meetings. Then I can say, 'I am ready to compromise but public opinion must be considered'. We shall stand firm in Morocco although we might seem to draw back a step. You may be sure that our Morocco policy will please you.

The German foreign secretary, in conversation with an extreme German nationalist, April 1911.

Source B

The only real crisis in Anglo–German relations between 1904 and 1914 happened in 1911 because of the way in which German political leaders tried to resolve the Moroccan crisis that was causing trouble between us and the French. The German foreign secretary lacked sufficient understanding of Britain, like so many German diplomats. He did harm by his careless handling of the situation. At his suggestion, the German chancellor sent the gunboat Panther to the Moroccan port of Agadir in 1911. He left the British government in the dark when it asked the reason and did not reply for several weeks. The result was that Lloyd George delivered a speech which had been drawn up in the British Cabinet in which he warned Germany that British power would be on the side of France in the event of a challenge. I was aware of this mistaken policy as soon as I learned that we had not previously come to an agreement with Britain. The result was that our prestige suffered a blow throughout the whole world and German public opinion disapproved.

The German naval secretary Admiral von Tirpitz, in his memoirs, published in 1919.

Instability in the Balkans

For centuries, Turkey had controlled a vast empire, stretching from its borders with Austria in the west and Russia in the north, to Persia in the east. This great empire began to decline in the 17th century, but survived into the 19th century largely because other European powers could not agree about how it should be divided.

Turkey was the main loser in international diplomacy at the end of the 19th century, but the new Balkan states that emerged – including Bulgaria, Montenegro and Serbia – now threatened peace. Each of the new countries recognised the danger of being overtaken by other Balkan states. The peace settlements to solve the crises were widely regarded as temporary because they did not solve the underlying problems caused by the ambitions of the small states and the concerns of the larger countries.

Figure 4.6 A map showing the borders of the Balkan states in 1913

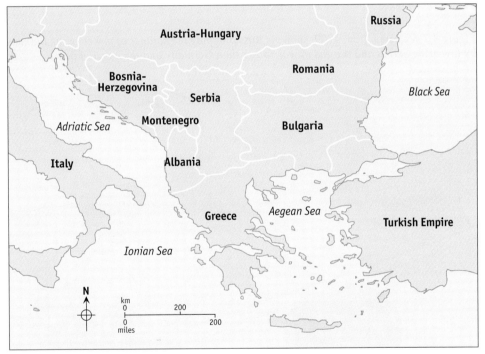

Balkan nationalism

Turkey's weak control of the Balkans led to an increase in nationalism towards the end of the 19th century. There were few natural frontiers to form the boundaries of new countries and it was a region of different racial groups, cultures and religions. These groups agitated for freedom from Turkish rule, but they also fought amongst themselves. Austria-Hungary and Russia both believed the situation in the Balkans was dangerous, but they also saw an opportunity in the form of a power vacuum that each country wanted to fill. This set the two nations on a collision course.

Austria had lost its leading role in Germany to Bismarck's Prussia, but it might still remain a major power if it controlled the Balkans. The region posed a threat to Austria because the growth of separatism and nationalism there might spread to the Austro-Hungarian Empire, which was itself populated by many different racial groups, including Croats, Slavs and Serbs.

Russia had lost the Crimean War in the mid 19th century and the Russo–Japanese War in 1905. It had not been able to extend its influence in the Mediterranean and more eastern regions. It had cultural and religious links with the Slavs, especially the Serbs – the largest Slav group – and consequently there was a strong body of support in Russia for a policy that would make Russia the leading Slav state.

Britain, France and Germany had no direct interests in the Balkans, but France was allied to Russia and Germany to Austria. This meant that they could not avoid becoming involved. Britain tended to be anti-Russian until an entente was established in the early 20th century, but the British continued to avoid direct involvement, urging negotiation when problems appeared.

Figure 4.7 A cartoon from 1909, showing Russia tipping the balance of power in the Balkans by favouring Serbia and the god of war rather than Germany and the angel of peace

Crises in the Balkans before 1914

In 1908–09, Austria-Hungary annexed Bosnia, which was mostly populated by Serbs. The Serbs in Bosnia and Serbia, as well as their ally Russia, were greatly angered by this move. In the tension that followed, Germany backed Austria and the two countries threatened to invade Serbia. This potential disaster involved the same nations as the crisis that developed in 1914; however, in this instance Serbia and Russia backed down and the situation was resolved peacefully. While Germany and Austria-Hungary took this to mean that Russia would not go to war in a similar situation in the future, in fact Russia came to believe that it should never again back down.

In 1912, members of the Balkan League rose against Turkey. The crisis persuaded the Great Powers to hold a conference in London to resolve the problem before it developed into a European-wide conflict. As a result of the conference, Serbia made gains that persuaded its people that Austria was a power in decline. It thus saw an opportunity to unify Serbs living outside its boundaries, including those in Austrian Bosnia.

Note:
The Balkan League was a short-lived alliance established in 1912 between the states of Bulgaria, Greece, Montenegro and Serbia. It was formed by a series of **bilateral agreements** in which these countries agreed to support each other against Turkish rule.

bilateral agreements
Agreements made between two parties or countries.

Questions

1. How far did Turkey's lack of control over the Balkans lead to instability in the region?

2. How did tensions between the Balkans and other countries continue to build up to 1914?

3. Why were outside nations particularly interested in the political situation in the Balkans?

Reasons for the outbreak of war in 1914

Before the assassination of the heir to the Austro-Hungarian throne in Sarajevo in June 1914, all the major European powers were dealing with internal problems that seemed more pressing than the unrest in the Balkans. Some politicians suggested that the situation might develop into an armed conflict, but it seemed more likely that it would be settled by diplomacy as crises there had in the past. Therefore, the speed and implications of the consequences of the assassination took many people by surprise.

The Austrian ultimatum

Key figure

Gavrilo Princip (1894–1918)

Princip was a fanatical Serb nationalist born in Bosnia. He was part of a three-man assassination squad sent by the terrorist group the Black Hand to kill the Austrian archduke, Franz Ferdinand. Princip was supposed to kill himself after assassinating the royal couple, but he failed to do so. He died of tuberculosis in prison in 1918.

Gavrilo Princip, a member of the extreme nationalist group the Black Hand, was there at the failure of the first attempt to kill the archduke in Sarajevo, when a grenade just wounded an Austro-Hungarian officer. Later that day, the archduke decided to visit the officer in hospital, but his driver was unfamiliar with the streets and took a wrong turn. Princip found himself unexpectedly next to the archduke's car, and seized the chance to succeed where his squad had failed earlier.

Note:
The Black Hand society, known originally as Union or Death, was founded in 1911. Its aim was the unity of all Serbs in Austria-Hungary, Serbia and other states. Its programme stated: 'This organisation prefers terrorist action to cultural activities. It will therefore remain secret.' Serbia arrested and executed several Black Hand leaders soon after the war broke out.

Princip's action gave Austria-Hungary an opportunity to crush Serbia's power and end the threat that nationalism in the region posed to its empire. It had no desire to seek another moderate, negotiated settlement. Austria-Hungary therefore responded to the outrage on 23 July by issuing Serbia with a series of demands, with a deadline for agreement within 48 hours. The ultimatum accused the Serbian government of supporting the murderers; it demanded that Serbia prosecute all those involved in the assassination and end all anti-Austrian propaganda; Austrian officials were to be allowed to enter Serbia to ensure that this was done. In addition, the Serbian government was ordered to publish its acceptance of Austria-Hungary's demands.

The Serbian government responded two days later. It accepted most of the demands, but it denied responsibility for the murder and suggested that an international judgment be reached by either The Hague Tribunal or a meeting of the Great Powers. Events developed rapidly after this, and within a week much of Europe had been drawn into the dispute:

- Russia intervened on Serbia's behalf. On 29 July, it mobilised its army to put pressure on Austria-Hungary.
- Germany urged Austria-Hungary not to back down. On 30 July, German forces began to mobilise in reaction to Russia's mobilisation.
- France was not concerned with rivalries in the Balkans, but it was a long-time enemy of Germany, and in support of its ally Russia, French forces were mobilised on 1 August.

Note:
The Hague Tribunal was also called the Permanent Court of Arbitration. It was established in 1899 and was replaced by the Permanent Court of International Justice, or World Court, in 1922, after the conclusion of the First World War.

After the shocking crime of 28 June, I can describe the atmosphere in Serbia. Relations between Austria and Serbia were poisoned on the Serbian side by extreme nationalism, hateful and strong. Proof of this can be had easily everywhere among all parties, in political circles as well as among the lower classes. It is well-known that the policy of Serbia is to abolish the Austrian Monarchy as a Great Power. The hatred of Austria has been further intensified as a result of the latest events which influence political opinion here. The crime at Sarajevo has aroused among the Serbians an expectation that the Austrian Empire will fall to pieces very soon. They had set their hopes on this even before the murder of the Archduke Franz Ferdinand. Austria appears to the Serbians as powerless, and as scarcely worthy of waging war with. Contempt is mingled with hatred. The Serbians believe that Austria is ripe for destruction, and she will fall without trouble under the control of the Great Serbian Empire, which will happen in the immediate future. Newspapers, even those which are not the most extreme, discuss the powerlessness and weakness of the Austrian Monarchy every day. They insult its officials without reserve and without fear of reprimand. They do not even stop short of the exalted person of our ruler. Even the official newspaper refers to the internal condition of Austria as the true cause of this wicked crime.

The Austrian foreign minister, accusing Serbia of seeking the destruction of Austria-Hungary, 21 July 1914.

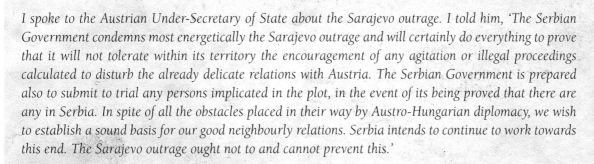

I spoke to the Austrian Under-Secretary of State about the Sarajevo outrage. I told him, 'The Serbian Government condemns most energetically the Sarajevo outrage and will certainly do everything to prove that it will not tolerate within its territory the encouragement of any agitation or illegal proceedings calculated to disturb the already delicate relations with Austria. The Serbian Government is prepared also to submit to trial any persons implicated in the plot, in the event of its being proved that there are any in Serbia. In spite of all the obstacles placed in their way by Austro-Hungarian diplomacy, we wish to establish a sound basis for our good neighbourly relations. Serbia intends to continue to work towards this end. The Sarajevo outrage ought not to and cannot prevent this.'

The Serbian ambassador to Austria, claiming that Serbia wanted good relations with Austria, 30 July 1914.

Britain and Germany by 1914

As other European countries prepared for war, Britain still hoped to remain on the sidelines. Although many historians have emphasised the tensions between Britain and Germany at the beginning of the 20th century, relations between them were actually improving by 1914. Despite Britain's membership of the Triple Entente with France and Russia, many British politicians did not believe that this would require their country to go to war alongside them. After the assassination in Sarajevo, the British government called for negotiations without indicating clearly which outcome it favoured.

By 1914, the naval race had soured relations between Britain and Germany, but they also had different international priorities. Britain was uneasy about getting drawn into the politics of continental Europe. Germany focused less on becoming a world power because its attempts to establish an empire beyond its own borders had not enjoyed much success. Despite this, there was much to suggest that Britain and Germany would do everything possible to avoid war with each other:

- The two countries had close trade links. Influential businessmen in Britain did not favour an expensive war with Germany.
- Britain was uneasy about an alliance with Russia and regarded the Entente Cordiale as an agreement with France that did not necessarily involve fighting a war.
- Britain was not interested in the Balkan region and favoured a negotiated settlement to the Sarajevo crisis.
- Germany's priorities were to keep France weak, to neutralise Russia and keep Austria-Hungary as an ally, to avoid being encircled. Britain was not seen as a major problem.

The invasion of Belgium

Germany's concern had always been the prospect of war on two fronts: against France in the west and Russia in the east. In 1905, therefore, the German military developed the Schlieffen Plan, which was based on the assumption that, because of its vast size, Russia would take longer to mobilise – and longer to defeat in a war – than France. The plan imagined a quick and overwhelming attack on the French army. By the time Russia was ready to fight a war, Germany would have more than enough soldiers in place in the east to defeat it.

The French frontier with Germany was heavily defended and would probably not allow Germany a swift victory. The alternative was to attack northern France through Belgium – a militarily weak country that would not be able to withstand the might of the German army. This was therefore made part of the Schlieffen Plan. However, such a manoeuvre posed a political problem for Germany: Belgian neutrality was protected by a series of treaties established in 1839, by which both France and Britain were committed to the defence of Belgium in the event on an attack. Despite this, the Schlieffen Plan formed the basis of Germany's strategy in 1914. It assumed that:

- Russia would take at least six weeks to mobilise
- France could be defeated in six weeks
- Belgium would be too weak to resist a German invasion
- Britain might protest, but would not go to war over Belgium.

Figure 4.8 The Schlieffen Plan

> ## Note:
> The German army swept through Belgium and entered France in 1914, but the Schlieffen Plan fell apart under battle conditions. French resistance was heavier than expected and the Germans made changes that weakened the advance. As a result, the German army and its British and French enemies were involved in trench warfare for four years.

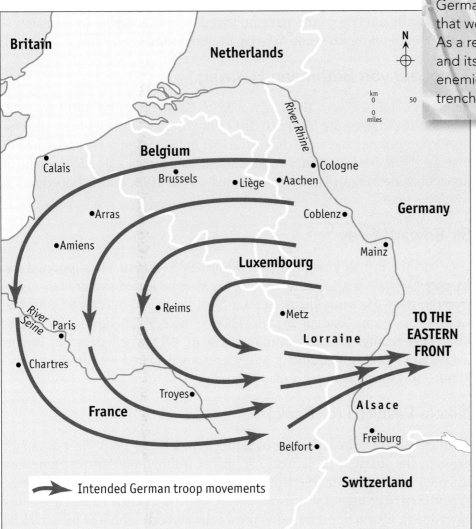

Germany's most serious error at this point was assuming that Britain would remain uninvolved, when in fact the invasion of Belgium proved to be the decisive factor in British entry into the war. Many people believed that it was a matter of honour to protect 'little Belgium', which was also important geographically. Britain's military strength relied on the navy, to protect its empire and to safeguard it against invasion; Belgium – situated on the North Sea – could be a potentially dangerous base for the Germany navy. The invasion of Belgium thus persuaded reluctant British politicians to go to war.

European politicians in 1914

Several European politicians played a leading role in the diplomatic manoeuvres leading up to the outbreak of war in 1914. Some of these key players are outlined below.

Count Leopold Berchtold

Berchtold was the Austro-Hungarian foreign minister from 1912 to 1915. He was a hardliner against Serbia before war broke out in 1914, and supported Austria-Hungary's ultimatum after the assassination of Archduke Franz Ferdinand. He would have preferred to invade Serbia immediately – without even taking the time to issue an ultimatum.

Theobald von Bethmann-Hollweg

Bethmann-Hollweg was the chancellor of Germany from 1909 to 1917. He came under pressure from extreme right-wing and militaristic groups for his foreign policies and from the liberals for his domestic policies. He had to manage the Kaiser's tendency to pursue extreme policies abroad. In spite of his doubts, Bethmann-Hollweg supported war in 1914, but he hoped that it would be brief.

Sir Edward Grey

Grey was the British foreign minister from 1905 to 1916. He supported the Entente Cordiale with France, mainly because he feared the growth of the German navy. He said: 'If the German fleet becomes superior to ours, the German army can conquer Britain. There is no corresponding risk of this kind to Germany.' He did not make clear in 1914 whether or not Britain would go to war with Germany until Germany declared war on Russia and France, and subsequently invaded Belgium.

Nikola Pashitch (or Pasic)

Pashitch was the prime minister of Serbia from 1912 to 1918. He was caught between the strength of Serbian nationalist feeling and Austria-Hungary's reaction, which regarded Serbian ambitions as a threat to its own security. When Franz Ferdinand was assassinated, Austria blamed Pashitch and his government. Pashitch promised to prosecute anybody who was proven to be involved, but events soon moved out of his control.

Raymond Poincaré

Poincaré was president of France from 1913 to 1920. He pursued strongly anti-German and pro-Russian policies. He sought good relations with Britain and tried to turn the Entente Cordiale into a firm alliance.

Sergei Sazonov

Sazonov was the Russian foreign minister from 1910 to 1916. He opposed Austro-Hungarian influence in the Balkans before the First World War, but some in Russia believed that he was too moderate and wanted him to do more to assert Russian influence in the region.

Declarations of war

Austria first declared war on Serbia. Then Russia mobilised its army on the frontiers of Austria and Germany. Germany declared war on Russia and France, as well as on Belgium. With that, Britain declared war on Germany. Within six weeks of the assassination in Sarajevo, the conflict had spread across Europe. Some of the countries involved, including Britain and France, had little interest in the Balkans and despite tensions in that region for years, none had developed into major crises. So why did a European war break out so quickly in 1914?

- Austria-Hungary was determined to crush Serbia, punishing it for its anti-Austrian campaign. It was confident that Serbia, much weaker militarily, would back down. Even if Serbia did not, Austria-Hungary believed it would win a quick war with Germany's support.
- Germany had only one reliable ally (Austria-Hungary) and it was not a strong power. Even with German support, urgent action against Serbia would demonstrate that Austria-Hungary was still a power to be reckoned with.
- Russia's friendship with Serbia was likely to cause a war with Germany. This would involve France in the action, with the result that Germany would face a war on two fronts.
- Serbia was a small country, but was encouraged by its gains in previous Balkans crises. The majority of the country was nationalist but there were divisions about the best way to act. Some were convinced that Austria-Hungary was in its final stage of decline; others were more realistic.
- Russia believed that it had made too many concessions in the past – now it must take a stand against Austria and Germany. Russia and Serbia had common interests.
- France was keen to keep Russia as an ally against Germany, so it had to make a stand against Austro-Hungarian intervention in Serbia.
- Britain's desire for a balance of power meant that it did not wish Austria and Germany or France and Russia to dominate Europe. The ententes with France and Russia did not oblige Britain to go to war with Austria, but the British did not make clear what solution they favoured beyond the hope that the crisis would remain a local one. In the end, Belgian independence was more important than events in the Balkans as a matter of honour and for strategic reasons.

Note:
Britain had long been concerned with Belgium and Holland, as these were places from which an invasion of England could be launched. Britain would not accept the French invasion of Belgium after 1792 and this was a major cause of conflict with France until 1814. In 1839, Britain signed the Treaty of London, guaranteeing Belgian independence.

Some historians believe that Russia's move to mobilise its army was a more significant short-term cause of the First World War than Austria-Hungary's ultimatum to Serbia. Certainly, Germany took Russian mobilisation to be a declaration of war. However, every country feared being attacked first, and Russia's great size and poor communications system meant that it would need longer to prepare for war than other countries. Other historians argue that the main cause of the First World War was fear – each of the Great Powers was afraid that it would lose influence unless it took a firm stand:

- Austria feared that it would lose its position as a Great Power if Serbia escaped punishment.
- Britain believed that it was threatened by the German invasion of Belgium and the growth of the German navy.
- France believed that it was necessary to resist German ambitions and, if possible, recover Alsace and Lorraine.
- Germany was afraid that it was being encircled by Russia and France. It had to support Austria, its only important ally.
- Russia saw itself as the champion of the Slavs and was afraid that it had seemed weak in previous Balkan crises.

There were only six weeks between the murder of Franz Ferdinand and the outbreak of a general war that changed Europe and the world beyond. What began as a local dispute in the Balkans widened to included conflicts about the alliance system, the arms race, nationalism and imperialism. One historian wrote: 'At successive signals, the five Great Powers, like the heavy steam trains of the time, pulled out onto their predestined collision courses.'

Figure 4.9 An official in Berlin reads out the announcement that Germany is at war in 1914

Outbreak and outcomes

During those vital six weeks, most Austro-Hungarian politicians were determined to go to war to end their problems with Serbia. However, statesmen in other countries assumed that diplomacy would calm the tensions. Britain was preoccupied with domestic problems, especially demands for Home Rule in Ireland. There were large groups of socialists in France and Germany who spoke out against war, and the Kaiser seemed so convinced that this would not develop into a major conflict that he went on a sailing holiday! But public opinion can change quickly, and even authoritarian rulers such as the tsar of Russia had to take note of popular demands for action.

At the start, it was widely assumed that the war would be a fast-moving affair involving a series of battles between rival cavalry units. Most people believed it would be 'over by Christmas'. Within a few months, however, it became clear that this outlook was vastly optimistic. The conflict rapidly became a **war of attrition**, in which soldiers of all nationalities found themselves trapped in trenches, risking their lives in order to gain a few metres of land. Modern weaponry had rendered traditional methods of warfare obsolete.

war of attrition
A conflict in which each side tries to wear down and slowly destroy its enemy by a process of constant attacks and steady killing.

Ultimately, the First World War lasted 52 months and caused the death of more than 30 million people, many of them civilians. All of the European countries that fought suffered heavy casualties – more than in any previous war. Societies became disjointed and economies were ruined. The German Kaiser, the Austrian emperor and the Russian tsar all lost their thrones, and their countries became republics. The post-war conference at Versailles decided that Germany bore most responsibility for the war and deserved most punishment, but the other defeated nations also suffered. The provinces of Alsace and Lorraine were returned to France. Germany had to pay a huge amount in reparations and was allowed to maintain only a small army. Its overseas empire was shared amongst the victorious powers. The Austro-Hungarian Empire was divided into new countries. Russia became a communist state led by Lenin and the Bolsheviks. France and Britain won militarily but their victory came at a high price.

The politicians who agreed the post-war settlements tried to ensure that this would be the 'war to end all wars'. Twenty years later, the old allies were once again united against Germany in the Second World War.

Historical debate

Historians have much debated the causes of the First World War. There are numerous contributory factors behind the war, ranging from the French defeat in the Franco–Prussian War in 1871 to the diplomatic efforts following Archduke Franz Ferdinand's assassination in 1914. Some historians have argued that the First World War was not inevitable, and that ultimately it was Germany and Austria's bid to control the Balkans and the Middle East that drew Russia and its allies into the conflict. Other historians have seen the alliance system itself as dragging Europe into war, while still others have argued that this is an oversimplification, as the main purpose of the alliances was defensive. The fact remains that the First World War was the culmination of many different factors feeding into one another.

Questions

1 Which do you think was stronger in 1914, the Triple Entente or the Triple Alliance? Why?

2 Below is a list of causes of the First World War. Rank these in order of significance (where 1 is the most significant and 6 is the least) and give brief reasons for the positioning of each reason in your list:

- the alliance system in Europe
- the naval and arms races
- the invasion of Belgium
- the assassination of the Austrian archduke
- imperial rivalries
- Russian mobilisation

3 What does Source A below reveal about relations between Britain and Germany before the First World War?

Source A

In 1908, I discussed the European situation with Bethmann Hollweg, the German Chancellor. He was very bitter about what he called 'the encirclement of Germany with an iron ring by France, Russia and Britain.' I did my best to assure him that Britain did not have the slightest desire to enter into any hostile agreement against Germany. We were most anxious to live in peace and as good neighbours with his great country. However, I told him that Britain was very uneasy about the growth of the German navy, which was a threat to Britain. Britain was an island and completely dependent on the sea for its existence. Bethmann Hollweg did not seem very enthusiastic about the German shipbuilding programme and he did his

best to convince me that the German people had no desire to attack Britain. But he was clear that Germany was very anxious about the agreements between Britain and France and Britain and Russia.

There was an extraordinary outburst when he repeated the claim about an iron ring. 'An iron ring', he repeated violently, shouting out the statement and waving his arms to everybody around us. 'Britain is embracing France. She is making friends with Russia. But it is not that you love each other; you hate Germany.' And he repeated and shouted the word 'hate' three times.

An extract from the memoirs of David Lloyd George, the British chancellor of the Exchequer in 1908, published in 1938.

Key issues

The key features of this chapter are:

- the development of the alliance system in Europe and how this contributed to the outbreak of the First World War

- how the rise of militarism and the arms race made war more likely

- the importance of the Balkans in the outbreak of war

- the significance of the assassination of the Austrian Archduke Franz Ferdinand in causing the war

- the war aims of the Entente Powers and the Central Powers.

Revision questions

1 Germany said that it never wished to replace British world power. Do you think this is true? Explain your answer.

2 Was Austria-Hungary or Russia more responsible for the failure to reach a peaceful resolution over the Balkan crisis of 1914?

3 Did the alliance system do more to safeguard or to threaten peace before 1914?

4 'France pursued warlike policies from 1900 to 1914.' How far do you agree with this statement?

Further reading

Culpin, C. and Darby, G. *The Origins of the First World War*. London, UK. Longman. 1998.

Henig, R. *The Origins of the First World War*. London, UK. Routledge. 2001.

Ross, S. *The Causes of World War I*. London, UK. Wayland. 2002.

Advanced reading

Joll, J. and Martel, G. *The Origins of the First World War*. London, UK. Longman. 2006.

Chapter

5 The Russian Revolution
1905–17

Key questions

- What were the causes and immediate outcomes of the 1905 Revolution?
- What were the strengths and weaknesses of Romanov rule from 1906 to 1914?
- Why was there a revolution in February 1917?
- Why did the Bolsheviks gain power in October 1917?

Content summary

- The position and policies of Nicholas II, and how they generated social and political instability.
- Bloody Sunday and wider risings in 1905.
- The October Manifesto, its implementation and its effects.
- Romanov rule from 1906 to 1914, including the reforms of Witte and Stolypin, and the extent of opposition from different sectors of Russian society.
- The causes of the February Revolution in 1917, including the effects of the First World War, the abdication of Nicholas II and the installation of the Provisional Government.
- How the Bolsheviks gained power in October 1917, and the crises faced by the Provisional Government; Lenin's leadership and the October Revolution.

Timeline

Nov 1894	Nicholas II becomes tsar of Russia
Feb 1904	Russo–Japanese War begins
Jan 1905	Start of the 1905 Revolution
Oct 1905	October Manifesto issued
Nov 1905	Sergei Witte becomes prime minister
Apr 1906	New constitution introduced – the Fundamental Laws; First Duma convened
Jul 1906	Pyotr Stolypin becomes prime minister
Sep 1911	Stolypin assassinated
Jul 1914	First World War begins
Mar 1917	Nicholas II abdicates; Provisional Government established
Oct 1917	October Revolution led by Lenin
Jul 1918	Nicholas II and family murdered by Bolsheviks

Introduction

In 1900, the power of the three great monarchies of continental Europe – Austria-Hungary, Germany and Russia – seemed secure. Nobody would have guessed that within 20 years they would all have disappeared.

At the turn of the century, Russia was the largest state in Europe, with a population of around 130 million. From 1894, the country was ruled by Tsar Nicholas II – an absolute monarch with unlimited power. Nicholas was determined to model his government on the example of his father, Alexander III, who staunchly opposed any reform to the inequalities that plagued Russian society. Nicholas was poorly educated and – with the exception of Sergei Witte – he chose ministers who were mostly incompetent. Many local officials were equally unsuitable for their positions.

Peasants and workers were dissatisfied with their conditions, and a revolution broke out in 1905. Soon the troubles spread throughout Russia and extended to the middle classes. Nicholas II survived, thanks to the support of the army, but he wasted the opportunity to introduce significant reforms. From 1906 to 1914, Russia seemed calm on the surface while the police and the army maintained order; opposition groups were divided and disorganised.

At the outbreak of the First World War in 1914, most Russians supported their country's involvement in the conflict. However, Russia's military failures soon revealed the incompetence of its government. After a series of heavy defeats, and with the Russian army in retreat, national morale suffered. Nicholas II's decision to go to the front and take personal charge of the troops backfired because there were no capable people to govern in his place. Most importantly, by this time the hardships suffered by the soldiers had lost the tsar their support. In February 1917, another revolution broke out. Nicholas II abdicated.

Chaos continued throughout 1917. The Provisional Government, led by Alexander Kerensky, faced immense problems over demands by the peasantry for the distribution of land, as well as the devastation caused by the war. In November, Vladimir Lenin led the Bolsheviks in yet another revolution. They took over the Provisional Government and from 1917 to 1924, Lenin and the Bolsheviks governed Russia. They ended the war with Germany, set up a one-party state and carried out far-reaching economic changes. But success was not easy, and between 1918 and 1921 a bloody civil war raged throughout Russia.

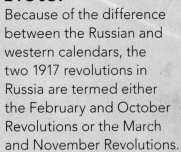

Note:

Because of the difference between the Russian and western calendars, the two 1917 revolutions in Russia are termed either the February and October Revolutions or the March and November Revolutions.

Russia at the beginning of the 20th century

At the start of the 20th century, Russia contained a large number of racial groups. In fact, only 45% of the population were ethnic Russians. The rest comprised Armenians, Balts, Georgians, Slavs, Poles and Ukrainians, as well as many Asiatic peoples. Each of these groups was proud of its nationality, language, history and religion, and for many years the only force unifying these disparate peoples was loyalty to the tsar. This was sufficient most of the time, but the general attitude towards their ruler changed when Nicholas II came to the throne. In particular, he alienated the different ethnic groups through his policy of 'Russification' – enforcing the Russian language as well as Orthodox religion and laws throughout the land.

Nicholas II

Nicholas II was of the royal Romanov dynasty that had ruled Russia for nearly 300 years. He became tsar in 1894, announcing: 'I shall maintain the principle of autocracy just as firmly as did my unforgettable father.' He kept this promise throughout his reign – resisting change however much circumstances within Russia altered. Nicholas was a devoted husband and father, but he was disastrously out of touch with the feelings of his subjects. When a revolution broke out in 1905, he granted some reforms. However, he showed his true attitude shortly afterwards by reasserting his power in the Fundamental Laws (see page 147). By 1917, when a further revolution swept Russia, Nicholas had lost so much support that he was forced to abdicate. He and his family were captured by the Bolsheviks and killed in 1918.

Figure 5.1 A map showing the expansion of the Russian Empire between 1795 and 1914

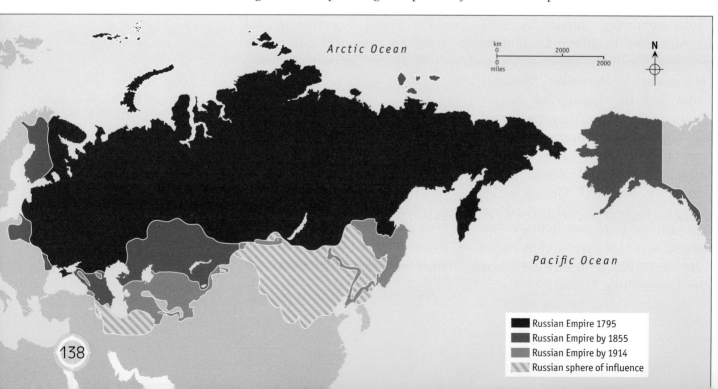

Russian Empire 1795
Russian Empire by 1855
Russian Empire by 1914
Russian sphere of influence

The social hierarchy in Russia

The vast majority of Russians were peasants. In theory, peasants were free (that is, they were not bound to a landlord as peasants had been for much of history), but in practice the emancipation of 1861 had brought few changes. It did little to improve their lives because most were still burdened with redemption payments for the land they had been granted. Most peasants were loyal to the tsar, but disliked the officials who demanded taxes and forced service from them. Peasants rioted in protest against these burdens, but they were not *revolutionary* – they saw no alternative to tsarist rule and their aims were social and economic, rather than political. There were no political parties in Russia as there were in western European countries. Scattered groups wanted change, but only a very small minority of extremists sought to overthrow the tsar.

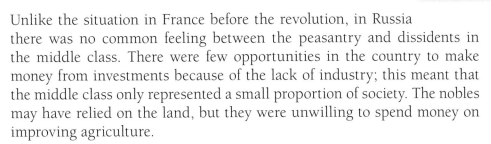

Note:
Tsar Alexander II emancipated (freed) the peasants or serfs in 1861. They could own property and marry without a landlord's permission, but they were not allowed to leave the peasant community freely. They had to make payments for 49 years for the land that they received. This land was often of poor quality, and emancipation still left most peasants in poverty.

Unlike the situation in France before the revolution, in Russia there was no common feeling between the peasantry and dissidents in the middle class. There were few opportunities in the country to make money from investments because of the lack of industry; this meant that the middle class only represented a small proportion of society. The nobles may have relied on the land, but they were unwilling to spend money on improving agriculture.

The peasantry itself was not a single unified group, and landholdings and farming included different factors:

- The soil – some farmed fertile land, others laboured on arid ground. The second group had more grievances than the first because of the hardship that they suffered.
- The extent to which peasants owned land directly or held it in common within the **communes** or *mirs*. The *mirs* controlled the amount of land that each peasant farmed, which was often insufficient.
- The interests of larger landowners were different because they could make profits from surplus production. There was the possibility of additional employment in small industries to supplement their incomes.
- Farming methods varied from the Baltic states in the west to Siberia in the east, as well as from north to south. The Baltic peasantry benefited from better land. Those in Siberia lived in particularly harsh conditions.
- Some communes were near markets in towns and cities where produce could be sold. Others were remote and had no incentive to produce more than they needed for their own survival.

communes
Communes or *mirs* were groups or communities of peasant farmers in Russia, prior to the 1917 Revolution. They were essentially agricultural co-operatives, with farmland divided up among the commune households.

The condition of the peasantry was perhaps Russia's most serious problem. Famines were frequent and due to a poor transport infrastructure, the government could not move food from places where it was plentiful to those where it was lacking. There was widespread poverty, and production levels were low. Peasants were encouraged to move from the west of Russia, where the problems were worst, to Siberia, where land was plentiful but natural conditions were too harsh to support a prosperous agriculture. In 1893, a Land Bank was founded to provide money for local communities and individual peasants to buy land. In 1905, redemption payments were cancelled, but in reality this made little difference to the peasants.

Economic structure

In spite of the problems of regions such as the inhospitable Siberia, Russia should have had enough agricultural resources to feed its population adequately. However, several factors stunted the economy:

- Agricultural methods were underdeveloped; neither the mass of the peasantry nor the landowners were interested in any form of modernisation to improve output.
- Russia did export wheat, and by the end of the 19th century grain exports were second only to those from America. However, profits did not benefit the peasantry and the central government was too inefficient to impose taxes on the landowners.
- In 1870, Russia had less rail track than Britain, France and Germany – the leading industrial countries. By 1910, more had been built, but Russia's vast size meant that the railways were still only thinly spread throughout the country.

This expanded railway system, along with increased industry, did help Russia to export more wheat, which benefited foreign trade. However, the money was not equally shared. The government's revenues were limited by the taxation system: income and land were taxed less than indirect taxes on commodities and food, and this system disadvantaged the peasants and the poor who lived in towns. Just as in France before 1789, the wealthier classes were taxed comparatively less.

The system by which taxes were collected was also inefficient. The lower classes complained about their heavy burden, but most taxes disappeared into the pockets of tax collectors and other middle-men before reaching the central government. The regime also did not spend its money wisely. Funds were allocated generously to the army and to the police, but little was spent on improving the economy. Nicholas II was simply not interested in modernisation or reform, and remained firmly committed to **autocracy**. The result was that the general Russian populace began to feel alienated from their leader.

autocracy
A system of rule where one person holds total and supreme power, and can make decisions without the approval of any other legal body.

Questions

1 What were living conditions like for the peasantry in Russia before the 1905 Revolution?

2 What were the social instabilities in Russian society at the start of the 20th century?

The causes and immediate outcomes of the 1905 Revolution

The position and policies of Nicholas II

Nicholas II was set on following the hardline policies of his father, Alexander III. Alexander had opposed any reforms in Russia, believing they threatened his own power and the ancient traditions on which the Romanov dynasty had been built. He considered the innovations being developed in the West as unsuitable for his own country.

Nicholas II believed that the reforms introduced by his grandfather Alexander II in the mid 19th century – especially the emancipation of the serfs – had weakened Russia. The tsar appointed and dismissed ministers, and there was no parliament to limit his authority. At the start of Nicholas's reign in 1894, the Zemstva, which had also been set up by Alexander II, maintained some responsibilities, but these were always under the supervision of the tsar's officials. The army put down violent unrest and the police kept political dissidents under control. The Orthodox Church, and especially its leading official **Konstantin Pobedonostsev**, fully supported the tsar's rule.

The tsar was personally a kind man, devoted to his wife, Alexandra, and his children. His only son, Alexei, suffered from the blood disorder haemophilia, and it was doubtful that he would survive into adulthood. This situation clearly left doubts over the succession to the throne, and played a significant part in the instability of Nicholas' regime.

Nicholas himself had little education, but he could speak English, French and German (in fact he preferred these languages to his own, believing that Russian was the language of peasants). Such qualities might have made him an amiable and respected local nobleman, but he lacked many of the qualities required in an effective ruler:

- He was isolated at court and uninterested in matters of government; he preferred to go hunting than to attend ministerial meetings.
- He could be swayed easily by advice, usually from courtiers, who also opposed reforms.
- His ministers were typically chosen because of their social position rather than for their abilities. These men competed for the attention of the tsar rather than co-operating with each other or offering objective advice.

Note:

The Zemstva were councils set up by Alexander II to give peasants and urban workers some responsibility in local administration. They were run by elected leaders and their responsibilities included education, health and local transport, for which small amounts of taxes could be raised. Alexander III and Nicholas II could not reverse the emancipation of the serfs, but they did their best to weaken the Zemstva.

Key figure

Konstantin Pobedonostsev (1827–1907)

Pobedonostsev, who had served Alexander III, was the leading official at the beginning of the reign of Nicholas II. He supported Nicholas in his opposition to any type of reform. Pobedonostsev was a high-ranking member of the Orthodox Church, and anyone with alternative religious sympathies was regarded as subversive. Pobedonostsev died in 1907, the determined enemy of all the reformers in Russia.

The State Council had no powers. Its members were mostly old men who were appointed because of long service to the state rather than for their vigour and skill in managing affairs. They were usually appointed for life by the tsar, but he could dismiss them if he wished. Members thus tended to give him the advice that they knew would be welcomed, rather than what they truly believed to be in Russia's best interests.

The members of the Senate were also appointed by the tsar. This body was supposed to oversee administration, but the system was confused and the powers of the Senate were unclear. There were many local officials whose responsibilities were also uncertain. Russia was made up of 97 administrative regions – far more than was necessary to govern even such a large country. The Zemstva provided a form of self-government for villages and some larger areas where the Russian population lived, but the system was not adopted in areas populated by ethnic minorities. The limited powers of the Zemstva could be overruled by governors and other officials who generally opposed reform. Towns and large cities were governed by appointed rather than elected officials. Overall, Russia was administered much less efficiently than the more modern states in western Europe.

Witte's reforms

The one forward-thinking Russian statesman at this time was **Sergei Witte**, who believed that the answer to Russia's problems lay in foreign loans and foreign exports. The country was rich in raw materials, but lacked the factories and railways required to produce and export manufactured goods. Building these would require huge sums of money, but Russia did not have the funds for this investment. Wealthy nobles were not interested in industry, dismissing it as undignified.

Witte increased taxes and raised money abroad by giving investors high rates of interest. Under him, the Trans-Siberian Railway was inaugurated and the coal industry grew in Ukraine. However, Witte's policies also caused problems. Twice as much was spent on repaying the foreign loans as was expended on education. Taxes were increased to repay the loans and this rise in tax affected the peasants most severely. Nicholas II gave Witte little support, and he was despised amongst members of the court and other nobility, who considered his ideas dangerous. After falling from grace, Witte was recalled briefly as prime minister at a time of crisis after the 1905 Revolution, mostly to negotiate a loan from France. His support for reforms was still unpopular and he was dismissed as soon as the loan was secured.

The positive results of Witte's reforms were that industry and the railways grew. The negative results were that the country's national debt increased and the standard of living of most the population declined. At the turn of the century these problems were certainly serious, but there was no indication that they would be fatal for Nicholas II. The situation was no worse than it had been for many years, and most people believed that the

Key figure

Sergei Witte (1849–1915)

Witte was one of the rare officials in Nicholas II's government who supported reform. As minister of finance from 1892 to 1903, Witte was convinced that rapid industrialisation was the solution to the country's economic problems. Nicholas II never supported Witte's ideas and dismissed him, only to recall him briefly as prime minister after the 1905 Revolution.

tsarist government could survive as long as it did not have to face a major crisis such as a foreign war. Assassins were always a danger to autocratic monarchs, but Nicholas II's police kept a vigilant eye on potential terrorists.

War with Japan

By 1900, China was extremely weak – suffering from internal conflict and poor government. Both Japan and Russia saw the possibility of expanding their influence in Manchuria, eastern China, and Korea. Port Arthur in Manchuria offered Russia an ice-free harbour, which would be useful because its other ports were either in the Arctic north or on the Black Sea, with difficult access to other oceans. Japan suggested that Russia could take control of Manchuria if Japan itself could have Korea. However, these negotiations broke down and war broke out in 1904, after Japan attacked Port Arthur.

In the course of the Russo–Japanese War, the poor quality of the Russian navy was demonstrated when ships had to be sent from the Baltic in the west to confront the Japanese navy. The fleet suffered a devastating defeat at the Battle of Tsushima on 27–28 May 1905 – in a stunning victory for the Japanese, two-thirds of the Russian fleet was destroyed, demoralising the surviving Russian sailors. The Russian army, larger than the Japanese but inferior in quality, failed to prevent the capture of Mukden, the capital of Manchuria. Ultimately, Russia had to agree a humiliating peace in the Treaty of Portsmouth in 1905.

> **Note:**
> There were a number of assassinations of leading figures in the late 19th century. The most famous in Russia was the murder of Tsar Alexander II, who was killed by a bomb in 1881, after surviving several earlier attempts on his life.

Figure 5.2 A map showing the progress of the Russo–Japanese War, 1904–05

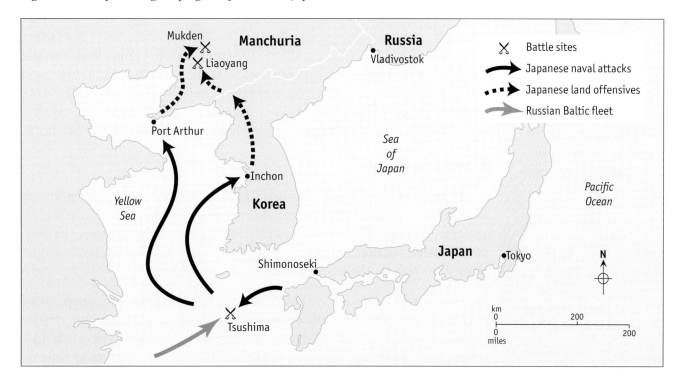

There were several significant consequences of this war:

- Japan began to be regarded as a more modern and efficient state – the first in Asia to defeat a European country.
- Russia's weaknesses were revealed. It turned its international interests from the east to the Balkans, with consequences that eventually led to the First World War.
- Internally, the defeat was a serious blow to the prestige of the tsarist government.
- The Russo–Japanese war was a major cause of the 1905 Revolution.

The 1905 Revolution

The Russian Revolution of 1905 was not a sudden event, but rather the culmination of years of discontent caused by several factors:

- The poor economic condition of the peasantry, who had seen little improvement in their lives following emancipation.
- The autocratic nature of Nicholas II's rule, which distanced him from the population.
- An economic recession in the early years of the 20th century, which resulted in high rates of unemployment.
- Growing nationalist unrest among racial groups such as the Finns, Balts, Armenians and Georgians, who resented the policy of Russification (see page 138).
- Other groups within the empire wanted a more democratic form of government. Some demanded socialism.
- Mass unrest was met with ruthless repression, causing further resentment.

Although revolutionary groups existed in Russia, they were not solely responsible for the 1905 Revolution. **Vladimir Ilyich Lenin**, leader of the small Bolshevik Party – a breakaway faction of the Russian Social Democratic Labour Party (SDLP) – was in exile at the time, and played no part in the events of 1905. Other revolutionary figures were more directly involved, notably **Leon Trotsky**, who encouraged the revolution from his base in St Petersburg.

Bloody Sunday

On 22 January 1905, a priest named Father Gapon led a non-violent march in Moscow to petition the tsar for land reforms and an assembly elected by universal suffrage. The crowd was dispersed violently by Cossack soldiers. The incident became known as 'Bloody Sunday' and the Russian people blamed the tsar for the extreme reaction of the soldiers.

The events of Bloody Sunday showed the extent of Nicholas II's unpopularity as the 1905 Revolution took hold. Strikes began in Moscow and rapidly spread to other cities. Some of the middle classes supported this protest, and industrial workers organised themselves into trade unions.

Key figures

Vladimir Ilyich Lenin (1870–1924)

Lenin was first sentenced to exile in Siberia and then lived in western Europe. He returned to Russia during the February Revolution. He opposed the Provisional Government and played a decisive role in the October Revolution of 1917. He governed Russia from this point until his death in 1924.

Leon Trotsky (1879–1940)

After the 1905 Revolution, Trotsky was sentenced to internal exile, but he escaped abroad. In 1917, he joined Lenin and played a key role in the Bolsheviks' seizure of power and later in the organisation of the Red Army against the Whites. When Lenin died in 1924, Trotsky lost a power struggle with Stalin. He was expelled from the Bolshevik Party and exiled from Russia.

Sailors on the battleship *Potemkin* mutinied, and the government feared more unrest among sailors and soldiers. However, the revolutionaries were largely disorganised, with no central co-ordination, and fortunately for the tsar, the army remained loyal to him at this point.

Today is the twelfth anniversary of 'Bloody Sunday', which is rightly regarded as the beginning of the Russian revolution. Thousands of workers—not political radicals, but loyal God-fearing subjects—led by the priest Gapon, streamed from all parts of the capital to its centre, to the square in front of the Winter Palace, to submit a petition to the Tsar. The workers carried religious icons. In a letter to the Tsar, their leader, Gapon, had guaranteed his personal safety and asked him to appear before the people.

Troops were called out. The Cossack cavalry attacked the crowd with drawn swords. They fired on the unarmed workers, who on their bended knees implored the Cossacks to allow them to go to the Tsar. Over one thousand were killed and over two thousand wounded on that day, according to police reports. The indignation of the workers was indescribable.

I shall quote a few passages from the workers' petition. It begins with the following words: 'We workers, inhabitants of St. Petersburg, have come to Thee. We are unfortunate, despised slaves, weighed down by despotism and tyranny. Our patience is exhausted, we stopped work and begged our masters to give us only that without which life is a torment. But this was refused. To the employers everything seemed unlawful. We are here, many thousands of us. Like the whole of the Russian people, we have no human rights whatever. Owing to the deeds of Thy officials we have become slaves.'

The petition contained these demands: amnesty, civil liberties, fair wages, the gradual transfer of the land to the people, a representative assembly on the basis of universal and equal suffrage. It ends with the following words:

'Sir, do not refuse aid to Thy people! Demolish the wall that separates Thee from Thy people. Order and promise that our requests will be granted, and Thou wilt make Russia happy. If not, we are ready to die on this very spot. We have only two roads: freedom and happiness, or the grave.'

Extract from a speech delivered in 1917 by revolutionary leader Vladimir Ilyich Lenin, on the anniversary of the start of the 1905 Revolution.

The October Manifesto

As unrest continued, Nicholas II was persuaded – reluctantly – to make concessions to the masses. These were delivered in the October Manifesto, which promised free speech and an elected assembly called the Duma (from *dumat*, which means 'to think'), whose agreement would be needed before any laws could be passed.

Note:
Although Nicholas II initially promised greater liberties and said the Duma would have the power to act to ensure these liberties were upheld, he did not allow the Duma to elect its own ministers, and he claimed the right to discharge the council whenever he wanted.

Reaction to the October Manifesto was divided. Many of the rebels felt that their voices had been heard, and that the landowners would have to accept their demands. However, a minority of extreme revolutionaries – including the Bolsheviks – felt that the Manifesto did not go far enough in addressing the grievances of the Russian people. There was some armed resistance, but the tsar's soldiers suppressed this, and it seemed for a time that stability would return to Russia.

Figure 5.3 Workers and students at a rally a day after the announcement of the October Manifesto in 1905

The disturbances and unrest in St Petersburg, Moscow and in many other parts of our country have filled my heart with great and profound sorrow. The welfare of the Russian Tsar and His people is inseparable and he feels the national sorrow. The present disturbances could give rise to national instability and present a threat to the unity of our country. The oath which I took as Tsar compels me to use all my strength, intelligence and power to put a speedy end to this unrest which is so dangerous for the state. The relevant authorities have been ordered to take measures to deal with direct outbreaks of disorder and violence and to protect people who only want to go about their daily business in peace. However, in view of the need to carry out quickly measures to pacify the country, I have decided that the work of the government must be unified. I have therefore ordered the government to take the following measures in fulfilment of my unbending will:

1 Fundamental civil freedoms will be granted to the population, including real elections which have already been organised.
2 It is established as an unshakeable rule that no law can come into force without its approval by the state Duma. Representatives of the people will be given the opportunity to take real part in the supervision of the legality of government bodies.
3 Personal liberty, freedom of conscience, speech, assembly and association will be guaranteed.

Participation in the Duma will be granted to those classes of the population which are at present deprived of voting powers, as far as it is possible in the short period before the Duma meets, and this will lead to the development of a universal franchise. There will be no delay to the Duma. We call on all true sons of Russia to remember the homeland, to help put a stop to this unprecedented unrest and to devote all their strength to the restoration of peace to their native land.

An extract from the October Manifesto, 1905.

Nicholas II's insincerity in issuing this decree soon became apparent, though. He proved unwilling to enforce the reforms that he had promised and issued the Fundamental Laws, which asserted his full autocratic powers. The police and the army continued to harass real or imagined critics of the tsarist regime; it is estimated that 15,000 people were killed and 70,000 arrested within a year.

The Duma

Although the Duma was an elected body, it did not represent a democracy. When the first Duma met in 1906, it represented a minority of the population. The franchise was restricted to landowners, and only a few peasants who owned land could vote. The Duma's powers were limited to control of a small part of the budget but, even so, Nicholas II ignored it and it was dissolved within two months. The second Duma met for a few months in 1907. After the franchise was changed to give even more representation to landowners, the third Duma lasted longer – from 1907 to 1912 – but it still achieved little. Nicholas retained power whilst the opposition Cadets (broadly democrats) and Decembrists (inspired by a revolt against Tsar Nicholas I in the early 19th century) could not agree on a common programme, other than to make no concessions to the peasantry. The fourth Duma had just been convened when the First World War broke out.

Some historians have argued that Nicholas II missed an opportunity in 1906 to carry through the reforms that would have made Russia a more modern and stable country. However, despots rarely prove willing to surrender any of their power, and Nicholas II was particularly reactionary. It soon became apparent that the reforms were largely cosmetic. The very factors that had caused the 1905 Revolution remained largely unresolved even after the tsar had put down the revolution and attempted to implement reforms. Nicholas II's treatment of the Duma showed his contempt for representative government, and his refusal to provide any sort of leadership laid the foundations for future troubles.

Questions

1. Do you think that 1906 was a missed opportunity for the tsar?

2. To what extent did the 1905 Revolution critically weaken Nicholas II's hold over the Russian Empire?

3. What do you think was the most important cause of the 1905 Revolution?

> **Note:**
> The first statement of the Fundamental Laws was that 'supreme autocratic power belongs to the tsar'. This denied the hopes of those who saw the Duma as a means of bringing more representative government to Russia. The tsar could introduce laws and could veto those passed by the Duma. Ministers were still appointed by the tsar, who controlled military and foreign affairs. The Duma had no way of enforcing its decisions.

The strengths and weaknesses of Romanov rule 1906–14

The 1905 Revolution shook Russia, but the tsar still enjoyed considerable support. In reality, there were very few republicans, and they were confined to tiny groups of radicals. The reaction to the October Manifesto showed that almost everybody wanted a settlement with Nicholas II. The Romanovs had ruled Russia since 1613, and not many people could see an alternative to tsarist rule. Many people regarded democracy as 'un-Russian' – a foreign system that would not suit their country.

Stolypin's reforms

Nicholas II took a positive step in 1906 when he appointed **Pyotr Stolypin** as minister of the interior and, later, as prime minister. Stolypin saw agriculture as the primary problem and wanted to work towards improving the peasants' situation However, he also believed in strict law and order, and he ruthlessly repressed any peasant uprisings. 'Stolypin's Necktie' (death by hanging) was used widely to punish rebels after the 1905 Revolution.

Agricultural reform

Although Stolypin sought reform, he was not a democrat. He supported changes in the franchise to weaken the troublesome Duma, and placed it under the control of landowners.

Having restored political order, he pursued a policy of social and economic reform. He believed that the most beneficial change would be to encourage the growth of a wealthy peasant class, or *kulaks*, saying that Russia should 'bet on the strong'. The *mirs* – peasant commune villages – oversaw the work of peasants and were generally restrictive. They directed what land a peasant could work and which crops could be grown, limiting the ability of an ambitious peasant to make improvements. Stolypin wanted to make peasants independent of the *mirs*. This would allow them to put together their individual strips of land and therefore work them more efficiently. The *kulaks* became a newly independent and comparatively wealthy class, but the experiment did not last long enough to transform Russia.

Key figure

Pyotr Stolypin (1862–1911)

Stolypin came from a noble family, but unlike many of his class, he demonstrated an awareness of the hardships that most Russians faced. He was also unusual amongst his class for his willingness to embrace reform. As well as being prime minister, Stolypin served as leader of the third Duma, and aimed to counter unrest by undertaking reforms that could vastly improve life for the peasants in Russia.

Note:

After the October Revolution of 1917, Lenin tried to suppress the *kulaks*, but without much success. It was Stalin who succeeded in eliminating them. After he came to power, more than 5 million *kulaks* were killed or sent to labour camps.

A Peasant Land Bank lent peasants money to buy their land. Those who had little or poor land were encouraged to move to unfarmed land in the east. Many peasants took advantage of these developments, as a result of which Russia began to experience regional changes. In places such as Ukraine and Crimea in the south, where the land was fertile, peasants had an incentive to secure their own land. In the harsh north and east, there was no such incentive. Agricultural production increased in the most favourable regions, making the *kulaks* more prosperous. It also benefited the government and those who exported wheat.

Exact figures are difficult to calculate, but output might have increased by 14% between 1900 and 1914, and the income of some landowners and *kulaks* rose by as much as 80%. However, some historians believe that most of the increase was the result of a series of naturally good harvests rather than Stolypin's reforms, and point out that many Russians did not benefit from these policies. Whatever the reason, agriculture – so vital to the Russian economy – was improving by 1914.

Industrialisation

Stolypin's interests went beyond agricultural reform. Industry boomed, and trade with Britain, France and Germany increased substantially. Russia had vast natural resources of coal, oil, metals and wood. Textiles were produced in greater quantities. Some believed that Russia was entering a period of industrial revolution like that in the West in the 19th century.

However, these developments came at a price. The government's attempts to prevent peasants moving to urban areas in the hope of jobs and a better standard of living did not work. As more people moved to towns and cities, living conditions there worsened. The urban population nearly doubled in the generation before the outbreak of the First World War. The **proletariat** lived in squalid housing and unhealthy conditions. There was very little medical care and standards of education were very low. Workers had virtually no rights. Trade unions were banned and the police cracked down on protests.

proletariat
An alternative name for the industrial working class. They generally had no wealth or property, and their only source of income was their own labour.

In the absence of a Russian middle class, the country's reliance on loans gave power to banks. Monopolies weakened the efforts of small businessmen to become more prosperous. Russia was thus benefiting economically from industrialisation, but was suffering socially.

In some ways this was a similar situation to that in the industrialising countries of western Europe a century earlier. But while they often acted reluctantly, the governments of Britain, France and Prussia usually conceded enough to avoid large-scale revolutions. In Russia, Nicholas II saw no need for any political concessions apart from the façade of the Duma. Most of the reforms the people demanded (a maximum working week, factory inspections to ensure that laws were enforced, some health and insurance provision) would have seemed moderate in western Europe. To the tsar, such demands were radical.

Mikhail Bakunin (1814–76)

Bakunin was the son of a wealthy Russian nobleman. He was a leading anarchist, opposing all forms of government, including Marx's socialist form of rule. He spent much of his life outside Russia to avoid prosecution, but his ideas gained a wide following within Russia, especially among young radicals.

anarchism
A political philosophy that believes that no form of government is necessary or desirable, and which encourages a society of workers living in voluntary associations without any form of leadership hierarchy.

Opposition to the tsar

Industrialisation brought a level of prosperity to Russia, but it also created problems for an authoritarian and inefficient government. Between 1909 and 1914, strikes became more common, which provoked increasingly violent efforts to suppress them. This only encouraged further protests. Shop workers and railway employees went on strike; university students staged protests; even sailors in the navy began to demonstrate dissatisfaction with their situation.

Unrest also simmered amongst the peasantry. Some who had bought their land found they could not keep up their repayments, and arrears to the Peasant Land Bank (see page 149) increased. Many peasants started to feel that their conditions were worse than they had been before the reforms were introduced. In the midst of this discontent, radical philosophies such as Marxism (see page 59) began to develop and gain popularity. The revolutionary **Mikhail Bakunin** encouraged **anarchism**, in which the state would disappear and workers would co-operate voluntarily. Bakunin disagreed fundamentally with Marxism, claiming that such a system would lead to the suppression of the agricultural and industrial poor.

Note:
One significant example of violence against strikers during this period was the massacre in the Lena gold mine in 1912. During the strike, 270 miners were killed and almost as many were wounded by tsarist soldiers.

Figure 5.4 The massacre at the Lena gold mine in April 1912

Other radical groups also became more outspoken. The Land and Liberty movement advocated a rural revolution to win power for the mass of the peasantry, who were disfranchised and living in poverty. The revolutionary activist **Georgi Plekhanov** was forced to flee from Russia after police persecution. He realised the impossibility of a peasant-led movement and later became a Marxist. Other radical Russians also sought refuge abroad, especially in Switzerland, where they plotted uprisings in Russia. Among these exiled radicals was Vladimir Lenin.

Unrest was seeping into Russia, weakening the foundations of tsarism. The police and the army could keep radicals under control but they could not eliminate them altogether. The exile of Lenin and other revolutionaries kept them out the clutches of tsarism, but it allowed them to continue their work abroad, where they gained increasing support. Radicals in internal exile in remote parts of Siberia still managed to spread their ideas and keep contact with others. Censorship was evaded and illegal newspapers, pamphlets and books were distributed widely.

Despite these threats, there was still no real challenge to the power of the tsar. Before the First World War broke out, Nicholas II could rely on the loyalty of the police and on the army, and despite the harsh conditions in which they lived, most people still felt a respect for the traditions of the monarchy. However, the events of 1905 were not forgotten and as Russia became embroiled in war, hardships increased and discontent grew stronger.

> **Key figure**
>
> **Georgi Plekhanov (1856–1918)**
>
> Plekhanov was a Russian Marxist who spent more than 30 years in exile. He supported the Russian Social Democratic Party and opposed Lenin's decision to break with it and set up a separate Bolshevik Party. In October 1917, he criticised the seizure of power by Lenin and the Bolsheviks, but died the following year.

Historical debate

Historians interpret the period from 1906 to 1914 in Russia in different ways. Traditional Soviet historians and some others believed that the fall of tsarism and the triumph of the Bolsheviks were inevitable according to Marxist theories. However, most modern historians do not subscribe to this view. They believe that during this period, the tsar ruled over a fragile society. Tensions within destabilised the state and the war caused the decrepit structure to collapse. Some historians believe Russia was mostly stable, with an improving economy and a government that controlled dissent. They believe the monarchy could have survived if it had not been for the catastrophe of the First World War.

Questions

1. What could Nicholas II have done to prevent revolution in 1905?

2. Do you think he was prepared to do this, based on the information in this section and any wider reading? Explain your reasons.

3. What were the goals of the proletariat and why did they find it difficult to achieve these?

The causes of the February Revolution in 1917

From 1906 to 1914, an uneasy peace existed in Russia. The 1905 Revolution had caused alarm amongst the liberals, and army generals and the police took steps to eliminate the opposition. By 1911, the tsar had lost confidence in Stolypin, and the same year the minister was murdered in mysterious circumstances. The tsar demonstrated no sorrow over Stolypin's death, and quickly replaced him with Ivan Goremykin. Goremykin was an extreme conservative, who fully believed in the authoritarian rights of the tsar and was more than willing to go along with his leader's conservative policies. In 1913, Russia celebrated the 300th anniversary of the Romanov regime, and despite the unrest simmering in the country, the tsar felt no threat. He saw no reason why his dynasty would not last for another three centuries – but in little more than three years, it had ceased to exist.

Rasputin

One significant factor in the decline of the tsar's reputation was his association with **Grigori Rasputin**. A self-professed healer, Rasputin seemed able to calm the young tsarevich, Alexei, during his frequent periods of illness, and this made him a great favourite of the tsar's wife in particular. However, Rasputin's lack of education and lowly origins meant he was despised by members of the royal court, and many grew concerned over the influence he seemed to have on the tsar and tsarina. Alexandra defended Rasputin fiercely: courtiers who were appalled at his crude manners fell out of favour; critical ministers were dismissed.

Before the First World War, Rasputin's unpopularity was confined to the court and higher circles of government. However, when Nicholas II set off for the front to take charge of the Russian army during the war, Alexandra was left in control of the country. She sought Rasputin's advice on many matters and this brought him to the attention of the wider public, where he proved equally unpopular. He was murdered in 1916 – not by political radicals striking a blow against the monarchy, but by a group of conservative courtiers who wanted to save the tsar's reputation.

The impact of the First World War

Russia claimed that it did not go to war in 1914 to win territory, but rather to protect Serbia – a small state with a population of fellow Slavs – from what Russians believed to be the unreasonable and warlike demands of Austria-Hungary, backed by Germany. These intentions seemed honourable to the Russian people, as their country had a long history of tension with Austria-Hungary. In turn, Austria-Hungary believed that Russia was using Serbia to

Key figure

Grigori Rasputin (1869–1916)

Rasputin came from Siberia. He was illiterate and had a reputation as a drunkard, a womaniser and a petty criminal. He spent a few months in a monastery, but had too little education to become a monk. He described himself as a holy man and healer. Rasputin arrived in St Petersburg in 1903, and came to the attention of the royal family, who hoped he could heal their son. He was murdered by a courtier in 1916.

Figure 5.5 A cartoon from 1916 commenting on Rasputin's control over the tsar and tsarina

extend its influence in the Balkans and to benefit from the break-up of the Austro-Hungarian Empire. However, it was Germany that ended up as the real threat to Russia.

The start of the war

The Russian military was in a mixed position at the start of the conflict. Defeat by Japan in 1904–05 had been a spur to addressing the deficiencies in the Russian army and navy, and considerable sums of money had been spent both enlarging and improving the armed forces. In 1914, the Russian army was three times the size of Germany's, with a significantly higher number of large guns. But Russia faced serious potential problems. To begin with, it would take much longer for Russia to mobilise its army than it would other countries, significantly Germany. In addition, although the Russian railway system was expanded before the war with financial assistance from its ally France, transport problems were far from resolved and there were still not enough railway lines to efficiently transport large numbers of troops and war supplies.

Note:
The army's budget was increased from 473 million roubles in 1907 to 700 million roubles in 1913, and there were plans to spend much more. The navy's budget was doubled during the same period.

These fears proved well-founded when war was officially declared. Russian mobilisation was slow and the Russian army was not in place as quickly as German troops. Large numbers of soldiers and weapons were kept in strongpoints behind the front lines.

It was clear that the increased expenditure on the military had not made the army capable of fighting a modern war. It still relied on its cavalry, which was not only ineffective against modern weapons like machine guns, but also caused problems because horses required large quantities of food and transport – both of which were more urgently needed elsewhere. Brave cavalry charges resulted in wholesale slaughter. Most soldiers relied on bayonet charges, which meant they were lost to gunfire before they could reach the enemy. Methods of modern warfare had not yet been instilled in the Russian army.

The course of the war

The conflict began badly for Russia, and despite some early victories against the Austro-Hungarian army, and a success against Turkey, it soon became clear that Russia would not be able to defeat Germany in an offensive war. It would have to resort to defensive tactics, for which it was neither well trained nor well suited.

Note:
The Battle of Tannenberg between Russia and Germany in the opening days of the First World War highlighted the weakness of the Russian army. The overwhelming victory of the German army showed its superiority in weapons, tactics and speed. A quarter of a million Russian soldiers were killed or captured.

The human cost of the war steadily mounted for Russia, as well as its cost in resources. The peasant majority of ordinary soldiers were short of clothes, food, weapons and ammunition. Guns and shells were piled up, unable to reach the front lines due to the inefficient system of transport and the vast distances to be travelled. Losses in 1916 alone amounted to a million men. Weak army generals did not modify their tactics of throwing masses of badly equipped soldiers against steady gunfire.

Because of repeated military failures, in 1915 Nicholas II decided to go to the front to take personal charge of his armies. This was a fatal mistake – the tsar had no military skill or training, and his presence inspired neither army generals nor common soldiers. His absence at court also left a power vacuum in Russia.

The effects of the war

The tsarina, Alexandra, was left in charge of the government, but she was incapable of exercising power effectively. Her German heritage caused her to be viewed with suspicion, and some even accused her of being a German spy. As a woman, she found she had little power or influence over traditionally minded ministers. Her reliance on Rasputin (see page 153) increased her unpopularity. As the Russian army crumbled in the face of its enemies on the front lines, back home the Romanov government disintegrated.

Russia possessed industries, the railway system had been enlarged and, in peacetime, the harvests were sufficient to feed the population. The major problem during the First World War was a lack of organisation. The railways could not transport food and supplies from areas of plenty to where there was need. Food was plentiful in some regions and lacking in others. This was most severe in the cities and towns, where the poorest suffered from famine while crops rotted in the fields and warehouses, or were fed to animals to avoid being wasted. The number of farm animals increased while the number of deaths by starvation also grew.

Inflation raised prices, which affected the lower classes in towns and the countryside. Strikes spread in major cities such as Moscow and St Petersburg (now renamed Petrograd). Unrest was not confined to the lower classes. Courtiers and generals expressed dissatisfaction and the Duma criticised economic policies. Its members were not revolutionaries – in fact most were conservative – but they wanted a more efficient tsarist government.

Figure 5.6 Russian soldiers enjoy a hot meal before getting on trains to the front lines in 1915

The abdication of Nicholas II

Traditional Russian Marxists argued that the fall of the Romanov regime and the triumph of the Bolsheviks were inevitable because of the backward state of Russia and the efficiency of Lenin and his followers. However, most historians now argue against this. They emphasise the importance of the war as an immediate cause of the fall of Nicholas II.

Perhaps the most crucial development in 1917 was a series of army mutinies. Conditions at the front were unbearable and stories spread of hardships at home. Soldiers drifted back to their homes in large numbers, afraid that their families would die if they did not return to help them. They became a focal point of dissatisfaction in the major cities. Sergei Khabalov, the governor of Petrograd, proclaimed martial law and ordered soldiers to restore order. The soldiers refused and opened fire on officers. Even the Cossacks – once the most loyal of the Romanovs' soldiers – turned against Nicholas II. Without army support, Nicholas II abdicated quietly in February 1917. Unrealistic as ever, he blamed 'treason, cowardice and deceit'.

> By the Grace of God, We, Nicholas II, to all our faithful subjects be it known:
>
> In the days of a great struggle against a foreign enemy who has been endeavouring for three years to enslave our country, it pleased God to send Russia a further painful trial.
>
> Internal troubles threatened to have a fatal effect on the further progress of this obstinate war. The destinies of Russia, the honour of her heroic army, the happiness of the people, and the whole future of our beloved country demand that the war should be conducted at all costs to a victorious end.
>
> The cruel enemy is making his last efforts and the moment is near when our valiant army, in cooperation with our glorious allies, will finally overthrow the enemy. In these decisive days in the life of Russia we have thought that we owed to our people the close union and organisation of all its forces to achieve a rapid victory. Therefore in agreement with the Duma, we have recognised that it is for the good of the country that we should abdicate the crown of the Russian state and lay down the supreme power.

The abdication of Nicholas II, February 1917.

Note:

After the October Revolution, Nicholas II, the tsarina and their five children were imprisoned by the Bolsheviks in the remote town of Ekaterinburg. They were executed in 1918. The bodies of the royal family have recently been identified and buried with religious and state honours in Russia.

Figure 5.7 Nicholas II and his family in March 1917, shortly after his abdication

Members of the Duma, supported by middle-class liberals and nobles, wished for a government headed by Prince Lvov, but he stood no chance of success. A member of the Duma and a liberal, Lvov was determined to continue the war, but he had no clear ideas for reform. Power quickly passed to a Provisional Government, led by the liberal **Alexander Kerensky**.

Questions

1. Carry out some further research into the political situation in Russia at the time of the tsar's abdication. What groups were in place to take power at that time?

2. Which of these groups do you think was in the best position to bring about the revolution that Russia needed in order to reform?

Key figure

Alexander Kerensky (1881–1970)

Kerensky trained as a lawyer and became minister of justice and then prime minister when the Provisional Government was established in Russia. He was a popular leader and tried to hold together the different factions. However, he lacked Lenin's ruthlessness and was not able to deal with his country's problems. He decided to continue the war and postponed land reforms, while the economy got worse. After the October Revolution, he moved to western Europe and then to the United States, where he lived until his death in 1970.

The Bolsheviks' rise to power

Ultimately, it was a small group of communists known as the Bolsheviks who came to power in Russia after the fall of the Romanovs. But their victory was not an easy one, and only came about after further revolution and years of civil war. Their eventual success was due in large part to the strong leadership of Vladimir Ilyich Lenin (see page 144).

Lenin's leadership

Lenin was born in 1870 to a lower middle class family. His father was a minor government official and Lenin trained as a lawyer. He became a revolutionary when his brother was executed after being accused of involvement in a plot to assassinate Alexander III.

Lenin's life followed a similar course to that of many other Russian revolutionaries of the era: internal exile in Siberia followed by voluntary exile abroad for much of the period from 1900 to 1917. He eventually proved to be an effective organiser, although there was little evidence for this before 1917.

Note:

During his membership of the Social Democratic Party, Lenin edited *Iskra* ('The Spark'), a newspaper that was smuggled into Russia. His books such as *The Development of Capitalism in Russia* (1899), *What Is To Be Done?* (1902) and *The State and Revolution*, written just before the Bolsheviks' revolutionary victory in 1917, were all extremely important to the movement that he led.

Lenin's skills

One of Lenin's greatest strengths was his ability to be both idealistic and practical, and his government of Russia after 1917 showed a willingness to compromise when necessary. His adaptation of Marxism gave rise to a new political philosophy that became known as 'Marxist–Leninism'. Lenin aimed to incite a revolution that would bring down the tsarist autocracy, but ironically he did not tolerate any challenges to his own leadership. He was a skilled orator – a fact that contributed to his success in 1917 – but more importantly in developing the Bolshevik movement, he was also a talented writer and a profound political thinker.

Lenin reached two decisions that shaped the future of Russia. Firstly, he appreciated the importance of organisation and discipline within a revolutionary party. The disorganised and fragmented radical groups had achieved very little and spent a great deal of time quarrelling amongst themselves. Secondly, he recognised the value of the industrial working classes in securing the success of any revolution. He believed that the peasantry would not be able to mount a united challenge to the tsarist regime. The proletariat worked in factories and lived in towns. As far as Lenin was concerned, it was more likely that they could be shaped into an effective revolutionary weapon.

Developments in 1903

The second congress of the Social Democrats met in London in 1903. Lenin, supported by Plekhanov (see page 151), decided to restrict membership of the party to those who were active in the cause of revolution and socialism. This would necessarily be a minority. Lenin wanted a revolution in Russia to defeat tsarism. Trotsky (see page 144) and Julius Martov – a Russian politician who was also exiled for his beliefs on reform – disagreed with these steps, believing that revolutionary success depended on a wider rather than a more restricted membership. They took the longer-term view of Marxism: that capitalism had to collapse from within before communism could triumph.

The deciding vote was very close – Lenin's group won by two votes. They took the name the Bolsheviks (a word meaning 'the majority'). Martov and Trotsky's group, the minority, became the Mensheviks. Despite their victory, however, the Bolsheviks were not popular. Many in the party feared that Lenin would be a dictatorial leader.

Lenin and the 1905 Revolution

The Bolsheviks and the Mensheviks were caught unawares by the 1905 Revolution in Russia. However, when the unrest broke out, Trotsky and other Mensheviks and radicals tried to promote strikes and other workers' actions. Workers' committees (soviets) were set up in factories. In fact, in terms of the 1905 Revolution, Lenin was the right man in the wrong place. He was in exile and returned to Russia 11 months after Bloody Sunday – too late to play an effective role in the revolution.

At the start of 1917, the exiled Lenin could not influence affairs in Russia. A month before the February Revolution, he commented that such an event might not take place during his lifetime. Events moved more quickly than he, and most others, anticipated.

Note:
After the party split in 1903, the Mensheviks continued to campaign for a more moderate approach to reform (although they still believed that revolution was necessary). Unlike the Bolsheviks, the Mensheviks were willing to work together with the liberal left to establish a temporary capitalist society, before this would evolve into a socialist structure. After the October Revolution, the Mensheviks attempted to establish themselves as a formal opposition party, but they were suppressed and many leading Mensheviks went into exile.

Crises of the Provisional Government

Kerensky, the head of the Provisional Government after the February Revolution in 1917, was more reformer than radical, favouring a republic of moderate policies. The Provisional Government kept Russia in the First World War and attempted to balance the conflicting demands of reforming and radical factions. However, such a balance proved impossible to maintain.

Russia was internally unstable, and the Provisional Government lacked the strength to restore order. Popular uprisings and army unrest were not uncommon in Europe at this time – Germany in particular experienced widespread disorder throughout 1918, as it became clear that the war was no longer going in its favour. However, a unique characteristic of the unrest

Figure 5.8 Alexander Kerensky
in 1917

in Russia was the formation of the soviets (councils of workers). These spread from the cities to villages in the countryside, as well as the army. The soviets were not highly organised, but they were sufficiently co-ordinated to represent a major threat to the Provisional Government. The problem of food distribution was not solved and peasants demanded that land was redistributed.

Meanwhile, the war went badly for Russia. The Provisional Government saw it as a matter of honour to continue fighting – and indeed it was pressed to do so by its allies. The government hoped that war might appeal to Russian nationalism and unite the country, but after a disastrous offensive against Germany it became clear that the army was in no condition to fight, and demands to make peace increased.

Lenin's return

Lenin now had a stroke of luck that he could not have calculated. His isolation in Switzerland ended when the Germans, intending to weaken Russia by stirring up disorder, transported him in a train (sealed to prevent observers), from Switzerland to the Russian frontier. The realistic Lenin quickly realised the potential power of the soviets. He saw them as an alternative to the Provisional Government, using the slogan 'All power to the soviets'. Bolshevik control of the soviets was seen as crucial, and soon his party dominated these councils in major cities.

In his 'April Theses', Lenin called for 'Peace, Land and Bread' to appeal to the wider population. Alexander Guchkov, the war minister, confessed that he was unable to govern his own ministry, and the army was under the influence of the soviets. Elections had been promised, but were not held – Kerensky and his associates knew that they would lose power to a group of people whom they regarded as a disorganised rabble.

The Provisional Government made a last effort to exert control against the Bolsheviks and their allies in the 'July Days'. Kerensky condemned Lenin as a German agent and spy. The Provisional Government gathered enough soldiers to put down disorder and Lenin had to leave the centre of action, fleeing to Finland.

Note:

'July Days' is the name given to 3–7 July, when workers and soldiers in Petrograd staged demonstrations against the Provisional Government. Many of the participants were armed, and the period marked a brief decline in Bolshevik power.

The Kornilov Affair

It was the Kornilov Affair that restored Lenin's fortunes. Lavr Kornilov, the commander-in-chief of the army, favoured strong action against the Bolsheviks and marched on Petrograd at the head of a troop of soldiers known as the 'Savage Division' because of its warlike reputation. It is uncertain how far Kerensky approved of the plan and how far Kornilov acted independently, but the scheme failed. Kerensky quickly accused Kornilov of attempting a takeover to establish a military dictatorship, and dismissed him from his post. The soldiers refused to back the government and many of them deserted. The Bolsheviks gained credit by leading resistance among the workers and soviets. Lenin was able to return to Russia.

This time Kerensky was portrayed as a German agent, plotting to surrender Moscow to the enemy. The Military Revolutionary Council, dominated by Bolsheviks, took control of Petrograd. Kerensky and the Provisional Government were aware of Lenin's intentions but were paralysed by a lack of support. A full revolution was imminent.

The October Revolution

The short-term causes of the October Revolution in 1917 can be summarised as follows:

- The Provisional Government had no control over events. It was discredited by disobedience from the soviets and by the Kornilov Affair.
- A Military Revolutionary Council (MRC) was established in Moscow, which acted as a rival government. It was controlled by Trotsky on behalf of the Bolsheviks.
- The Russian army was suffering huge losses in the ongoing war, and this made the Provisional Government even more unpopular.
- Kerensky could not deliver other reforms, such as the redistribution of land or a new constitution.

As the German army advanced, Kerensky could not provide enough soldiers to defend key points in the major cities. Rumours began to spread that he was preparing to abandon Petrograd to the Germans. Lenin overruled doubters among the Bolsheviks who believed that Russia was not ready for a revolution. He claimed that he was acting on behalf of the soviets and demanded that his supporters rise up at this critical juncture.

Taking swift action, the Bolsheviks gained control of Petrograd and seized the Winter Palace – the former residence of the tsar. The October Revolution was over within a few hours. The Bolsheviks claimed that it was a popular action, a revolution of the people. The reality was that few armed men took part and only about six people were killed. Lenin had succeeded in bringing about revolution, but it was doubtful whether he and the Bolsheviks would be able to hold on to power in the chaos that ensued.

Figure 5.9 *Soldiers and workers on the streets of Petrograd during the October Revolution in 1917*

The situation is critical in the extreme. In fact it is now absolutely clear that to delay the uprising would be fatal … With all my might I urge comrades to realise that everything now hangs by a thread. We are confronted by problems which are not to be solved by conferences but only by the masses and by the struggle of the armed people … We must at all costs, this very evening, this very night, arrest the government, having first disarmed the officers … We must not wait! We may lose everything!

Under no circumstances should power be left in the hands of Kerensky and his group, not under any circumstances. The matter must be decided without fail this very evening, or this very night … History will not forgive we revolutionaries for delaying when we could be victorious today (and we certainly will be victorious today), while we risk losing much tomorrow, in fact, the risk losing everything.

It would be an infinite crime on the part of the revolutionaries if we let the chance slip, knowing that the salvation of the revolution, the chance of peace, salvation from famine, and the transfer of the land to the peasants depend upon them … The government is tottering. It must be given the death-blow at all costs.

Vladimir Lenin, justifying the October Revolution, published in his *Collected Works* **in 1972.**

Figure 5.10 A map showing the unrest in Russia during 1917

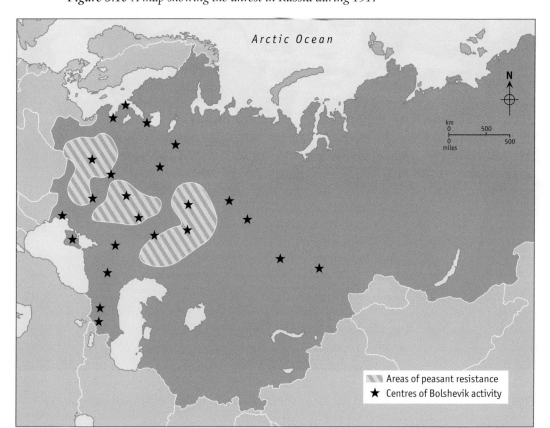

Areas of peasant resistance

★ Centres of Bolshevik activity

Conclusion

Karl Marx believed that economic forces were the determining factor in history. Changes in the economy gave power to classes and government, and then replaced them by others until the proletariat came to power and established its own dictatorship. It would overcome capitalism, which was dominated by the middle class (bourgeois). This meant that successful revolutions would occur in industrialised countries where members of the proletariat were most numerous. The revolutions would be followed by a state that gave priority to the needs of the workers. Wealth would be distributed more equally: 'From each according to his abilities, to each according to his needs.'

Russia was not a country that Marx thought suitable for revolution. Industrialised countries such as Britain and Germany were more likely, in his opinion. Russia was dominated by a rural economy and the mass of peasants was far larger than that of the industrial workers. There was little organisation among the proletariat. Trade unions had limited influence before 1914. Revolutionaries were scattered and mostly ineffective.

The most significant factor in the Russian Revolution was the First World War, which paralysed the authoritarian monarchy and let loose uncontrollable forces. The proletariat, through the soviets, was important but the revolutions of 1917 were also a movement of the peasantry and the army. Russia did not go through a process of middle-class capitalism as a halfway stage between authoritarian monarchy and communist rule. The aftermath of the October Revolution did not result in the triumph of the workers but in the victory of a small group of political activists. Russia saw the dictatorship of Lenin and Stalin, not the dictatorship of the proletariat.

Note:

Lenin was determined to end the war but did not find it easy to persuade all his colleagues. Trotsky favoured dragging out negotiations as long as possible so that Germany would agree to more lenient terms. Lenin was convinced that this approach would result in more German victories and might cause the collapse of the revolution.

Lenin did not find it easy to hold on to power. He had to deliver on his promises of 'Peace, Land and Bread'. Peace was achieved in 1918 through the Treaty of Brest-Litovsk with Germany, by which Russia had to give up huge areas of land, containing most of its coal mines and half its industries. Some of Lenin's Bolshevik colleagues wanted to fight on, but Lenin saw that this would be pointless. The new government's army (the Reds) fought a civil war against counter-revolutionary forces (the Whites) who were supported by some foreign countries, including Britain and France. After a bloody and dangerous struggle in which almost a million communist soldiers and millions more civilians died, the Reds were finally victorious in 1921.

'Land and Bread' posed economic problems in a bankrupt country. Lenin first introduced state control through War Communism and then a more relaxed New Economic Policy (NEP) which brought some improvements. He survived an assassination attempt but did not return to full health, suffering a series of stokes from 1921. By the time of his death in 1924, Lenin had secured the revolution and established a communist regime in Russia. But the Bolsheviks faced new problems under his successor, Joseph Stalin.

Questions

1. How dangerous was the 1905 Revolution to Nicholas II?

2. Which do you think was the more important factor in the Bolsheviks' victory in 1917 – the weakness of the Provisional Government, the effects of the First World War or Lenin's leadership? Give reasons for your choice.

Key issues

The key features of this chapter are:

- the policies of Nicholas II and how they weakened his own position; whether or not his downfall was inevitable

- the nature of the opposition to the tsar, and the reasons for the failure of the 1905 Revolution

- the long-term and short-term causes of the 1917 Revolution and the role of the First World War in forcing these events

- the reasons for the downfall of the Provisional Government and Lenin's success in bringing the Bolsheviks to power.

Revision questions

1 How far do you agree that Nicholas II missed the opportunity to make his government more secure after the 1905 Revolution?

2 How far did the reforms of Witte and Stolypin strengthen the tsarist regime?

3 Why was the First World War an important cause of the downfall of Nicholas II in February 1917?

4 Why did Lenin's Bolsheviks replace Kerensky's Provisional Government in October 1917?

Further reading

Bromley, J. *Russia 1848–1917*. London, UK. Heinemann. 2002.

Hutchinson, J. *Late Imperial Russia*. London, UK. Longman. 1999.

Waldron, P. *The End of Imperial Russia 1855–1917*. Basingstoke, UK. Palgrave Macmillan. 1997.

Advanced reading

Wade, R. S. *The Russian Revolution 1917*. Cambridge, UK. Cambridge University Press. 2005.

Chapter

6 Examination skills

Key questions

- What skills will be tested in examination, and how?
- What types of question will you be asked?
- How should these questions be addressed?
- How should you prepare for the examination?

Content summary

- Assessment Objectives – the skills being tested in examination.
- The different types of question you will face.
- General tips for preparing examination answers.
- Knowledge and understanding questions and how to address them.
- Analysis and evaluation questions and how to address them.
- Primary and secondary sources.
- Different types of historical source and how to use them effectively.
- Source-based questions and how to address them.
- Revision and preparation for the examination.
- General tips about examination techniques.

Introduction

In order to achieve success at AS Level History, you will need to develop skills that were, perhaps, less important in earlier examinations you may have taken. Generally, pre-AS Level examinations require you to demonstrate your knowledge and understanding of certain historical events. Now you will be required to *analyse* and *interpret* your knowledge in much greater depth.

This has implications for the way in which you study the subject. Your teacher will be able to help you by providing background knowledge, developing your historical skills and providing resources for you to work with. However, your teacher cannot tell you what to think or what opinions to have! At AS Level, you will have far more responsibility for developing your own ideas, views and judgements. To do this effectively, you need to acquire independent learning skills. In particular, this means reading as widely as possible around a topic, so that you gain access to different interpretations of the same issues and events. This will also give you an insight into the methods historians use to put across their ideas; you will be able to adapt these methods for your own use when answering examination questions.

History is not a series of universally accepted facts that, once learned, will provide you with a detailed and accurate understanding of the past. Just as historical events were perceived in many different (and often contradictory) ways by the people who experienced them at the time, so they have been interpreted in many different (and often contradictory) ways by people who have studied them subsequently. The historical debates discussed throughout the main chapters of this book have shown that historians are not all in agreement about the reasons for, or the significance of, certain key events.

Although history deals with facts, it is equally about opinions, perceptions, judgements, interpretations and prejudices. Many of the questions you will face in examination do not have *right* answers; they are asking for your *opinion/judgement* about a certain issue. Provided you can justify it – support it with appropriate and accurate use of evidence – your opinion is just as valid as any other. Sometimes, your friends and colleagues might disagree with your opinion and be able to provide convincing evidence to demonstrate why. Sometimes, they might convince you to change or refine your opinion. Sometimes, you will be able to convince them to change or refine theirs. Sometimes, you might just agree to differ. It is this ability to see things in different ways – and to have the confidence to use your knowledge and understanding to make judgements, form opinions and develop arguments – that makes history so interesting, challenging and exciting.

What skills will be tested in examination, and how?

During a lecture delivered in the late 1960s, the historian A. J. P. Taylor said: 'History is not about answering questions; it is about knowing what questions to ask.' This may seem like a rather strange statement – not least because your own success in your history examinations will depend on your ability to answer questions effectively. However, as you will discover in this chapter, there is much truth in what Taylor said. The most impressive answers to exam questions come from students who have done more than simply acquire knowledge – they have developed the skills required to analyse information, interrogate evidence and form their own reasoned opinions. In short, they know what questions to ask!

Examination questions are not designed to 'trick' you or catch you out. On the contrary, questions are carefully designed to give you the opportunity to demonstrate how well you have mastered the required historical skills (as outlined in the Assessment Objectives).

You will be confronted with three main types of question, which are outlined below.

> **Note:**
> Assessment Objectives are lists of the historical skills on which you will be tested in the examination. They can be found in the examination board's documentation for the particular course/syllabus you are following (available on the board's website).

Knowledge and understanding questions

Knowledge and understanding questions are testing your ability to:

- understand the question and its requirements
- recall and select relevant and appropriate material
- communicate your knowledge and understanding in a clear and effective manner.

> **Key point**
>
> These questions are testing *understanding* as well as *knowledge*. Remembering a relevant point is one thing; showing that you understand its significance is more important.

Analysis and evaluation questions

Analysis and evaluation questions are testing your ability to:

- understand the question and its requirements
- recall and select relevant and appropriate material
- analyse and evaluate this material in order to reach a focused, balanced and substantiated judgement
- communicate your argument in a clear and effective manner.

Key point

Your answer should contain a clear judgement/argument that is:
- focused – addresses the actual question set
- balanced – shows understanding of alternative viewpoints
- substantiated – supported by evidence.

Source-based questions

Source-based questions are testing your ability to:

- understand the question and its requirements
- comprehend source content in its historical setting
- analyse and evaluate source content
- reach a focused, balanced and substantiated judgement
- communicate your argument in a clear and effective manner.

Key point

Your answer should contain a clear judgement/argument that is:

- focused – addresses the actual question set
- balanced – shows understanding of alternative viewpoints
- substantiated – supported by evidence
- analytical – not dependent on a basic comprehension of source contents, but on a detailed evaluation of their reliability, and so on.

In this chapter, we will look at some examples of each type of question, analysing the skills you will need to apply in order to answer them effectively.

Knowledge and understanding questions

These questions usually require you to explain why a particular event took place or why a particular course of action was taken. For example, you might be asked the question:

Why was Louis XVI executed in 1793?

Here are two typical responses to this question.

Information on Louis XVI can be found on pages 8–17.

Response 1

> The French Revolution broke out in 1789. France was almost bankrupt and Louis XVI called a meeting of the Estates General to solve the problem. The members failed to agree and the situation quickly became more extreme. In Paris the Bastille was attacked and captured whilst there was disorder in the provinces. The members of the Third Estate in the Estates General, who were mostly members of the middle class or bourgeoisie, declared the formation of the Constituent Assembly, which issued the Declaration of the Rights of Man. The king and his family were taken forcibly from their palace to Paris, where they lived almost as prisoners. The king became more alarmed as violence and extremism spread throughout France, and he decided to flee abroad. However, he and his family were arrested at Varennes before they reached the border. This convinced the revolutionaries that the king could not be trusted. A new and more extreme group called the Jacobins, led by Maximilien Robespierre, had seized power. They believed that Louis XVI was a serious threat to the revolution, especially because France was now at war with powerful foreign monarchies. Their solution was to execute the king in 1793.

Response 2

> The most important reason why Louis XVI was executed in 1793 was that the king was distrusted whilst power was in the hands of a group, the Jacobins, who believed that violence was necessary to save the revolution from the king and his supporters. Louis XVI agreed reluctantly to the changes that had been introduced since 1789, such as the Declaration of the Rights of Man. The king regarded himself as the defender of the Roman

Catholic Church and was offended by the Civil Constitution of the Clergy, which severely restricted the rights of the Church. In addition, France was at war with neighbouring countries. Robespierre and his followers among the Jacobins believed that strong action was needed to save the revolution. They demanded the execution of Louis XVI and equally harsh measures against his followers. The death of the king shows the extent to which those who were now in power feared that the gains made during the revolution might be lost. The king was executed in 1793, but this event was only a part of the Reign of Terror that was unleashed by the Jacobins.

Both responses contain much the same basic information. Both are based on the recall and selection of accurate, appropriate and relevant factual material (*knowledge*). However, Response 2 demonstrates a greater *understanding* of how and why these factors led to Louis XVI's execution. The points it makes are fully explained and supported by evidence. The judgement is clear: 'The most important reason why …'. It shows how various factors link together – the basic instability in France, the king's reaction to the revolution, the reasons or fears of the radicals and the link with the wider Reign of Terror. On the other hand, Response 1 makes a number of rather vague and unexplained statements, which might imply that the writer does not fully understand the significance of the points made.

Try to write an analytical rather than a narrative answer. Narrative means telling the story for its own sake, without offering any analysis or evaluation of the events described. Lacking a historical argument, narrative answers tend to be about the *topic* generally, rather than the question itself. If provided at all, analysis is likely to be limited to a few comments in the conclusion. Under examination conditions, there is not enough time to write down everything about a topic – the *only* effective strategy is to construct an analysis, which considers ideas but does not waste too much time on description. Remember, it is important to refer to accurate knowledge, but knowledge *supports* explanation, not the other way around. Explanation without knowledge will result in only a vague answer. Generalisations without *any* exemplification should also be avoided.

So, the key points to remember when addressing this type of question are:

- You need to read the question carefully in order to ensure that you fully understand what it requires. *[Skill: comprehension]*
- You need to be able to recall and select appropriate factual material. *[Skills: knowledge and effective revision]*
- You need to show the relevance of this factual material to the question, something that Response 1 does not always achieve. *[Skill: understanding]*
- You should always prepare a brief plan before starting to write. A quick and easy way of doing this is to draw a table with two columns. Record the key points in the left column. In the right column, show how each key point helps to address the question. This serves three purposes:

  1 It ensures that you don't miss anything out, which is easy to do under examination pressure.
  2 It ensures that you keep fully focused on the requirements of the question.
  3 It ensures that you demonstrate the relevance of each point – you provide evidence that you understand how the point helps to answer the question.

Take the question:

Why did a revolution break out in Russia in February 1917?

A plan might look something like this:

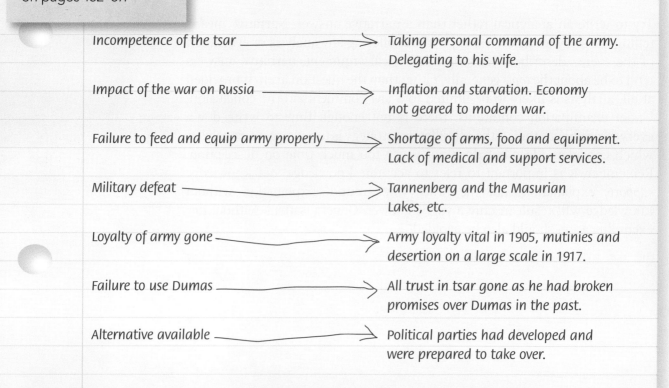

Information on the February Revolution in Russia can be found on pages 152–57.

Incompetence of the tsar	Taking personal command of the army. Delegating to his wife.
Impact of the war on Russia	Inflation and starvation. Economy not geared to modern war.
Failure to feed and equip army properly	Shortage of arms, food and equipment. Lack of medical and support services.
Military defeat	Tannenberg and the Masurian Lakes, etc.
Loyalty of army gone	Army loyalty vital in 1905, mutinies and desertion on a large scale in 1917.
Failure to use Dumas	All trust in tsar gone as he had broken promises over Dumas in the past.
Alternative available	Political parties had developed and were prepared to take over.

Your plan may not need to contain quite this much detail and can, of course, make use of abbreviations. The plan is entirely for your benefit – an examiner might look at it, but it will not be marked. One final point: do remember to *use* the plan when writing your response. It is amazing how often a perfectly good plan is followed by a poor answer that bears almost no relation to it!

Analysis and evaluation questions

These questions require you to do more than just demonstrate your knowledge and understanding. They require you to *use* your knowledge and understanding in order to develop a logical argument and make a reasoned judgement.

There are a number of tasks you need to perform *before* you start to answer this type of question. These are:

- identify the **factual material** you will need
- establish what **task** the question is asking you to carry out with that factual material
- develop a **plan** that lists the factual material so that it is fully focused on the requirements of the question
- reach a **judgement**
- decide how you are going to explain this judgement as an **argument** in your answer.

Let's look at these specifically, relating to the following question:

To what extent did the lower classes benefit from the Industrial Revolution by the middle of the 19th century? Refer to Britain and either France or Germany in your answer.

Factual material: effects of the Industrial Revolution on the lower classes.

Task: determine, justify and explain how far the lower classes benefited, or did not benefit.

Plan: this enables you to create a mind map with points on both sides of the argument. Remember that the plan is entirely for your benefit – it is up to you how much detail it includes and, indeed, what format it takes. An example is shown on page 176.

Information on the effects of the Industrial Revolution on difference classes can be found on pages 57–61.

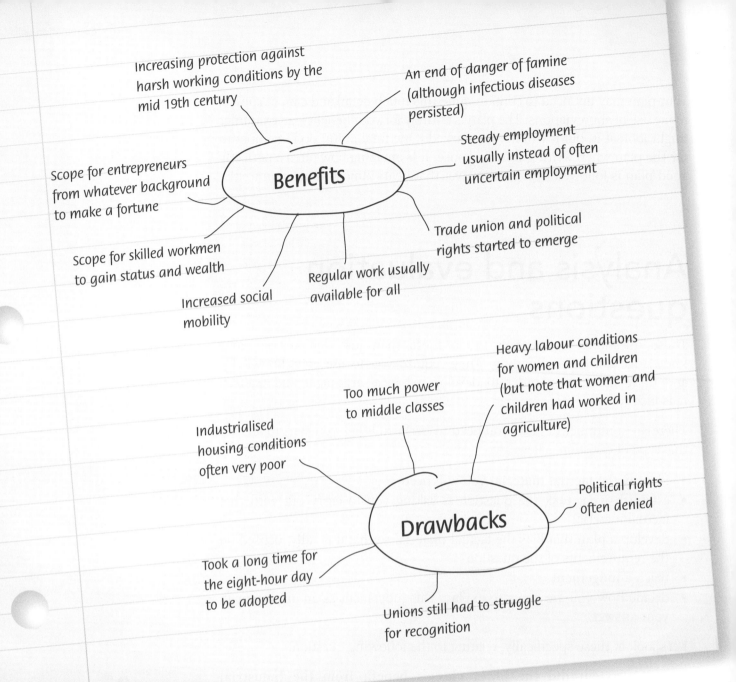

The mind map above contains:

Benefits
- Increasing protection against harsh working conditions by the mid 19th century
- An end of danger of famine (although infectious diseases persisted)
- Steady employment usually instead of often uncertain employment
- Trade union and political rights started to emerge
- Regular work usually available for all
- Increased social mobility
- Scope for skilled workmen to gain status and wealth
- Scope for entrepreneurs from whatever background to make a fortune

Drawbacks
- Too much power to middle classes
- Heavy labour conditions for women and children (but note that women and children had worked in agriculture)
- Political rights often denied
- Unions still had to struggle for recognition
- Took a long time for the eight-hour day to be adopted
- Industrialised housing conditions often very poor

Judgement: this type of question is asking you for an *opinion* – there is no 'right' answer and examiners do not have a preconceived idea of what a suitable judgement might be. They will not be assessing what your judgement is but how well you explain it and support it with valid evidence. A possible judgement might be: 'There were considerable benefits for the lower classes by the middle of the 19th century, but this overall judgement must be qualified in two ways. Firstly, it applies only to Britain. Developments in France and Germany were very different. Secondly, the gains were much less than in the second half of the century.'

Argument: there are a number of things to remember when constructing your answer:

- **Focus:** you must make sure that you address the question set. For example if you are asked the question 'Who of Cavour and Mazzini did more to unify Italy?' you will not get any credit for writing a great deal about other aspects of Italian unification.

- **Balance:** it is important that you demonstrate an understanding of both sides of the argument. You need to show how you have compared and weighed the evidence in order to reach your judgement. Therefore, your answer should not be based solely on the evidence that supports your conclusion.

- **Clarity:** in effect, you are aiming to convince the reader to agree with your judgement. It is crucial that your argument is communicated in a clear and obvious way.

- **Evidence:** for your argument to be convincing, it must be supported by evidence. Many examination essays contain *unsupported assertions* – these are statements/opinions for which no factual evidence is provided, and so should be avoided.

- **Consistency:** make sure that your argument remains consistent throughout. Examiners frequently come across essays that are contradictory, the first part seemingly arguing one thing and the second part apparently arguing the exact opposite. The reason for this is that the candidate is trying to show a balanced understanding, but has not actually weighed the evidence and come to a judgement. Such essays often conclude with a statement such as: 'So it is clear that the lower classes benefited more than the middle classes from the Industrial Revolution.' Since no explanation has been given to justify such a statement, it is an unsupported assertion.

- **Organisation:** do not repeat yourself. Make a point and then move on. This is not the same as comparing two points.

- **Planning:** all these points show just how important the planning stage is. Put simply, you need to know exactly what you are going to say *before* you start writing.

Note:

One of the most difficult skills to master is the ability to demonstrate an understanding of both sides of an argument without appearing to contradict yourself. Most students begin by outlining the evidence that supports their judgement and then refer to evidence that might disagree. This approach can easily undermine the strength of your argument and cause confusion to the reader. It is usually more effective to deal with the evidence that could be seen as disagreeing with your judgement first, and then explain why you find this less convincing than the evidence that supports your argument.

Below is a response to the question 'To what extent did the lower classes benefit from the Industrial Revolution by the middle of the 19th century? Refer to Britain and either France or Germany in your answer.'

> The Industrial Revolution brought many benefits to the lower classes in Europe. Before this, most of them were peasants working on the land, often exploited by landowners, living in poverty. The revolution meant much more regular work for men and their families, and it also offered a chance for the lower classes to rise up through the ranks of society. Men who gained necessary skills got higher wages and improved social status. Real wages rose and death rates dropped as there was a more regular supply of food. Increasingly, the lower classes joined trade unions, which helped to improve pay and working conditions. Laws were also passed which stopped too much exploitation of women and children. Political rights for the working classes often followed. The rapid growth of the population, with more children surviving and living longer shows how much the lower classes benefited. The wealth generated by the revolution led to the growth of cities which required builders, and railways, which required workers to operate them and led to even greater social mobility.

What are the *strengths* of this answer?

- It is clearly focused on the requirements of the question.
- It contains a clear, explicit and consistent argument.
- It provides some generalised evidence to support its argument.

What are the *weaknesses* of this answer?

- The major weakness is the fact that it lacks balance. It offers no evidence that might challenge its judgement. In order to demonstrate that the essay is based on balanced and objective consideration, it is necessary to show an understanding of how the Industrial Revolution negatively affected the lower classes, with an explanation as to why the chosen judgement has been reached. It just does not deal with the question on 'extent'.
- It makes no mention of the countries to which the argument applies. The question specifically asks for reference to Britain and *either* France *or* Germany, but the answer gives general statements.

Information on the February 1917 revolution in Russia can be found on pages 152–56.

Here is another similar type of question, although it is written in a rather different way:

'The main reason why the tsarist regime fell in February 1917 was Nicholas II's incompetence.' How far do you agree with this view?

In this case you are given an *opinion* ('the main reason why …') and your task is to decide the extent to which you agree with it.

Below is a high-quality response to this question. As you read though the response, bear in mind its strengths:

- It is clearly focused on the requirements of the question.
- It contains a clear, explicit and consistent argument.
- It provides evidence/knowledge to support its argument.
- It shows a clear judgement.

The panels next to each paragraph look at the response in more detail..

"

There are many reasons why the tsarist regime fell in 1917, but the principal one is the large number of bad decisions taken by the tsar himself. They range from the decision to go to war in the first place in 1914, his appointment of incompetent advisors and generals, and his decision to take personal command of his armies, to leaving his German wife and the sinister Rasputin in the capital, allegedly running the country. There were of course other factors that led to the collapse, such as the inevitable problems arising out of an autocratic regime, Russia's weak economy, alternative leadership developing in Russia and German military success. However the responsibility in this case must really lie with the man at the top – Nicholas II.

The tsar's own poor decision-making was the cause of most of his, and Russia's, problems. He made the decision to go to war in 1914; arguably his support for Serbia was a significant factor in the actual outbreak of war. It should be noted that the choice to go to war was popular in Russia in 1914, but its consequences were calamitous and ultimately fatal for Nicholas II. His previous decision in taking Russia to war had led to disaster for his army and navy, and humiliation for his country in the war with Japan. This had led to the first 'revolution' in 1905. Nicholas survived that crisis because the army remained loyal, and he promised to bring about reforms in Russia that would improve conditions for the people. His failure to follow through on these promises was an important reason why his situation was still weak in 1914, before the pressures of war weakened it further.

In the years before 1914, the tsar had many opportunities to improve his position, but with his careless treatment of the Dumas and his hypocrisy over the October Manifesto, he seemed to go out of his way to alienate liberal supporters and give ammunition to radicals such as the Bolsheviks and Mensheviks. With the exception of Stolypin he chose poor ministers, often for social reasons rather than because of their ability.

Paragraph 1
The opening paragraph provides an answer and reasons, and has a strong analytical focus. It shows an awareness of other factors that contributed to the fall of the tsarist regime, but states clearly the line that the essay will take. Many students write generalised introductions that merely repeat the question or give some background information about the topic. Such introductions are unnecessary and take up valuable writing time.

Paragraph 2
This paragraphs begins strongly. It makes the objective of the paragraph very obvious, and links back clearly to the opening paragraph.

Paragraph 3
Here, the answer continues to build on the argument stated in the opening paragraph, citing examples of Nicholas's poor decision-making.

Paragraph 4

There is a good level of detail in this paragraph, describing the effects of the war on Russia. There is rarely time in an exam to include every detail you might know, but this section reveals that the candidate has depth of knowledge as well as his or her own ideas.

It was the war years that really highlighted Nicholas's incompetence. He did not think about the implications of what he was doing when he ordered his army to mobilise. The Russian economy was unprepared for war, as was the army. The lessons of the disastrous Japanese war had not been learned. There were incompetent commanders, soldiers without food, arms and ammunition. There were no proper medical services for soldiers. The Germans quickly destroyed Russian armies in 1914 at the terrible battles of Tannenberg and the Masurian Lakes. The Germans discovered that Russian commanders did not use any code for their radio messages, so the enemy knew exactly what they were going to do. In some Russian regiments only a third of the men had rifles. Food for the soldiers rotted in railway sidings as the transport system just could not cope. Inflation and starvation began to affect the whole Russian population.

Paragraph 5

This argues convincingly that the tsar's decision to command the Russian army in person was a turning point in the ultimate fate of the tsarist regime, resulting in the loss of the military support that had helped him keep a grip on power up to this point.

In deciding to go to the front and command his armies personally, Nicholas made one of his worst decisions. Not only was he naturally indecisive, he was also ignorant of military matters and demonstrated little common sense. It meant that he could now personally be blamed for the continuing military failures. His incompetence all but guaranteed that the army, his major support in 1905, would turn against him or fail to support him in 1917. Leaving his German wife Alexandra and Rasputin running the country only deepened mistrust of the tsar, and made it even more clear to those who had supported him in the past that he and his regime had to go.

Paragraph 6

This creates balance by mentioning other factors in the fall of the tsarist regime. However, the word 'might' tells the reader that although the candidate has considered these factors, he or she still believes that the *main* reason was the tsar's incompetence.

It might possibly be unfair to see Nicholas's failures in this arena as the only cause of his downfall in 1917. The war was not entirely his fault. There had been some social and economic progress under Stolypin, but the Russian economy was still weak and underdeveloped. He could not be blamed for the fact that Russia was ill equipped to participate in a war of this magnitude. The German army was a great fighting machine that also had much success elsewhere on the Western front. At home, other possible leaders of Russia had emerged, and democratic ideas were spreading.

Paragraph 7

The conclusion summarises the argument and makes a clear final statement.

There is agreement amongst most historians that in 1914 the tsarist regime would survive if it continued to make social and economic progress and at least gave some authority to the Dumas. However, the decision to go to war and the bad management of the war ultimately led to the tsar's abdication in 1917. As Nicholas was responsible for both the decision and the subsequent poor leadership, it was his incompetence that largely led to his downfall.

Overview of the response

The response on the previous pages is based on detailed knowledge and understanding of events in Russia leading up to the 1917 Revolution. Rather than simply describing Tsar Nicholas II's policies, the response analyses them in a way that assesses how far his actions were responsible for the fall of the tsarist regime. There is a clear and consistent argument based on a balanced review of the evidence. The writer is in control of the argument throughout, guiding the reader towards acceptance of a particular conclusion. There are clear linking points between each paragraph – this enables the essay to flow, making it easy for the reader to follow the argument.

Summary

So, what are the key points to remember when answering analysis and evaluation questions?

- Don't simply provide the reader with a series of facts relating to the topic – use your knowledge to make a judgement, form an opinion and develop an argument.
- Communicate your argument in a clear and consistent manner.
- Ensure balance – demonstrate your understanding of both sides of the argument, but do so in a way that does not make your answer seem contradictory. Show, with supporting evidence, why one side of the argument is stronger than the other.
- Remain focused – ensure that each paragraph is making a point directly related to your judgement/argument. Do not drift off into irrelevance.
- Do not make unsupported assertions – ensure that any analytical point you make is backed up by factual evidence.
- Plan carefully *before* you start to write.
- Try to make your answer *flow*, for example by finding ways to link paragraphs together so that one leads logically into the next. This helps to keep the readers' interest and allows them to follow the argument you are making.

Note:
Mentioning the names of historians who hold particular views about an issue can be useful – it can add weight to your argument and suggests that you are widely read. However, this technique should be used with caution. It must be done accurately. You should also not do this too often, as it could imply that you are relying on the opinions of others rather than being able to form your own views on the subject.

Note:
An answer 'flows' when the argument is clear and each paragraph follows logically from the previous one. This makes it easier for the reader to understand and follow your line of reasoning. The reader is not suddenly confronted with an idea that seems to have no logical connection to what has gone before. The planning stage is crucial for this – you need to decide in what order to put your paragraphs and how you are going to link them together.

Source-based questions

In order to make judgements and form opinions about past events, historians need to gather as much information/evidence as possible. They use a variety of sources for this – written sources, speeches, photographs, cartoons, posters. Much of the evidence historians use is contradictory, reflecting the different opinions and perspectives of the people who produced the sources. Therefore, historians have to analyse these sources very carefully in order to form their own opinions/judgements about the past.

In much the same way, you will be faced with a variety of different historical sources in the examination. You will need to be able to analyse these sources in the light of your own subject knowledge. The key word here is *analyse*. This means going beyond basic comprehension of what a source is saying or showing, and asking yourself questions about how reliable the source is and why it appears to contradict what some other sources suggest.

At face value, the sources will provide material that supports or undermines the hypothesis. However, good candidates will demonstrate – by interpreting and evaluating the sources in their historical context – how to use the sources as evidence rather than merely as information. It should be stressed that these questions ask about the *sources* and their adequacy as evidence to test the hypothesis in the questions, rather than about the *events* with which the sources deal. Knowledge of the events is not the prime objective, although candidates should use their knowledge in order to cope more effectively with the sources.

Historical sources can be categorised under two broad headings: primary and secondary.

Primary sources

A primary source is one that was written/spoken/drawn at or very near the time of the historical event it is describing. It is usually the product of someone who was directly involved in the event or who was, in some sense, an eyewitness to the event.

Advantages of a primary source include:

- It provides a first-hand, contemporary account of the event.
- It provides an insight into the author's perceptions and emotions at the time of the event.
- If the source was created by someone who was directly involved in the event, it might give detailed 'inside' information that other people could not possibly know.

Disadvantages of a primary source include:

- The source gives us only the opinions of the person who created it; these may not be typical of the opinions prevalent at the time.
- If the source was created by someone who was directly involved in the event, it might contain bias, trying to convince the audience to agree with a particular line of argument.
- Eyewitnesses may not always be completely reliable – they might not have access to the full details of an event or they might be trying to impose their own opinions on the audience.

Secondary sources

A secondary source is one that was written/spoken/drawn significantly after the historical event it describes. It is usually the product of someone who was not directly involved in the event or someone who was not an eyewitness to the event.

Advantages of secondary sources include:

- Because they were created some time after the event they are describing, they can reflect the 'full picture' – they know how the event finally concluded and the impact it had. They have the advantage of hindsight.
- Many secondary sources have been produced by historians and academics. They are often the product of extensive research, including the use of primary sources.
- If the author was not directly involved in the event, there is less potential for bias.

Disadvantages of secondary sources include:

- The source gives us only the opinions of the person who created it; other people may have totally different interpretations.
- Secondary sources include biographies written years later by people who were directly involved in a particular event. This raises questions of reliability – the author's memory may not always be accurate; the author might want to exaggerate or downplay his or her role in an event.
- Secondary sources include accounts by eyewitnesses written years after the event. This also raises issues of reliability – was the author really an eyewitness? How accurate is the author's memory?

Note:
Primary sources reflect the customs and beliefs of the time and place from which they come. We should not be critical of the contents of a primary source just because they do not share our own values. For example, modern opinions about equal rights are very different from those that were widely accepted even 50 years ago.

Note:
Hindsight is the ability to look back at an event some time after it has occurred. With hindsight, it is easier to understand the reasons why an event took place, its significance and the impact that it had. It is important to remember that people living at the time of the event did not have the advantage of hindsight.

Note:
Do not assume that secondary sources are *less* useful than primary sources because they were not created by people who were directly involved in the event they are describing. Do not assume that secondary sources are *more* reliable than primary sources because they were created by people who were not directly involved in the event they are describing!

Assessing a source's reliability

It should be clear from the point above that historians have to be extremely careful when using sources, whether primary or secondary. They cannot afford to accept that everything a source tells them is completely reliable and true. People exaggerate. People tell lies. People have opinions that others may not share. People make mistakes.

Imagine you are out walking – lost in your own thoughts – when you suddenly hear a screeching of brakes and a thud behind you. As you turn in the direction the sound came from, you see a car drive quickly away and a pedestrian lying in the road. Your first priority, surely, would be to tend to the pedestrian, checking for injuries and calling for an ambulance or other assistance. When the police arrive, you would be classed as an 'eyewitness' to the accident, and they would want a statement from you.

But were you *really* an eyewitness? Did you really see the accident or did you just *hear* it? You saw the car drive quickly away, but does that mean it was going too fast when the accident occurred? How far might your sense of pity for the pedestrian affect your idea of what actually happened? Could you be certain that the pedestrian was not to blame for the accident? Would you be able to describe the car in detail and give the police its registration number? How far would your recollection of the event be blurred by your own shock? How and why might the statements of the car driver and the pedestrian differ from your own?

So, what can we, as historians, do to minimise the risk of drawing inaccurate conclusions from sources? There are a number of questions we need to ask in order to determine just how *reliable* a source is and to evaluate its provenance. For example:

- **Who** wrote it?
- **When** was it written?
- What is the **context**?
- Who was the intended **audience**?
- **Why** was it written? What was the author's **motive**?
- **What** does it actually say?
- **How** does what it says compare with our own **subject knowledge** and with **what other sources say**?

Note:
These example questions assume that the source is a written one, but the same principle applies for all sources, whether written, spoken, drawn, photographed, and so on.

Suppose, for example, that this is the statement given to police later in the day by the driver of the car involved in the accident you 'witnessed':

> *I was driving along the High Street, carefully and well within the speed limit. Suddenly, and without warning, a pedestrian walked out into the road from behind a parked lorry. There was absolutely no way I could have stopped in time to avoid hitting the pedestrian. In a state of panic, I did not stop. I drove away, but later reported to the local police station.*

- **WHO wrote it?** The driver of the car involved in the accident. The driver would clearly not wish to be blamed for causing the accident and therefore might have a reason for being less than honest.

- **WHEN was it written?** Later on the same day as the accident. By this time, the driver would have recovered from the initial shock, realising that there was no option but to report to the police. There would have been time for the driver to reflect on the incident and, possibly, develop an argument to lay blame for the accident on the pedestrian. Would the driver's memory be accurate?

- **What is the CONTEXT?** The driver reporting to the police to admit involvement in the accident.

- **Who was the intended AUDIENCE?** The police, who will make the final decision regarding who was to blame for the accident.

- **WHY was it written? What was the author's MOTIVE?** It is possible that, on reflection, the driver accepted the need to report involvement in the accident. It is also possible that the driver, realising that the police would eventually catch up with them, wanted to report the incident in order to clear their own name by laying blame on the pedestrian.

- **WHAT does it actually say?** The driver argues that they were not driving carelessly and that the accident was the pedestrian's fault (for walking out into the road from behind a lorry, without checking for traffic). They admit to leaving the scene of the accident out of panic.

- **HOW does it compare with what other sources say?** To find out whether the driver was telling the truth or simply lying in order to remove blame from themselves, the police would need to compare the statement with those of other witnesses and with other evidence. Other witnesses might, for example, be able to comment on how fast the car was going at the time of the accident and whether the pedestrian really did walk out into the road without due care and attention. Your own statement does not directly contradict what the driver says, although you did hear a screeching of brakes, which might suggest the car was going too fast. The police would be able to measure the length of any skid marks in order to work out the car's speed. The police might also be able to find out if there really was a lorry parked in the road as the driver suggests.

Now let's take a more specific example – a source revealing one view on the unification of Italy.

Source A

After the failure of the revolutions in 1848–49 two courses were open to us. We could give up all the hopes which had guided King Charles Albert and think only of the interests of Piedmont. On the other hand, we could, while accepting all the hardships, keep alive the faith that inspired the great actions of Charles Albert, and keep alive the hopes which were defeated in the revolutions. In recent years, therefore, we have acted as the spokesman and defender of the other peoples of Italy. This policy found one such opportunity by our intervention in the Crimean War. Our hopes were not disappointed because Piedmont gained credit. It was an outstanding fact that the cause of Italy was for the first time supported by an Italian power.

An extract from a speech by Count Cavour to the Piedmont parliament, 1858.

Information on the unification of Italy can be found on pages 95–104.

- **WHO wrote it?** Count Cavour, prime minister of Piedmont.
- **WHEN was it written?** 1858.
- **What is the CONTEXT?** The source dates from the period just after the Crimean War, in which Piedmont had allied with France and Britain. At around this time, Cavour was attempting to provoke war with Austria.
- **Who was the intended AUDIENCE?** The Piedmont parliament.
- **WHY was it written? What was the author's MOTIVE?** Cavour is encouraging his government to support the unity of the Italian states.
- **WHAT does it actually say?** The source acknowledges that previous nationalist actions had failed, but Cavour argues that Piedmont should continue to fight for this cause and that it should be the champion of other Italian states, which are less able to fight for themselves. Although intervention in the Crimean War was a success, he sees this as more of a victory for Piedmont than for Italy as a whole.
- **HOW does it compare with what other sources say?** Other sources may describe events from the perspective of foreign countries such as Austria, which had been a major power in the region. They could also be written by leaders of other Italian regions who resented the power Cavour exerted. Some sources may challenge Cavour's claim that Piedmont was acting on behalf of all the 'peoples of Italy' and suggest his actions were simply a way of extending Piedmont's own power and influence.

'Compare and contrast' questions

In examination, you may be asked to compare and contrast two or more different sources. Below are two more sources on the unification of Italy. (These extracts are taken from Cambridge International AS Level History 9389 Specimen Paper 1 Section A.)

Source B

Victor Emmanuel is a Catholic king but he forgets every religious principle, and despises every right of the Church, tramples upon every Church law and insults the head of the Catholic Church. He has now taken to himself the title of King of Italy; with which title he demonstrates his immoral ambition and insults the authority of the Papacy. The Pope has already solemnly protested as he saw successive attacks made upon his sovereignty. He must now make a fresh protest against the assumption of a title which tries to justify the iniquity of so many deeds. Therefore the Pope will never be able to recognise the title of King of Italy, claimed by the king of Piedmont, since it is opposed to justice and to the sacred property of the Church.

Pope Pius IX, protesting against Italian unification, 1861.

Source C

Italy is free, and nearly entirely united. The opinion of civilised nations is favourable to us. The just and liberal principles now dominant in European countries are favourable to us. Italy herself, too, will become a guarantee of order and peace, and will once more be an effective instrument of universal civilisation. These facts have inspired the nation with great confidence in its own destinies. I take pleasure in expressing to the first Parliament of Italy the joy I feel in my heart as king and soldier.

An extract from a speech given by Victor Emmanuel II as king of Italy, 1861.

We first need to go through the same process of source analysis:

- **Who?** Pope Pius IX and the king of the new united Italy, Victor Emmanuel.
- **When?** Both sources date from 1861.
- **Context?** Two opposing reactions to the recent political union of the Italian states as the Kingdom of Italy.
- **Audience?** Source B was a public protest against unification under a secular government. Source C was a speech delivered to parliament, celebrating unity.
- **Motive?** Each speaker is trying to convince his audience that his opinion is correct, to rally support for his own stance.

> **Note:**
> One of the most important skills for a historian is the ability to differentiate between fact and opinion. In Sources B and C, what are the opinions and what are the facts?

- **Content?** The pope objects to the unification of Italy under a secular government. Victor Emmanuel supports unification and talks of the role it will allow Italy to play on the international stage.
- **Subject knowledge?** We know that Pope Pius IX had previously followed some liberal policies, but that after his authority was challenged by the 1848 revolution he became a staunch advocate of traditional Catholic policy, strongly opposing liberalism and nationalism. Many Italians, and several other countries in Europe, supported the unification of Italy, and Victor Emmanuel's speech clearly reflects this attitude.

A straightforward way of comparing the views expressed in these two speeches is to devise a plan, such as the table below. This will allow you to quickly identify the differences and similarities between the attitudes of these two leaders.

Pope Pius IX	Victor Emmanuel
Written by a religious leader whose power was limited by unification.	Written by a secular leader whose power was extended by unification.
Strongly objects to unification.	Welcomes unification.
Claims that it violates the traditional rights and laws of the Church and that as a Catholic king, Victor Emmanuel should support these.	Claims that 'civilised nations' are in support of unification, and that it will allow Italy itself to ensure 'universal civilisation'.
Associates unity with liberalism (which he sees as a bad thing).	Associates unity with liberalism (which he sees as 'just').
Speaks of 'trampling' and 'attacks'.	Speaks of 'order' and 'peace'.
Sees himself as the rightful leader of Italy ('his sovereignty').	Sees himself as the rightful leader of a united Italy.
Believes that unification was driven by nothing more than Piedmont's unwarranted ambitions.	Believes that unification was driven by 'just principles' and the will of the Italian people.
Uses emotive language to get point across ('despises', 'tramples', 'insults', 'opposed to justice').	Uses emotive language to get point across ('confidence in its own destinies', 'the joy I feel in my heart').

Note:
Emotive language is that which is deliberately designed to play on the emotions of the reader. Emotive techniques can also be used in non-written sources, such as posters and cartoons. Identify the emotive language in Sources B and C.

Visual sources: posters

Visual sources should be approached in much the same way as textual sources. Look at this German poster from 1914.

What was its purpose? Why would someone go to the trouble and expense of having such posters printed and displayed in public places? Think of a modern advertising poster – its aim is to encourage the viewer to buy a particular product and it will use a variety of clever, often highly emotive, techniques to do this. A toothpaste advert, for example, might suggest that you will suffer from tooth decay, gum disease and bad breath if you don't use a particular brand. By implication, the advertisement is saying that this brand is more able to prevent these problems than any other.

This poster is not trying to sell a product; rather it is trying to persuade people to support Germany against Britain in the First World War. Posters usually contain very few words – sometimes none at all. The illustration is usually the main feature. Here, the soldiers can be identified as German by their uniforms. The impending attack on Britain is shown indirectly by the sea. Posters are not objective. They are simplified. Here, for example, there are no explanations of why Britain and Germany are at war, or of the problems facing Germany in invading Britain. The message is implicit in the artwork. Posters like this are valuable as sources because they show historians how governments or pressure groups tried to influence people.

Visual sources: photographs

Just as the German poster was a propaganda tool, so too is this photograph. It shows Tsar Nicholas II, dressed in battle uniform, on the front lines during the First World War. Behind him, hundreds of soldiers are gathered. It suggests that the tsar was a great leader, who felt the weight of his position in command of the Russian army. We know from other sources and our own knowledge that in fact Nicholas was a poor military leader. He inspired little confidence in his men, and had effectively abandoned government of his country to fight the war. This does not make the photograph any less useful as a historical source, as it tells us how Nicholas wanted to be viewed by his people – even how he viewed himself.

PUNCH, OR THE LONDON CHARIVARI.—August 12, 1914.

NO THOROUGHFARE

F.H.Townsend Aug. 1914

BRAVO, BELGIUM!

Visual sources: cartoons

Cartoons can be the most difficult sources to analyse. In most cases, they are created to achieve two things: to amuse and entertain the audience and to make a point and send the audience a message. To achieve this, they use symbolism and a subtle form of humour that may have been perfectly understandable to people at the time, but which might be less obvious to us.

Look again at this British cartoon from August 1914. In order to analyse the cartoon and understand its message, we need to go through much the same process as when dealing with other types of source.

Date? Published on 12 August 1914, in the middle of the German invasion of Belgium at the start of the war.

Context? Although tensions had been simmering since the assassination of the Austrian archduke Franz Ferdinand in July, the German invasion of Belgium came as a shock to the rest of the world. Belgium was a neutral country and did not have a strong enough fighting force to prevent the Germans from sweeping through the country and into France.

Provenance? Published in a British magazine and, therefore, intended for a British audience. Britain had a long-established pact to protect Belgian neutrality so when the German invasion began on 4 August, Britain declared war. Therefore, the cartoon has been drawn from the perspective of someone who is directly involved in the conflict rather than an observer.

Symbolism? The artist has depicted the two countries as stereotypes of their people: a Belgian shepherd boy and a larger, more elderly German, with sausages dangling from his pocket. (Even before 1914, British propaganda had shown Germany in the form of this 'Prussian bully', particularly in regard to its naval expansion.) Germany wields a large club against the small boy's stick. The German's shadow points threateningly towards the city in the background.

Message? The cartoon is a comment on Belgium's bravery in resisting the German invasion, despite its lack of military strength. It was also designed to encourage support for Britain's entry into the war, showing how Britain had to come to the aid of 'defenceless' Belgium against German aggression.

In examination, you may be asked to compare and contrast two cartoons like this. Essentially this is asking you to show and explain the similarities and differences between them. You can do this by asking the same type of questions as you would if you were comparing and contrasting written sources (see pages 186–88).

Cross-referencing between sources

One of the most important things to remember is that a source should never be used in isolation. It needs to be interpreted in the light of information obtained from other sources. There are three main reasons why cross-referencing between sources is so important:

- We can only judge how useful and reliable a source is by comparing it with what we already know and what other sources say.
- It can help us to solve mysteries or apparent contradictions.
- By using a combination of sources, we can often deduce things that *none* of the sources say when looked at individually.

Look at these sources from German chancellor Otto von Bismarck.

Source A

Germany is clearly too small for both Prussia and Austria … Austria will remain the only state to whom we can permanently lose or from whom we can permanently gain. I am convinced that, in the not too distant future, we shall have to fight for our existence against Austria. It is not within our power to avoid that. The course of events in Germany has no other solution.

Otto von Bismarck, in a letter to his friend Minister von Manteuffel, 1856.

Source B

I think it more useful to continue for a while the present marriage [with Austria] despite small domestic quarrels, and if a divorce becomes necessary, to take the prospects as they then prevail rather than to cut the bond now, with all the disadvantages of obvious perfidy, and without now having the certainty of finding better conditions in a new relationship later.

Bismarck, in a letter to the Prussian ambassador in Paris, 1865.

There seems to be a contradiction between Sources A and B. In Source A, Bismarck claims that war with Austria is inevitable and that Prussia has no choice but to fight for 'permanent gain' in Germany. In Source B, Bismarck suggests that he has no intention of waging war with Austria. He refers to Prussia and Austria as experiencing merely 'small domestic quarrels'. How can we explain this apparent contradiction?

The first thing to note is that Source A is dated 1856 while Source B comes from nearly a decade later, in 1865. Much had changed in the intervening period, most notably the fact that by the time he wrote the letter in Source B, Bismarck was no longer merely a politician, but prime minister of Prussia. His words therefore carried greater weight. We must also take into account the recipients of each of these dispatches. Source A was a private letter, whereas Source B was a letter to a Prussian official in a country with which Bismarck hoped to secure an alliance.

From our own knowledge we know that despite Bismarck's claims in Source B, Prussia in fact fought and won a war against Austria in 1866. Other sources also suggest that Bismarck deliberately provoked the conflict, for example by continuing to deny Austria admittance to the Zollverein. Linking these sources and using our own knowledge, therefore, can help us reach certain conclusions about the reliability of such sources, and may reveal something about Bismarck's character and attitude that the sources alone do not explicitly state.

Addressing source-based questions: a summary

The key things you need to remember when addressing a source-based question are as follows:

Comprehension: you need to establish what the source is saying.

Reliability: don't simply accept what the source is saying. You need to test how reliable it is by:

- comparing what it says with what other sources say and with your own subject knowledge
- looking carefully at who wrote (drew/said) it, when, why and for what purpose/audience
- establishing if there are any reasons to doubt the reliability of the source.

Interpretation: what can you learn from the source, taking into account your judgement about how reliable it is?

Objectivity: always look at a source objectively and with an open mind. Do not make assumptions. For example:

- Don't assume that a source must be biased because it was written by a certain person at a certain time. These points might establish a motive for bias, but they do not necessarily prove that it is biased.
- Never make unsupported assertions. A statement such as 'Source A is biased' must be accompanied by evidence/examples to demonstrate how it is biased, together with reasons to explain *why* it is biased.

Comparing sources: if you are asked to compare and/or contrast two sources, make sure that you analyse both sources before you start to write your answer. Record your findings on a simple plan.

Draw conclusions: what can you learn from your analysis of the source? How does it enhance your knowledge and understanding of a particular topic or event?

Examination technique

This section offers a few general points about how you should approach the examination. Some of them might seem obvious, but it is as well to remember that, under the pressures of an examination, we are all capable of being careless. It is best to be aware of the pitfalls so that we are less likely to make costly mistakes.

Preparation

It is essential that you are fully prepared for the examination. In particular, make sure you know:

Note:
All this information will be freely available on the examination board's website. You will be able to access sample/past exam papers, examiners' mark schemes and so on. These things are also available in hard copy.

- what topics the questions will be about
- what form the questions will take
- how many questions you will have to answer
- how long you will have to complete all your answers
- what the examiners will be looking for when assessing your answers.

One of the most important things to do is to look carefully at past or sample examination papers and their mark schemes. This will give you a clear insight into the type of questions you will face and, equally importantly, how the examiners mark them.

Equipment

Make sure that you arrive at the examination with all the equipment you are likely to need. Always ensure that you have more than one pen. Find out exactly what you are allowed and not allowed to take into the examination room. Different centres have their own rules about this, but there are also very clear guidelines issued by examination boards.

Rubric

All examination papers contain *rubric* – this provides you with information (such as how long you have to complete the exam) and instructions (such as how many questions you need to answer). Always:

- check the title of the examination paper to ensure you have been given the right one
- check how long the exam lasts
- read *all* the instructions carefully and make sure you follow them.

Question selection

Obviously this is not an issue if you have to answer all of the questions on the examination paper. However, here is some advice if you have the opportunity to select which questions to answer:

- Read *all parts of all questions* carefully *before* making your selection.
- Don't select a question simply because it happens to be about a topic on which you feel confident; just because you know a lot about the topic is no guarantee that you understand the question and can answer it effectively. Select by *task* (what the question is asking you to do) rather than by *topic* (basic subject matter).
- If questions consist of more than one part, make sure that you can answer *all parts* of it. For example, do not select a two-part question if you are confident about Part (a) but know nothing about (or are confused by) Part (b). By doing this you would immediately be reducing the number of marks you could achieve.
- Decide the order in which you are going to address the questions. Do not leave the question you feel most confident about until last – you don't want to run out of time on your best question.
- Make sure that you number your answers correctly (you don't need to waste time writing out the whole question). Make it as easy as possible for the examiner to understand what you are doing.

Timing

It is a good idea to work out how long you have to complete each question/part of a question. Make a note of it and make every effort to keep to this timing. What should you do if the examination is nearing its end and you realise that you are not going to complete your final answer?

- Write a comment such as 'running out of time – hence notes'.
- Describe, in note form, what you would have written if time had permitted.
- Ensure that these notes will make sense to the examiner and are not just a list of facts – make them relevant to the actual question.

This approach will not get you as many marks as if you had completed your answer properly. However, the examiner *will* read them and *will* give you credit for them provided that they are accurate and relevant.

The best way to avoid the problem of running out of time is to ensure that you have had a great deal of practice in writing answers to examination questions under timed conditions.

Planning

Always ensure that you have planned each answer thoroughly *before* you start to write. When confronted with the time constraints of an examination, too many students assume that it is essential to start writing as quickly as possible. As a result, they are making their judgements and forming their arguments as they write – this invariably leads to confused, unbalanced or unfocused answers. Careful planning is not time wasted. It is time well spent.

Revision

It is widely assumed that the purpose of revision is to get information into your brain in preparation for the exam. In fact, if you have followed the course appropriately, all the information you will need for the examination is already there. The human brain, rather like a computer, never 'forgets' anything it has experienced. *The key purpose of revision, therefore, is not to put information into your brain, but to ensure that you can retrieve it again when it is required.* Revision should not be something you undertake in the last few days and hours before an examination; effective revision needs to be an ongoing process throughout the course.

How frustrating is it when you need an important document that you know is somewhere on your computer, but you can't access it because you can't remember what filename you gave it? It can take hours of tedious and unproductive searching before you locate it – but, once you do, everything you need is there. All you needed was a simple filename in order to access all the information you required. Revision needs to operate in much the same way; identifying the key points ('filenames') that will bring related information flooding back into your memory. The notes you make during the course therefore need to be very carefully planned and structured.

When taking notes from a book, most students simply copy out long passages. They convince themselves that this is essential to ensure that they don't miss anything important. In fact, this is a largely pointless exercise that is invariably undertaken without concentration, comprehension, analysis or discrimination. The outcome is a mass of continuous prose that the student has not really read or understood. This causes problems when it comes to revision. A more productive way of note-taking and revising is:

- Read a whole section of the book first without making any notes at all, ensuring that you fully understand what the author is trying to say.
- Identify and record the key points being made (just like computer *folders*).
- Under each of the key points, list the arguments/evidence the author uses to support it (like computer *files*).

Index

Acknowledgements

The volume editor and publishers acknowledge the following sources of copyright material and are grateful for the permissions granted. While every effort has been made, it has not always been possible to identify the sources of all the material used, or to trace all copyright holders. If any omissions are brought to our notice we will be happy to include the appropriate acknowledgement on reprinting.

The extracts from the specimen paper on p. 187 are reproduced by permission of Cambridge International Examinations.

Picture credits
p. 7 Corbis; p. 8 (t) Collections de Louis XIV, Louvre/Wikipedia; p. 8 (b) Wikipedia; p. 9 (t) Wikipedia; p. 9 (b) Wikipedia; p. 11 Bettmann/Corbis; p. 13 Time & Life Pictures/Getty Images; p. 15 Wikipedia; pp. 16–17 Interfoto/Alamy; p. 21 Library of Congress; p. 22 Bettmann/Corbis; p. 28 Mary Evans Picture Library; p. 33 Interfoto/Alamy; p. 37 Corbis; p. 39 Wikipedia; p. 40 Bettmann/Corbis; p. 43 Ullsteinbild/Topfoto; p. 45 Illustrated London News Ltd/Mary Evans Picture Library; p. 48 Georgios Kollidas/Shutterstock; p. 49 Bettmann/Corbis; p. 50 (l) Wikipedia; p. 50 (r) Mary Evans Picture Library; p. 51 (r) Wikipedia; p. 55 Tom Morgan/Mary Evans Picture Library; p. 59 Corbis; p. 61 Universal Images Group Limited/Alamy; p. 64 Mary Evans Picture Library; p. 66 Getty Images; p. 69 Getty Images; p. 73 Bettmann/Corbis; p. 74 Library of Congress; p. 75 (r) Wikipedia; p. 81 Getty Images; p. 84 Library of Congress; p. 85 Mary Evans Picture Library; p. 87 Wikipedia; pp. 88–89 Getty Images; p. 90 Bettmann/Corbis; p. 93 Mary Evans Picture Library/Alamy; p. 95 Antonio Abrignani /Shutterstock; p. 96 Neveshkin Nikolay/Shutterstock; p. 97 Library of Congress; p. 98 (t) Getty Images; p. 98 (b) Antonio Abrignani /Shutterstock; p. 99 Stocksnapper/Shutterstock; p. 101 Mary Evans Picture Library; p. 102 Antonio Abrignani/Shutterstock; p. 107 Time & Life Pictures/Getty Images; p. 108 Wikipedia; p. 110 Interfoto/Alamy; p. 118 Mary Evans Picture Library/Alamy; p. 124 Mary Evans Picture Library; p. 132 Suddeutsche Zeitung Photo/Mary Evans Picture Library; p. 142 Library of Congress; p. 144 Library of Congress; p. 146 Ullsteinbild/Topfoto; p. 148 Library of Congress; p. 150 (l) Wikipedia; p. 150 (r) ETAR-TASS Photo Agency/Alamy; p. 152 Wikipedia; p. 153 Topham Picturepoint/Topfoto; p. 155 Time & Life Pictures/Getty Images; p. 157 Hulton-Deutsch Collection/Corbis; p. 160 Mary Evans Picture Library/Alamy; p. 163 Alexander Meledin/Mary Evans Picture Library; p. 188 (t) Mary Evans Picture Library; p. 188 (b) Getty Images; p. 190 Time & Life Pictures/Getty Images.

Produced for Cambridge University Press by
White-Thomson Publishing
+44 (0)843 208 7460
www.wtpub.co.uk

Project editor: Sonya Newland
Designer: Clare Nicholas
Illustrator: Stefan Chabluk

Author **Russell Williams** is an experienced university lecturer and teacher. He is a senior examiner at A and AS Levels. The author of a number of textbooks that are sold around the world, he has also written many articles for A Level students.

Series editor **Patrick Walsh-Atkins** has an MA and D.Phil. in Modern History from Oxford University He has taught 15 to 18 year-olds history and politics in a number of schools in the UK. He has been an A Level examiner for many years, and is also the author of a variety of textbooks for A Level students.